Heidegger

Heidegger

An Introduction

Richard Polt

Cornell University Press
Ithaca, New York

First published 1999 by Cornell University Press.

Polt, Richard F. H., 1964–
    Heidegger: an introduction / Richard Polt.
        p.   cm.
    Includes bibliographical references and index.
    ISBN 978-0-8014-8564-0 (pbk. : alk. paper)
    1. Heidegger, Martin, 1889–1976.   I. Title.
B3279.H49P65   1999
193—dc21   98-30460
                                            CIP

Cornell University Press strives to use environmentally responsible suppliers and materials to the fullest extent possible in the publishing of its books. Such materials include vegetable-based, low-VOC inks and acid-free papers that are recycled, totally chlorine-free, or partly composed of nonwood fibers. For further information, visit our website at www.cornellpress.cornell.edu.

Paperback printing   10 9 8 7 6 5

Printed in United States of America

Contents

Preface   ix

1 The Question   1

2 Beginnings   8
The roots   8
Theory of theory   10
Dilthey and Husserl   12
Theory and life   16
Heidegger the teacher   19
Towards *Being and Time*   21

3 *Being and Time*: Introduction and Division I   23
The problem and the goal   24
§1: The mystery of Being   25
§2: Ourselves as the starting point   28
§3: Being and the sciences   32
§4: Being and human existence   33
§§5, 6 and 8: The plan of *Being and Time*   35
§7: The method of *Being and Time*   38
§§9–11: Existence and everydayness   43
§§12–13: Being-in-the-world and knowing   46
§§14–18: The world as a significant whole   49
§§19–21: The impoverished Cartesian "world"   55
§§22–24: Quantitative space and the space of appropriateness   59
§§25–27: Being-with and the "they"   60
§28: The basic features of Being-in   64
§§29–30: Attunement   65
§§31–33: Understanding, interpretation and assertion   68

§34: Discourse   74
§§35–38: Falling   75
§§39–42: Anxiety and care   76
§§43–44: Reality and truth   80

4   *Being and Time*: Division II and Beyond   85
§§46–53: Facing up to mortality   85
§§54–60: Owning up to indebtedness and responsibility   88
§63: Existentiell truth as the basis of existential truth   92
§§62, 64–65: Temporality as the key to the Being of Dasein   94
§§66–71: Reinterpreting everydayness in terms of temporality   98
§§72–77: History, heritage and fate   100
§§78–82: Primordial temporality and the ordinary concept of time   106
A glimpse of Division III   109

5   Later Heidegger   113
Signs of the turn   117
"What is Metaphysics?": nothingness and the disintegration
    of logic   121
"On the Essence of Truth": unconcealment and freedom   126
Introduction to Metaphysics: the history of the restriction of Being   130
"The Origin of the Work of Art": the clash of earth and world   134
Contributions to Philosophy: fragments of another beginning   140
    Machination and lived experience   141
    Being as appropriation   143
    Truth as sheltering   149
    The way from beings to Being   150
Heidegger's politics: facts and thoughts   152
"Letter on Humanism": existentialism, humanism and ethics   164
"The Question Concerning Technology": beings as
    manipulable resources   171
Poetry and language   174
The final analysis?   178

Selected Bibliography   181
Index   193

To my parents,
John H. R. Polt and Beverley A. H. Polt

Preface

The greatest danger in discussing a philosopher is that we will summarize the thinker's views without conveying the passion and wonder of the original thinking. As Heidegger puts it:

> The widespread sterility of academic philosophy courses is . . . caused by the attempt to instruct the students with the well-known broad brushstrokes, in possibly one semester, about everything in the world, or about even more than that. One is supposed to learn to swim, but only goes meandering on the riverbank, converses about the murmuring of the stream, and talks about the cities and towns the river passes. This guarantees that the spark never flashes over to the individual student, kindling a light in him which can never be extinguished.[1]

It may help if, from the very start, we give up the ambition to cover "everything in the world". This book does not try to say everything that could be said about Heidegger. Even my relatively detailed analysis of his masterwork, *Being and Time*, discusses only the points that, in my judgment, are most helpful to the beginning reader of that text. The purpose of this book is never to replace Heidegger, but to help his readers – especially those who are new to his writings – to read him with more confidence and insight. There can be no substitute for thinking through the thoughts of philosophers themselves.

I have presented not only Heidegger's positions, but also the questions that led him to his positions, and some of the further questions that can be asked. This approach is meant to encourage readers "to learn to swim" – to participate with Heidegger in the activity of thinking.

Heidegger usually does not write for beginners in philosophy. He assumes that his readers have wrestled with the history of Western thought – that they

1. *The Metaphysical Foundations of Logic*, tr. M. Heim (Bloomington, Indiana: Indiana University Press, 1984), p. 7.

have awakened to its possibilities and suspected its limitations. The more one knows about other philosophers, the more one is likely to get from his writings. However, it is not really necessary to study Aristotle for 10 to 15 years (as Heidegger once advised his students to do) in order to profit from Heidegger.[2] A relative novice in philosophy will find much that is stimulating and thought-provoking in his texts, and may even have an advantage over readers who are steeped in traditional philosophical concepts. This book presupposes as little specialized knowledge and vocabulary as possible, not only in order to be useful to a wide audience but also in order to encourage reflection – because the jargon of professional philosophers can be used as an excuse not to think.

I have written with an eye to the entire range of Heidegger's thought. *Being and Time* has been in print for over seven decades, but the greater part of his writings was unavailable until the publication of the *Gesamtausgabe*, or collected edition (Frankfurt am Main: Vittorio Klostermann, 1976–). The collected edition will eventually include some 100 volumes; over 50 have appeared to date. Most of the lecture courses of 1919–1944 have now been published, along with other important, previously unavailable texts, such as the complex manuscript of the late thirties titled *Contributions to Philosophy (On Appropriation)* and a volume of dialogues composed in 1944–45. These materials have given us invaluable assistance in understanding Heidegger's development and his concerns. It would be unhelpful and probably impossible to summarize all these texts in an introductory book, but I have used material from a wide variety of volumes of the *Gesamtausgabe*.

For the most part, this book proceeds in chronological order. Chapter 1 introduces Heidegger's central question, the question of Being, and makes some general observations about his way of doing philosophy. Chapter 2 looks at the beginnings of his thought, as well as his environment and personality. Chapters 3 and 4 take readers through *Being and Time*. These chapters are best read in conjunction with *Being and Time* itself. My analyses are detailed at first, but gradually leave more work to the readers, on the assumption that they have become familiar with Heidegger's style and approach. Chapter 5 considers some highlights of his later thought, providing guidelines for reading a number of important texts, including the *Contributions to Philosophy* and several shorter essays.

In notes, "GA" refers to the *Gesamtausgabe*. Full details on the collected edition and other texts cited, as well as suggestions for further reading, are in the bibliography.

In this as in other projects, I am grateful to Charles Guignon for his generous support and forthright judgments. His detailed comments on my manuscript were invaluable, as were those of Michael Baur, David Cooper, Lee Horvitz, Lou Matz, and John Shand.

2. *What is Called Thinking?* tr. F. D. Wieck & J. G. Gray (New York: Harper & Row, 1968), p. 73. Heidegger proposes this as a preparation for reading Nietzsche.

To Gregory Fried I owe many insights about Heidegger gained during years of friendship and conversation.

I also owe special thanks to the graduates of Xavier University who commented on my work: Edward B. George, Andrew Hill, David Imwalle, Jonathan J. Sanford, and Phillip Wodzinski. What a pleasure it is for a teacher to learn from his former students.

This book is dedicated to my parents, with deep appreciation for their love and encouragement.

Finally, I thank Julie Gifford, my wife, for supporting the writing of this book in so many ways.

CHAPTER ONE

The Question

Celebration . . . is self-restraint, is attentiveness, is questioning, is meditating, is awaiting, is the step over into the more wakeful glimpse of
the wonder – the wonder that a world is worlding around us at all,
that there are beings rather than nothing, that things are and we
ourselves are in their midst, that we ourselves are and yet barely
know who we are, and barely know that we do not know all this.
— Martin Heidegger[1]

Why is there something rather than nothing? Strange as this question is, it seems
oddly familiar. Puzzling though it is, it has a certain unique simplicity.

This is not to say that it can be answered in the way we might answer the
question, "Why do birds migrate to the same place every winter?" or "Why is
there more crime in the United States than in Japan?" These questions stand a
chance of being resolved by scientific research. But no scientific investigation
can tell us why there is something rather than nothing. Science describes the
things we find around us, and it explains how some of these things are caused
by others, but it cannot say why the whole exists. The Big Bang theory may be
correct – but it does not answer why there was a Big Bang rather than nothing.
We might say that God made the Big Bang. But then, why is there God? Perhaps God exists by necessity. However, few thinkers these days accept the
idea of a necessary being whose existence we can know and prove. Most
would agree that whatever we may propose as the cause of everything is itself
something whose existence stands in need of explanation. It looks very much
as if our question, "Why is there something rather than nothing?" reaches
beyond the power of human reason. It is beginning to seem that our question
simply cannot be answered at all.

1. *Hölderlins Hymne "Andenken"*, GA 52, p. 64. "GA" in notes will refer to Heidegger's
Gesamtausgabe, or collected edition (Frankfurt am Main: Vittorio Klostermann, 1976–).

1

Does this imply that it is meaningless? Some philosophers think so. We can construct arguments to show that the question never signified anything to begin with. We can argue that the word "nothing" in our question means precisely that – it means nothing at all. But when the arguments are done, the question sneaks back and seems significant after all. As cosmologist Stephen Hawking writes, once science has described how everything works, we will still want to ask: "What is it that breathes fire into the equations and makes a universe for them to describe . . . Why does the universe go to all the bother of existing?"[2]

For Heidegger, our question is deeply meaningful. He ends his 1929 essay "What is Metaphysics?" with it, and it opens his lecture course *Introduction to Metaphysics* (1935). More precisely, Heidegger asks: "Why are there beings at all, and not rather nothing?"

The term "beings" translates *das Seiende*, more literally "that which is". "Beings", and its synonym "entities", refer to anything at all that has existence of some sort. Clearly atoms and molecules are beings. Humans and dogs are beings, as are their properties and activities. Mathematical objects – hexagons, numbers, equations – are beings of some kind, although philosophers disagree on whether these beings exist apart from human thought or behavior. Even dragons are connected to beings – they themselves do not exist, but we can talk about dragons only because myths, images and concepts of dragons do exist, as do dragonlike animals, such as lizards. In fact, it seems that anything we can think about, speak about, or deal with involves beings in some way.

But if the question of why there are beings rather than nothing cannot be answered by pointing to any particular being as a cause, then how can it have any meaning? Maybe its meaning comes from the special character of its "why". Maybe the "why" in this question is not a search for a cause, but an act of celebration. When we ask the question, we celebrate the fact that anything exists at all. We *notice* this amazing fact. Normally the existence of things is so familiar to us that we take it for granted. But at certain moments, this most familiar of facts can become surprising. Ludwig Wittgenstein describes the experience this way: "*I wonder at the existence of the world.* And I am then inclined to use such phrases as 'how extraordinary that anything should exist' or 'how extraordinary that the world should exist'."[3]

Once we have noticed and celebrated the fact that beings *are*, we can take a step further – and everything depends on this step. We can ask: what does this "are" *mean*? What is it to *be*? Now we are asking what makes a being count as a being, instead of as nothing: on what basis do we understand beings *as* beings? Now we are asking not about beings, but about Being.

---

2. S. Hawking, *A Brief History of Time: From the Big Bang to Black Holes* (New York: Bantam, 1988), p. 174.
3. "A Lecture on Ethics" (1929), in *Philosophical Occasions, 1912–1951* (Indianapolis, Indiana: Hackett, 1993), p. 41. For Wittgenstein, these phrases are, strictly speaking, nonsense; but they reflect "a tendency in the human mind which I personally cannot help respecting deeply" (p. 44).

"Being" is our counterpart to the German expression *das Sein*, literally "the to-be". In English, the word *being* can refer either to something that is (an entity) or to the to-be (what it means for entities to exist). So, like many translators of Heidegger, I will capitalize "Being" in order to distinguish Being clearly from *a* being. (This is not Heidegger's practice, for in German, all nouns are capitalized – and one should beware of confusing Being with the supreme being, God.)

Being is not a being at all; it is what marks beings out as beings rather than nonbeings – what makes the difference, so to speak, between something and nothing. Another, similar phrase may serve just as well: *Being is the difference it makes that there is something rather than nothing.* Even if we cannot find a cause for the totality of beings, we can investigate the meaning of Being, for it *does* make a difference that there are beings rather than nothing. We can pay attention to this difference and describe it.

However, this question of the meaning of Being looks deceptively simple: to say that something "is" just seems to mean that it is there, given, on hand. In short, it is present instead of absent. Being is simply presence. Presence appears to be a very straightforward fact, so it may seem that the Being of a thing has next to no content, and is quite uninteresting.

But is the difference between presence and absence so trivial? If my house burns down, its absence is overwhelming. At the death of those we love, their absence attacks and gnaws at us. Are these just "subjective" responses that have nothing to do with the "objective" question of Being – or are they moments in which we realize that there are, in fact, crucial and rich distinctions between something and nothing?

We can also ask whether all the sorts of beings we have mentioned exist in the same *way*. Is a dog present in the same way as the dog's act of running is present? Is a myth present just as an atom is present, or a number is present? The particular difference it makes that there is a being rather than nothing may depend on what *sort* of being is in question. Presence begins to look complex – and puzzling.

And maybe some beings are not present at all. For instance, we constantly relate to possibilities – whenever we think of what we might do, consider what may happen to us or see where we can go. A possibility is something in the future, something that is not yet present and may never be present. However, we would hardly want to say that a possibility is *nothing*, since surely we are considering *something* when we consider possibilities. Similarly, we remember and investigate the past. The past is not present either. But if it were nothing whatsoever, it would make no sense for us to describe it, argue about it, reject it or long for it.

It turns out, then, that the meaning of Being is unclear, and it is very hard to define the boundary between beings and nothing. It also seems that in order to think about Being, we will have to think about temporality – for beings make a difference to us not only when they are present in the present, but also when they are in the past and future dimensions of the mysterious phenomenon called time.

Our initial question – why is there something rather than nothing? – has taken us to a second question: what does it mean to be? Now we can ask a third question: what is it about *our* condition that lets Being have a meaning for us? In other words, why does it make a difference to *us* that there is something rather than nothing? This is a crucial question about ourselves – for if we were indifferent to the difference between something and nothing, we would be sunk in oblivion. We constantly distinguish between something and nothing, by recognizing countless things as real while rejecting falsehoods and illusions. The process is at work not only in philosophy, but in the simplest everyday tasks: I recognize a pitcher as a being simply by reaching for its handle. It is clear that without our sensitivity to Being, we would not be human at all. Even for the most apathetic or shellshocked individual, Being means something – although it is hard to put this meaning into words.

We are now traveling the path of Heidegger's thought. For Heidegger, these three questions belong together in such a way that they can be called *the* question of Being: he wants to notice the wonder that there is something rather than nothing, to ask what difference this makes, and to ask how it can make a difference to us.

How does Heidegger answer the question of Being, then? What is his philosophy? He replies, "I have no philosophy at all".[4] But he is a philosopher nonetheless – because philosophy, for him, is not something one has, but something one does. It is not a theory or a set of principles, but the relentless and passionate devotion to a question. In a Heideggerian formula: "questioning is the piety of thought".[5] For Heidegger, providing an answer to the question of Being is less important than awakening us to it, and using it to bring us face to face with the riddles of our own history: "My essential intention is to first pose the problem and work it out in such a way that the essentials of the entire Western tradition will be concentrated in the simplicity of a basic problem."[6] Heidegger is remarkable not for his consistent answers, but for his persistent inquiry.

Having said this, we must add that he does try to respond to the question of Being in a particular direction. His thought develops throughout his life, but early in his philosophical career he seizes on some enduring guidelines.

First, as we implied above, Heidegger holds that presence is a rich and complex phenomenon – and even so, the meaning of Being is not exhausted by presence, or at least by any traditional understanding of presence. Roughly speaking, for ancient and medieval philosophy, to be is to be an enduringly present substance, or one of the attributes of such a substance. The most real being is an eternal substance – God. For much of modern philosophy, to be is to be either an object present in space and time as measured by quantitative

---

4. *History of the Concept of Time: Prolegomena*, tr. T. Kisiel (Bloomington, Indiana: Indiana University Press, 1985), pp. 301–2.
5. "The Question Concerning Technology", in *Basic Writings*, D. F. Krell (ed.), 2d edn (San Francisco, California: HarperSanFrancisco, 1993), p. 341.
6. *The Metaphysical Foundations of Logic*, p. 132.

natural science, or a subject, a mind, that is capable of self-consciousness, or self-presence. According to Heidegger, these traditional approaches may be appropriate to some beings, but they misinterpret others. In particular, they fail to describe *our own* Being. We are neither present substances, nor present objects, nor present subjects: we are beings whose past and future collaborate to let us deal with all the other beings we encounter around us. (Readers of Heidegger have come to use the expression "metaphysics of presence" to describe the philosophical tradition that Heidegger is criticizing.)

But if Being is not presence, what *is* it? *Being and Time*, which was supposed to answer this question, faltered and was left unfinished. Later, Heidegger increasingly stressed that the meaning of Being evolves in the course of history. Furthermore, Being is intrinsically mysterious and self-concealing. For these reasons, he does not provide us with a straightforward answer to the question of the meaning of Being.

He does, however, believe that we must call into question the metaphysics of presence – for this tradition has pernicious consequences. It dulls us to the depth of experience and restricts us to impoverished ways of thinking and acting. In particular, if we identify Being with presence, we can become obsessed with getting beings to present themselves to us perfectly and in a definitive way – with *re*presenting beings accurately and effectively. We try, by means of philosophy, science or technology, to achieve complete insight into things and thereby gain complete control over them. According to Heidegger, this ideal is incompatible with the nature of understanding; understanding is always a finite, historically situated interpretation. Heidegger does affirm that there is truth, and he does hold that some interpretations (including his own) are better than others – but no interpretation is *final*. Heidegger is a relentless enemy of ahistorical, absolutist concepts of truth.

This brings us to his most important guideline of all: it is our own *temporality* that makes us sensitive to Being. "Temporal" in Heidegger does not mean "temporary". He is not interested in the fact that we are impermanent so much as in the fact that we are *historical*: we are rooted in a past and thrust into a future. We inherit a past tradition that we share with others, and we pursue future possibilities that define us as individuals. As we do so, the world opens up for us, and beings get understood; it makes a difference to us that there is something rather than nothing. Our historicity, then, does not cut us off from reality – to the contrary, it opens us up to the meaning of Being.

But according to Heidegger, many of the philosophical errors he combats are rooted in a tendency we have to ignore our historicity. It can be difficult and disturbing to face our own temporality and to experience the mystery of Being. It is easier to slip back into an everyday state of complacency and routine. Rather than wrestling with who we are and what it means to be, we would prefer to concentrate on manipulating and measuring present beings. In philosophy, this self-deceptive absorption in the present leads to a metaphysics of presence, which only encourages the self-deception. Heidegger consistently points to the difference between this everyday state of oblivion and a state in which we genuinely face up to our condition. In *Being and Time*, he calls this the difference between *inauthenticity* and *authenticity*.

We have now touched on Heidegger's basic question, the question of Being, and on some of the enduring guidelines that orient his response to that question. But no less distinctive than his questions and answers is his *style* of philosophizing.

Heidegger is steeped in the Western philosophical tradition and is capable of erudite textual and conceptual analysis. But he also recognizes that real life may elude traditional concepts. Like Pascal, Kierkegaard, Nietzsche, or Unamuno, Heidegger senses that the philosophical tradition is out of touch with life as it is lived.[7] These other thinkers, however, have tended to make wholesale attacks on the tradition without descending to a detailed and thorough critique of it. They have been deliberately unsystematic, in an attempt to break free of the dead weight of traditional concepts. Heidegger shares these thinkers' desire to capture the concrete textures and tensions of experience – but he also respects the tradition with which he is struggling. He is willing and able to carry out painstaking, close readings of Aristotle or Kant, for example. In *Being and Time* he weaves an intricate conceptual web in order to address what may be the oldest philosophical topic of all – Being. Heidegger is convinced that matters of vital importance are at stake in the tradition. If we think tenaciously until we uncover the roots of traditional problems and concepts, we can bring philosophy back to the basic and urgent realities of our human condition.

In this way, Heidegger unites historical research with original thinking. In English-speaking countries, doing "history of philosophy" is often distinguished from working on "problems". The first involves reconstructing the arguments that philosophers have made in the past; the second involves developing one's own arguments and responding to the arguments of one's contemporaries. Heidegger undercuts this opposition in two ways.

First, he insists that in order to understand the history of philosophy properly, we have to philosophize. For instance, when interpreting a Platonic dialogue, he explains that his goal is to "see the content that is genuinely and ultimately at issue, so that from it as from a unitary source the understanding of every single sentence will be nourished".[8] Understanding what a text is about requires us to think for ourselves about the topic under discussion. In fact, it may mean that we have to think farther than the original author did. Heidegger's goal is to discover what lies "unsaid" and "unthought" in the background of what an author says and thinks.

---

7. For representative statements from these thinkers, see Blaise Pascal, *Pensées*; Søren Kierkegaard, *Concluding Unscientific Postscript*; Friedrich Nietzsche, *Twilight of the Idols*; Miguel de Unamuno, *The Tragic Sense of Life*. Several translations of each text are available.

8. Heidegger, *Plato's Sophist*, tr. R. Rojcewicz & A. Schuwer (Bloomington, Indiana: Indiana University Press, 1997), p. 160 (translation modified).

Conversely, he holds that in order to philosophize properly, we have to understand the history of philosophy. Otherwise, we will just reproduce hackneyed, traditional patterns of thought. In philosophy, it is especially true that to be ignorant of history is to be condemned to repeat it. When we return to the historical sources of our concepts and our concerns, we become aware of the motivations behind these concepts and the alternatives to them. We become more, not less, capable of original thinking.

Heidegger titles one collection of his essays *Holzwege* (*Woodpaths*). In German, to be on a *Holzweg* is to be on a dead-end trail. But dead ends are not worthless. If we follow a path to its end and are forced to return, we are different, even wiser, than we were before we took this path. We have come to know the lay of the land and our own capacities. We know much more about the woods, even if we have never gotten out of them.

One may disagree with every claim found in Heidegger's writings. They may all be dead ends. But they are still worth reading, because they have the potential to reveal a host of fundamental, interconnected problems. As Heidegger likes to put it, the task of a philosopher is to alert us to what is worthy of questioning. That he certainly does.

CHAPTER TWO

Beginnings

The roots

The quiet Swabian town of Messkirch is the home of St. Martin's, one of the ornate Catholic churches that grace many southern German villages. In the shadow of the church, a massive statue of a soldier stands atop a column inscribed, "To our dead heroes of the World War 1914–1918". A less somber monument honors a local celebrity, the composer Conradin Kreutzer. Just a few steps away, a plaque bearing a poor likeness of the other well-known Messkircher, Martin Heidegger, marks the house in which the thinker spent his boyhood. His father, Friedrich Heidegger, was the sexton who looked after St. Martin's Church. A brief climb takes a visitor to the hilltop graveyard that contains the Heidegger family plot. All but one of the tombstones in the plot are marked with crosses. The stone inscribed "Martin Heidegger, 1889–1976" is marked with a star, recalling a line written by the philosopher in 1947: "To think is to confine yourself to a single thought that one day stands still like a star in the world's sky."[1]

Heidegger was born and is buried in this rural, conservative, pious town. But is this fact relevant to understanding his philosophy? On the occasion of the 175th anniversary of the birth of Conradin Kreutzer, in 1955, Heidegger claimed in a memorial address in Messkirch: "The greater the master, the more completely his person vanishes behind his work."[2] However, he himself had written in 1921: "I work concretely and factically out of my 'I am', out of my intellectual and wholly factic origin, milieu, life-contexts, and whatever is available to me from these as a vital experience in which I live."[3] In 1929, he makes

1. "The Thinker as Poet", in *Poetry, Language, Thought*, tr. A. Hofstadter (New York: Harper & Row, 1971), p. 4.
2. "Memorial Address", in *Discourse on Thinking*, tr. J. M. Anderson and E. H. Freund (New York: Harper & Row, 1966), p. 44.
3. Letter to Karl Löwith, August 19, 1921, in *Im Gespräch der Zeit*, D. Papenfuss & O. Pöggeler (eds), **2** of *Zur philosophischen Aktualität Martin Heideggers* (Frankfurt am Main: Vittorio

this point more generally: "every metaphysical question can be asked only in such a way that the questioner as such is present together with the question, that is, is placed in question."[4] Philosophy, for Heidegger, is not a matter of exercising one's pure reason in isolation from concrete circumstance. Thought, like all human activity, is historical and builds on one's own particular heritage. Even in his 1955 memorial address, he quotes the regional poet Johann Peter Hebel: "We are like plants which – whether we like to admit it to ourselves or not – must with our roots rise out of the earth in order to bloom in the ether and to bear fruit."[5]

There are good Heideggerian grounds, then, for paying attention to Heidegger's roots – his circumstances and his character. Of course, we should not *reduce* the philosophy to the philosopher's personality, as if the thought were just a symptom of the thinker's habits and neuroses. This approach prevents us from experiencing the philosophy as true or false, as relevant to our own lives. Instead, we have to consider Heidegger's beginnings as we work to discover what is illuminating about his thought and what is misleading. For our beginnings both illuminate and hide our world, opening up certain dimensions of life at the same time as they close off others. To use one of Heidegger's preferred words, our origin opens a "clearing", an open space within which things are revealed to us – but this clearing is always surrounded by the dark woods, the realm of the concealed and inaccessible.

Heidegger's background made him especially sympathetic to the traditional world of the German country. He heard the promises and demands of Christianity, its interpretation of life and history as a drama of sin and redemption.[6] He was familiar with the centuries-old routines of everyday labor. He knew the countryside cultivated by the farmers and he loved to ski and hike through the landscape of the Black Forest. These dimensions of experience – guilt, the struggle for authenticity, handicraft, nature – would become focuses of his thought.

Just as Heidegger's beginnings revealed traditional rural life to him, they closed him off to urban modernity. His background turned him against the big city, with its emphasis on efficiency and productivity, its culture of news and novelty, and its cosmopolitanism. He always remained deeply suspicious of machinery, journalism and liberal democracy, and retained his attachment to the countryside. When asked to leave the University of Freiburg and teach in Berlin in 1933, he refused. In an essay composed on this occasion, "Why do I

Klostermann, 1990), pp. 27–32; quoted and translated in T. Kisiel, *The Genesis of Heidegger's Being and Time* (Berkeley, California: University of California Press, 1993), p. 78.

4. "What is Metaphysics?" in *Basic Writings*, p. 93.

5. "Memorial Address", in *Discourse on Thinking*, p. 47.

6. In 1937 or 1938 he reflects that his thought has involved "a confrontation with Christianity [that] is a preservation of my ownmost origin–my parents' house, my home and youth – and *also* a painful separation from it. Only someone who has been rooted this way in a real, lived, Catholic world can glimpse some of the necessities that worked like subterranean tremors upon the path of my questioning up to now". *Besinnung*, GA 66, p. 415.

Stay in the Provinces?" he explains that his "philosophical work . . . belongs right in the midst of the peasants' work".[7]

If it were not for Heidegger's extraordinary gifts, his circumstances would simply have led him towards provincial conservatism. But he was restless, intelligent and inquisitive, naturally inclined not only to defend what he knew, but to work to understand it. Young Martin must have seemed destined for the scholarly, self-disciplined piety of the Jesuit order, and it was no surprise when he entered a Jesuit seminary in 1909. However, he left after only two weeks. His heart was not strong enough, it was said. Whether this problem was purely physical or also spiritual, he chose to pursue theology in a strictly academic way, at the University of Freiburg. By 1911, he had discovered his true calling: he enrolled as a student of philosophy.

As a philosopher, Heidegger would ask questions that are rooted in his origins. What are the limitations of the worldview of modern science and technology? What aspects of human life and nature does it overlook? How does Western intellectual history lead to this narrow understanding? Can we discover more promising alternatives by reinvigorating one of the earliest Western questions – the question of Being?

Theory of theory

"To tell the truth, I am not really interested in my development", confessed Heidegger in 1927.[8] Why, then, should *we* be interested? It is not essential for the beginner to know the details of Heidegger's early development, and *Being and Time* can be understood well without this background knowledge. However, some acquaintance with Heidegger's earliest thought will help to clarify the sources of important concepts and themes in *Being and Time*. It is especially valuable to see that young Heidegger begins with a point of view that he will reject in his mature thought. Above all, having a sense of his development helps us understand *Being and Time* not as a perfect and independent whole, but as part of an ongoing philosophical path. We turn now to the start of this path.

In 1911, Heidegger officially became a student of philosophy. But he had already been reading about the problem of Being for some time. He knew Franz Brentano's *On the Several Senses of Being in Aristotle* (1862) and *On Being* (1896) by the Freiburg theologian Carl Braig. "The following question concerned me in a quite vague manner: If Being is predicated in manifold meanings, then what is its leading fundamental meaning? What does Being mean?"[9] Heidegger

7. "Why do I Stay in the Provinces?" in *Heidegger: The Man and the Thinker*, T. Sheehan (ed.) (Chicago, Illinois: Precedent, 1981), p. 28.
8. Letter to Karl Löwith, August 20, 1927, quoted and translated in Kisiel, *The Genesis of Heidegger's* Being and Time, p. 19.
9. "My Way to Phenomenology", in *On Time and Being*, tr. J. Stambaugh (New York: Harper & Row, 1972), p. 74.

now plunged into the study of Aristotle himself and of his medieval interpreters. He studied under the neo-Kantian Heinrich Rickert and was fascinated by a difficult book published in 1900 by Edmund Husserl, titled *Logical Investigations*.

The German educational system requires that prospective university teachers produce two substantial theses, a dissertation and a *Habilitationsschrift*. The industrious Heidegger finished his dissertation in 1913 and titled it *The Theory of Judgment in Psychologism: A Critical-Positive Contribution to Logic*. His *Habilitationsschrift* (1916) was titled *Duns Scotus' Theory of Categories and Meaning*.[10] There is no need for us to review the complexities of these early works. But it can be helpful to look at some basic features of young Heidegger's philosophical orientation, as they will help us understand the dramatic shift that was soon to occur in his thought.

The shift is indeed dramatic, for the mature Heidegger is famous for his explorations of the history of language and his plays on words, and he is infamous for his pronouncement that "the idea of 'logic' itself disintegrates in the turbulence of a more original questioning".[11] But young Heidegger calls his dissertation a "contribution to logic", and he seems to identify logic with philosophy itself. He often stresses that logic has nothing to do with grammar or etymology: the meaning of a statement is independent of the peculiarities of the language in which it is expressed.[12] Heidegger sounds like many of today's analytic philosophers when he says it is the logician's duty to strive for "unambiguous definitions and clarifications of the meanings of words".[13]

What does Heidegger mean by "logic"? Today we usually think of logic primarily as formal, symbolic logic. Heidegger is aware of the advances in symbolic logic made by Frege and Russell, but he thinks that this approach to logical problems is too limited.[14] Logic in the broader sense studies "the conditions of knowing in general. Logic is theory of theory".[15] In other words, the job of logic is to explain how theoretical claims can be meaningful and true. For instance, we might consider the statement, "Human beings have descended from apes". An evolutionary biologist would investigate whether the claim is true or false, but a logician, according to young Heidegger, should ask how it is *possible* for the claim to communicate something meaningful, to relate to reality, and to be either correct or incorrect. This concept of logic is broad enough to include what today we might call philosophy of science, philosophy of mind, epistemology and philosophy of language.

It even includes metaphysics, in the sense of a theory about what sorts of things there are and what kind of Being they have. For Heidegger adopts the view that the propositions expressed by our theoretical assertions have a special sort of Being, "validity" (*Geltung*, not to be confused with what in

10. Neither text has been published in English translation. The originals can be found in *Frühe Schriften*, GA 1.
11. "What is Metaphysics?" in *Basic Writings*, p. 107. We will take a close look at this claim in Chapter 5.
12. GA 1, pp. 32, 103, 302, 338, 340.   13. *Ibid.*, p. 186.
14. *Ibid.*, pp. 42–3.   15. *Ibid.*, p. 23.

11

English we call the validity or logical consistency of an argument). Validity is an atemporal mode of Being which should be distinguished from the ordinary, time-bound "existence" of ourselves, our statements and thoughts, and the objects that we usually discuss.[16] When I say, "Human beings have descended from apes", my mental state at that moment and my utterance of these English words are real, existing events. The descent of humans from apes is also a real, existing fact. But the *proposition* that my words *express* is "valid": it is an ideal meaning that is timelessly true, independently of whether anyone is thinking about it or expressing it. When we know something about an object, we do so by way of a leap to the realm of validity:

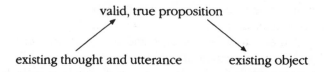

This "theory of theory" makes a strict distinction between acts of thought and the propositions they express. Accordingly, Heidegger (following Rickert and Husserl) comes out strongly against psychologism, the claim that logic is nothing but the study of how people actually happen to think. Instead, logic studies how we *ought* to think in order to conform to the principles of the timeless realm of validity. Heidegger is confident that we will discover that "definite basic principles of all knowing, the logical principles, guide knowledge on to unshakeable, absolutely valid paths".[17] He hopes that the study of these logical principles will give us the key to "the whole domain of 'Being'".[18]

But not long after subscribing to such views, Heidegger will vehemently denounce them. The crucial assumption he will reject is that we are connected to things primarily through *theoretical knowledge*. According to the mature Heidegger, the truth of scientific statements about objects depends on a much more basic "unconcealment". Before theory ever comes along, the world is opened up for us by "life", which is situated and historical. Our obsession with theoretical propositions, then, dangerously alienates us from the human condition; it dismisses the richness of pre-scientific experience, which originally makes the world meaningful for us. We can now see how Heidegger came to develop this position.

Dilthey and Husserl

When he published his *Habilitationsschrift* in 1916, Heidegger added an afterword that expressed impatience with the standard, "all too traditional way of handling *logic*"[19] and asserted that meaning must be understood in its connection with "*essentially historical spirit*".[20] A sea change was underway, in

16. *Ibid.*, pp. 22, 24.   17. *Ibid.*, p. 7.   18. *Ibid.*, p. 186.
19. *Ibid.*, p. 410, note.   20. *Ibid.*, p. 407.

Heidegger's personal and intellectual life as well as in Europe itself. War had broken out in 1914. Heidegger began teaching at the University of Freiburg in 1915. In 1916, he was called to serve as military censor at the Freiburg post office. In 1917 he entered into his lifelong marriage to Elfride Petri. Martin was Catholic, Elfride was Lutheran, but as Elfride was soon to admit, "My husband has lost his religious faith, and I have failed to find mine".[21] In 1918, Heidegger was sent to the front to serve at a meteorological station (he never saw combat). He returned in 1919 to give impassioned lectures on the essence of philosophy and the university.[22] In 1919 and 1920, the Heideggers' two sons, Jörg and Hermann, were born.

Heidegger's reading and thinking had broadened during these years. He turned away from the systematic, metaphysical Christianity of the scholastics towards the passionate and personal Christianity of Paul, Augustine, and Luther. "The system", he wrote, "totally excludes an original and genuine experience of religious value."[23] While continuing his intensive study of Aristotle, he was increasingly attracted to writers who had explored the extremes of human experience in literature and philosophy: Kierkegaard, Dostoyevsky, Nietzsche. Most important of all were two thinkers whose works Heidegger had studied for several years, but who now became vitally important for his own thought: Wilhelm Dilthey (1833–1911) and Edmund Husserl (1859–1939).

Dilthey was a wide-ranging philosopher and intellectual historian who was especially concerned with the objects and methods of the "human sciences", such as history, psychology and sociology. According to Dilthey, these disciplines should not take the natural sciences as their model, because while physics or chemistry study ahistorical objects, the objects of the human sciences – we ourselves – are essentially historical. In works such as *Introduction to the Human Sciences* (1883), Dilthey set himself the task of interpreting "'life' itself in its structures, as the basic reality of history", as Heidegger puts it.[24] In addition, Dilthey was concerned not only with interpreting life, but also with hermeneutics, or the theory of interpretation itself. A number of Dilthey's basic concepts were to inspire Heidegger's analysis of human existence in *Being and Time*.[25]

As for Husserl, Heidegger had been fascinated for some time by his work, but he had understood little of it.

21. H. Ott, *Heidegger: A Political Life*, tr. A. Blunden (New York: BasicBooks, 1993), p. 109.
22. For a fascinating list of Heidegger's courses and seminars from 1915 to 1930, see Kisiel, *The Genesis of Heidegger's* Being and Time, pp. 469–76. Kisiel's book also provides summaries of many of these lecture courses.
23. Unpublished note, circa 1917, quoted in Kisiel, *The Genesis of Heidegger's* Being and Time, p. 73.
24. *History of the Concept of Time*, p. 17. A good secondary source on Dilthey is R. A. Makkreel, *Dilthey: Philosopher of the Human Studies* (Princeton, New Jersey: Princeton University Press, 1975). On the relation between Dilthey and Heidegger, see C. Bambach, *Heidegger, Dilthey, and the Crisis of Historicism* (Ithaca, New York: Cornell University Press, 1995), esp. Chapters 4 and 5.
25. See Kisiel, *The Genesis of Heidegger's* Being and Time, Chapter 7.

My perplexity decreased slowly, my confusion dissolved laboriously, only after I met Husserl personally in his workshop. Husserl came to Freiburg in 1916 as Heinrich Rickert's successor. . . . Husserl's teaching took place in the form of a step-by-step training in phenomenological "seeing" which at the same time demanded that one relinquish the untested use of philosophical knowledge.[26]

Soon Heidegger was working as Husserl's most trusted assistant, and Heidegger would play a crucial role in the development of the phenomenological movement led by Husserl. It was only when Husserl read *Being and Time* – which was dedicated to him – that he realized how far his protégé had deviated from his own thought.

We can indicate only a few main features of the thought of Husserl, who is arguably the single most influential figure in twentieth-century continental philosophy.[27] Husserl struggled throughout his life to define phenomenology and develop it in detail. But the basic idea is straightforward: phenomenology is the description of phenomena. In other words, before we ask what really *exists* and why, we should focus on what actually *shows* itself to us, and notice *how* it displays itself, looking for patterns in this display. This approach can be applied to any conscious experience whatsoever, because all acts of consciousness are *about* something that shows itself to us, something that can be investigated as a phenomenon. (Husserl refers to this essential directedness of consciousness as *intentionality*.) Even if I am conscious of something absent, such as my lost watch, the watch still shows itself to me – as a missing and desired object. Phenomenology can thus investigate any experience at all.

A phenomenologist confronted with a portrait can ask, for example: What is it about this phenomenon that presents it as a picture of a person rather than as a person in the flesh? What features present it as a work of art? As a good or bad one? We can also focus on ourselves as conscious of this phenomenon, and ask: what distinguishes our *experience* as an experience of a representational work of art?

For Husserl, phenomenology must seek the *essential* aspects of phenomena – necessary, universal structures, such as the essence of art or the essence of representation. For years, Husserl hoped to establish phenomenology as a science of these essences. This science would provide a foundation for all other sciences, and would help to save Western culture from relativism, skepticism and historicism.

At least two of Husserl's concepts were to prove especially important for Heidegger: the concepts of *evidence* and *categorial intuition*. "Evidence" is

26. "My Way to Phenomenology", in *On Time and Being*, p. 78.
27. One good introduction to Husserl is J. J. Kockelmans, *Edmund Husserl's Phenomenology* (West Lafayette, Indiana: Purdue University Press, 1994). On phenomenology in general, see H. Spiegelberg, *The Phenomenological Movement: A Historical Introduction*, 3d edn (The Hague: Martinus Nijhoff, 1982). For Heidegger's own account of the beginnings of phenomenology and the phenomenological problems that he viewed as decisive, see the "Preliminary Part" of his 1925 lecture course *History of the Concept of Time*.

Husserl's technical term for a state in which a phenomenon shows itself to consciousness. Perfect or "adequate" evidence would be a condition in which something would show itself completely; no aspect of it would remain hidden. Husserl writes: "This final fulfilment represents an ideal of perfection . . . this limiting case is *evidence or knowledge in the pregnant sense of the word* . . . The *varying notions of truth*, which all must be built up on one single, selfsame phenomenological situation, here reach complete clearness."[28] For Heidegger, this idea that truth means self-showing, or *unconcealment*, was very powerful.[29] But he was to argue, against Husserl, that things can unconceal themselves to us only because we are profoundly historical, and that *perfect* unconcealment is impossible; truth is necessarily accompanied by untruth.

The notion of "categorial intuition", presented in the Sixth Logical Investigation, fascinated Heidegger and other students of Husserl long after Husserl himself had abandoned it.[30] We saw that according to Husserl, all acts of consciousness are directed towards something that can be investigated as a phenomenon, something that shows itself to us – in other words, something that we "intuit". Some forms of intuition are sensory: we intuit the redness of an apple through vision. But when we think, "Here is an apple", we are conscious of more than sensations. *Here* as opposed to elsewhere, *unity* ("an" apple), and *Being* (the "is") are fundamental features of our experience that cannot be perceived through the senses, argues Husserl: "I can see colour, but not *being*-coloured. I can feel smoothness, but not *being*-smooth."[31] But phenomena such as Being must *somehow* show themselves to us. This means that we must have a power of "categorial intuition": the "categorial" aspects of experience, the fundamental structures that shape what we encounter, can show themselves to us. This opens up the possibility of investigating Being as a phenomenon. As Heidegger puts it, "there are acts [of consciousness] in which ideal constituents [such as Being] show themselves in themselves, [ideal constituents] which are not constructs of these acts, functions of thinking or of the subject."[32] Being is not something that we have invented or that we project on to the world; it is a phenomenon that is given to us and that we can investigate.

Husserl and Dilthey would seem to be two completely different thinkers: Husserl, who began as a mathematician, tries to escape historical particularity and looks for absolute knowledge of essences, while Dilthey is interested in how to interpret thoroughly historical realities. But Heidegger reports that when Dilthey read Husserl's *Logical Investigations*, at the age of 70, he recognized

an inner kinship with its basic direction . . . In a letter to Husserl, he compared their work to boring into a mountain from opposite sides until they break through and meet each other. Dilthey here found an

28. E. Husserl, *Logical Investigations*, tr. A. J. Findlay (London: Routledge & Kegan Paul, 1970), p. 670 (translation modified).
29. "My Way to Phenomenology", in *On Time and Being*, p. 79.
30. "My Way to Phenomenology", pp. 78–9.
31. Husserl, *Logical Investigations*, p. 780.   32. *History of the Concept of Time*, p. 71.

initial fulfillment of what he had sought for decades . . . a fundamental science of life itself.[33]

However, the two philosophers were still approaching life from opposite directions, and it was the question of history that divided them the most. On this point, Heidegger sided with Dilthey: "Husserl's position toward the problem of history . . . must be described as impossible, rightly evoking Dilthey's dismay."[34]

Heidegger's own philosophy, as it now began to emerge, can be seen as a creative combination of Dilthey and Husserl. Heidegger unites the systematic rigor of Husserl with Dilthey's sensitivity to concrete existence in order to develop a phenomenology of historical life. In doing so, he rejects his own early "logic" in favor of the view that theoretical truth is secondary to our non-theoretical openness to beings.

Theory and life

One of Heidegger's earliest lecture courses is also one of his most dramatic: "The Idea of Philosophy and the Problem of Worldviews", delivered in the "war emergency semester" of 1919. Here Heidegger rejects his own early opinions, without ever mentioning that he held them himself: "Logic has actually been referred to as theory of theory. Is there such a thing? What if that were an illusion?"[35]

A main target of his scorn is his early notion of "validity", which he will continue to attack in several texts of the 1920s. He calls the concept "a tangle of confusions, perplexity and dogmatism".[36] The main problem is that valid propositions are supposed to be "timeless", while our thoughts and utterances are supposed to be "temporal". But when we probe a little deeper, we find that we cannot give a satisfactory account of what it is to *be* in these two modes. What does it really mean to be "timeless" and "temporal", and why are we using time to make a distinction between types of Being?[37] Furthermore, how is it that the temporal and timeless realms can connect?[38] (In our diagram on p. 12, we drew arrows connecting the two, but what are these arrows supposed to mean?) Heidegger concludes that the whole idea of an atemporal realm of validity is "an invention that is no less doubtful than medieval

33. *Ibid.*, p. 24.   34. *Ibid.*, p. 119.
35. *Die Idee der Philosophie und das Weltanschauungsproblem*, in *Zur Bestimmung der Philosophie*, GA 56/57, p. 96. (I was not able to consult the new translation of this important volume: *Towards the Definition of Philosophy*, tr. T. Sadler [London: Athlone, 1998].)
36. *Logik: Die Frage nach der Wahrheit*, GA 21, p. 79.
37. *Being and Time*, tr. J. Macquarrie & E. Robinson (New York: Harper & Row, 1962), p. 39/18. Throughout this book, references to *Being and Time* will provide, first, a page number in the Macquarrie and Robinson translation, and then the corresponding page number from *Sein und Zeit*, 14th edn (Tübingen: Niemeyer, 1977).
38. *Ibid.*, p. 259/216.

speculation about angels".[39] The distinction between validity and ordinary existence is an artificial notion that leads to insoluble problems: "first one constructs these two domains, and then a gap between them; and now, one looks for the bridge".[40]

If theoretical statements such as "human beings have descended from apes" do not get their meaning by expressing timelessly valid propositions, how *do* they get their meaning? Heidegger proposes that we have to look at the roots of theory in life. Human life, in all its concrete individuality and historical situatedness, is the origin of theoretical truth. For instance, before a scientific statement about evolution can make any sense to me, I need to have experienced both human beings and apes. This basic experience is not a *theoretical* experience: it is not just looking and taking notes. It has to be an experience that is relevant to me *as an individual*, that forms a meaningful part of *my own life*. In Heidegger's words, he is interested in "the full, concrete, and historically factical self that is accessible to itself in its historically concrete experience of itself".[41] I learn what it is to be human not by measuring and scrutinizing examples of *homo sapiens*, but by *being* human. If I then become an anthropologist, who does measure and scrutinize *homo sapiens*, my theoretical insights will grow *from* my own, living experience.

If life is more basic than theory, then a "theory of theory" is at best a superficial pursuit that fails to illuminate the roots of theory in life. There must be a way of understanding life that does not theoreticize it. This would be "a non-theoretical science, a genuine *primordial* science, from which the theoretical itself takes its origin".[42] Heidegger's goal is to develop a phenomenology of concrete existence – or, to borrow another bit of jargon from the title of an early lecture course, a "hermeneutics of facticity".[43]

We cannot go into the particulars of Heidegger's early work on this project, but we should pause to consider a methodological problem that is intimately connected to the issues we have been discussing: how can we philosophize or phenomenologize about life without *theorizing* about it, and thus obliterating its unique, concrete texture?[44] Isn't understanding *necessarily* theoretical? This would mean that a "non-theoretical science" is nonsense. For example, even if we describe life as "full, concrete, and historically factical", are these concepts themselves not theoretical generalizations? It appears that the concreteness of life is exactly what resists being expressed and understood.

To resolve the problem, we have to develop a new way of using concepts that Heidegger calls "formal indication". In this way of thinking and speaking,

---

39. *The Basic Problems of Phenomenology*, tr. A. Hofstadter (Bloomington, Indiana: Indiana University Press, 1982), p. 215.
40. GA 21, p. 92.
41. "Comments on Karl Jaspers's *Psychology of Worldviews*" (1919–21), tr. J. van Buren, in *Pathmarks*, W. McNeill (ed.) (Cambridge: Cambridge University Press, 1998), p. 26.
42. GA 56/57, p. 96.   43. *Ontologie (Hermeneutik der Faktizität)*, GA 63.
44. GA 56/57, pp. 100–1. For a summary of this passage, see Kisiel, *The Genesis of Heidegger's Being and Time*, p. 48.

we use concepts to *indicate* something that is already familiar to us from our own experience. "Formally indicative" concepts do not capture the essence of a thing and explain it with perfect theoretical clarity; they *allude* to a phenomenon in our lives and encourage us to live in such a way that we pay closer attention to it.[45]

For example, in 1919 Heidegger declares: "As I live in an environment, it signifies to me overall and always, it is all worldly, '*it worlds*' . . ."[46] Heidegger's listeners were struck by the phrase *es weltet*, "it worlds" or "it's worlding". But what does it mean? Obviously it is not a scientific statement. It does not clearly *explain* anything. It is an attempt to *indicate* something more basic than science – the sheer fact that we find ourselves in a meaningful world.

In English-speaking philosophy, there are two traditions that sometimes coexist peacefully and sometimes are at war – but which are both hostile to what Heidegger is trying to do. The first tradition treats philosophy as a theoretical science that ideally should be as unambiguous and certain as mathematics. Heidegger, however, claims that the theoretical way of thinking would falsify the phenomenon he is trying to think about – the pre-theoretical *roots* of theory. The second tradition is a common-sense tradition: it insists on stating things in ordinary language with everyday concepts. But Heidegger believes that ordinary language is usually misguided and shallow. We need to find seeds of illumination in ordinary language, and then use them creatively in an attempt to show what cannot be said directly. For instance, impersonal constructions such as "it's raining" and "it's thundering" can inspire a creative phrase such as "it's worlding". Readers of Heidegger have to brace themselves for many such innovations, and they may have to give up some of their preconceived notions about language and philosophy.

Wittgenstein writes at the end of his *Tractatus Logico-Philosophicus*, "What we cannot speak about we must pass over in silence".[47] Heidegger is closer to Wittgenstein on more points than one might expect, but on this point he disagrees. He might say: what we cannot speak about theoretically, we must indicate formally.

Heidegger never gave up the goal of understanding how theoretical truth is rooted in a more fundamental "unconcealment" that is central to our existence. This is one way of interpreting the main goal of *Being and Time*. But before we turn to the composition of that book, let us glimpse what it was like to study with Heidegger in the early and mid-1920s, when he was struggling towards his masterpiece.

45. For a good explanation, see *The Fundamental Concepts of Metaphysics: World, Finitude, Solitude*, tr. W. McNeill & N. Walker (Bloomington, Indiana: Indiana University Press, 1995), pp. 296–7. The expression "formal indication" is also used in several other texts of the 1920s, including *Being and Time*. For detailed references and interpretations, see Kisiel, *The Genesis of Heidegger's* Being and Time, pp. 48–59, 164–171.
46. GA 56/57, p. 73.
47. *Tractatus Logico-Philosophicus*, tr. D. F. Pears & B. F. McGuinness (London: Routledge & Kegan Paul, 1961), p. 151.

Heidegger the teacher

During his early years of teaching (at the University of Freiburg in 1919–1923 and the University of Marburg in 1923–1928) Heidegger lectured on everything from phenomenology to neo-Platonism. He also conducted intensive seminars on thinkers such as Aristotle, Aquinas, Descartes, Kant and Hegel, where he trained students to wrestle with the problems that these thinkers faced. Walter Biemel recalls:

> It sometimes happened that, in one semester, we read and tried to understand only two or three pages of a philosopher. But through these pages, which Heidegger had selected carefully, he was so able in leading us to the very core of the thinking of the philosopher we happened to be studying that we achieved greater understanding of it than some gain through years of study.[48]

As a rule, Heidegger wrote out his lectures word for word, and most are available today as volumes of his collected writings. They are composed in a highly individual voice. Heidegger rarely refers to himself in the first person, but his tone can be fiercely proud. Humor is rare, but sarcasm abounds. He has nothing but scorn for those who work within established conceptual schemes, and he is eager to awaken his students to the urgency of philosophical questioning. As Karl Löwith observes, "only one half of him was an academic. The other – and probably greater – half was a militant and preacher who knew how to interest people by antagonizing them, and whose discontent with the epoch and himself was driving him on".[49] However, Heidegger's lectures never degenerate into mere rhetoric: they pursue real problems through the thickets of challenging texts.

In the classroom, Heidegger was nothing short of electrifying. Hans-Georg Gadamer remembers, "He demonstrated a well-integrated spiritual energy laced with such a plain power of verbal expression and such a radical simplicity of questions".[50]

> What he provided was the full investment of his energy, and what brilliant energy it was. It was the energy of a revolutionary thinker who himself visibly shrank from the boldness of his increasingly radical questions and who was so filled with the passion of his thinking that he conveyed to his listeners a fascination that was not to be broken . . . Who among those who then followed him can forget the breathtaking swirl of questions that he developed in the introductory

---

48. W. Biemel, *Martin Heidegger: An Illustrated Study*, tr. J. L. Mehta (New York: Harcourt Brace Jovanovich, 1976), p. 8.
49. K. Löwith, *My Life in Germany Before and After 1933: A Report*, tr. E. King (Urbana, Illinois: University of Illinois Press, 1994), p. 28.
50. Hans-Georg Gadamer, *Philosophical Apprenticeships*, tr. R. R. Sullivan (Cambridge, Massachusetts: MIT Press, 1985), p. 19.

hours of the semester only to entangle himself in the second or third of these questions and then, in the final hours of the semester, to roll up deep-dark clouds of sentences from which the lightning flashed to leave us half stunned?[51]

Löwith, another distinguished student of Heidegger, provides a similar account:

We nicknamed Heidegger "the little magician from Messkirch" . . . His lecturing method consisted in constructing an edifice of ideas, which he himself then dismantled again so as to baffle fascinated listeners, only to leave them up in the air. This art of enchantment sometimes had the most disturbing effects in that it attracted more or less psychopathic personalities, and one female student committed suicide three years after such guessing games.[52]

Hannah Arendt, who first heard Heidegger as a gifted young woman of 18, also felt his charisma (and fortunately did not commit suicide):

People followed the rumor about Heidegger in order to learn thinking. What was experienced was that thinking as pure activity . . . can become a passion which not so much rules and oppresses all other capacities and gifts, as it orders them and prevails through them. We are so accustomed to the old opposition of reason versus passion, spirit versus life, that the idea of a *passionate* thinking, in which thinking and aliveness become one, takes us somewhat aback.[53]

For Arendt and Heidegger, the passion was to involve more than thinking: in 1925 they entered into an affair that was to last until around 1930. Arendt was repelled by Heidegger's behavior in 1933–34, when he served as the National Socialist rector of the University of Freiburg. But the two resumed a friendship after the war, and Arendt was instrumental in publishing Heidegger's works in translation in the United States. Her own philosophy shows the influence of Heidegger's thought.[54]

Heidegger made an impact not only on his students, but on his colleagues. These included important theologians such as Paul Tillich and Rudolf Bultmann, who adopted much of Heidegger's language in order to discuss religious experience.

Every aspect of Heidegger's personality was distinctive – from his ideas to his clothing. Early on, he adopted a peculiar way of dressing, known to his

51. *Ibid.*, p. 48 (translation modified).
52. Löwith, *My Life in Germany Before and After 1933*, pp. 44–5.
53. H. Arendt, "Martin Heidegger at 80", in *Heidegger and Modern Philosophy*, M. Murray (ed.) (New Haven, Connecticut: Yale University Press, 1978), p. 297.
54. On the personal relationship between the two thinkers, see E. Ettinger, *Hannah Arendt/ Martin Heidegger* (New Haven, Connecticut: Yale University Press, 1995). An excellent work on their intellectual relationship is D. Villa, *Heidegger and Arendt: The Fate of the Political* (Princeton, New Jersey: Princeton University Press, 1996).

students as "the existential outfit". Gadamer writes, "It was a piece of clothing designed by the painter Otto Ubbelohde, one that tended slightly to a rural folk style, and in it Heidegger in fact had something of the modest magnificence of a farmer dressed up for Sunday."[55] Löwith sees in it something more sinister:

> He wore a kind of Black Forest farmer's jacket with broad lapels and a semi-militaristic collar, and knee-length breeches, both made from dark-brown cloth . . . [it] amused us then, but at that time we did not recognize it as a peculiar temporary compromise between the conventional suit and the uniform of the SA [Hitler's storm troops].[56]

Heidegger naturally attracted imitators. Students who mimicked Heidegger's passionate tones were said to be "Heideggerized".[57] Heideggerization continues to this day, even though Heidegger himself always tried to encourage independent thought. It seems that philosophers who want no following always attract followers. As Gadamer puts it, "Moths fly into the light".[58]

Towards *Being and Time*

Heidegger published nothing between his *Habilitationsschrift* (1916) and *Being and Time* (1927). Husserl described the situation well: this "highly original personality" "does not want to publish yet", because he is still "struggling, searching for himself and laboriously shaping his own unique style".[59] But although Heidegger's thoughts were not in print, he was writing and lecturing at an intense pace.

The recently discovered 1922 essay "Phenomenological Interpretations with Respect to Aristotle: Indication of the Hermeneutical Situation"[60] was meant as an introduction to a projected book that would present a phenomenological reading of Aristotle. It is not primarily about Aristotle, but about Heidegger's own approach to the human condition. Heidegger sent the essay to Paul Natorp at the University of Marburg, and on the strength of this piece Heidegger secured a teaching position there in 1923. This document reflects the fact that Heidegger's rereading of ancient philosophy played an invaluable role in his own development; as I have pointed out, history of philosophy and systematic thought are always intertwined for Heidegger. The text is as cumbersome and jargon-laden as its title. What makes it so important is that it is the first statement of several crucial themes of *Being and Time*, including the distinction

55. Gadamer, *Philosophical Apprenticeships*, p. 49.
56. Löwith, *My Life in Germany Before and After 1933*, p. 45.
57. Gadamer, *Philosophical Apprenticeships*, p. 46.   58. *Ibid.*, p. 50.
59. Letter from Husserl to Natorp, February 1, 1922, quoted in Kisiel, *The Genesis of Heidegger's* Being and Time, pp. 248–9.
60. "Phenomenological Interpretations with Respect to Aristotle: Indication of the Hermeneutical Situation", tr. M. Baur, *Man and World* **25**, 1992, pp. 355–93.

between authentic and inauthentic existence and the project of deconstructing the history of metaphysics.

Another landmark is the lecture "The Concept of Time" (1924).[61] It can be recommended to beginners as an introduction to Heidegger's views on the difference between the temporality of human existence and time as conceived in natural science.

According to Theodore Kisiel, we can distinguish three separate stages in the composition of *Being and Time* itself.[62] In the final product, these stages blend into each other almost seamlessly. Heidegger's first efforts focused on the historical character of human existence; naturally enough, he borrowed heavily from Dilthey. The second draft oriented the book towards the question of Being in general, and gave it a Husserlian, phenomenological emphasis.[63] The third draft focused on time; now Heidegger, who had recently been delving into Kant's *Critique of Pure Reason*, gave the book some Kantian twists. Although Heidegger has often been called an existentialist, most of the language of "existence" was added to his book only in this final draft. *Existenzphilosophie* had been afoot in Germany ever since the publication of his friend Karl Jaspers' *Psychology of Worldviews* in 1919, but Heidegger was always reluctant to associate himself with the trend. We will discuss this topic further in Chapter 5.

Composing *Being and Time* was an arduous task, but the motto "publish or perish" applied as well in the Germany of the 1920s as it does today. Heidegger came under increasing pressure to get his work into print. In January 1926, authorities in Berlin rejected the University of Marburg's proposal to grant Heidegger a tenured full professorship, in view of his "not very large literary accomplishments".[64] In a burst of activity in March 1926, he managed to complete most of the first two divisions of the first part of a work intended to have two parts, of three divisions each. In June, the university renewed its request to appoint Heidegger to a chair in philosophy – and in November, the Berlin bureaucracy renewed its rejection. Meanwhile, the completed portions of *Being and Time* were going to press. They finally appeared in April 1927, as part of the *Yearbook for Philosophy and Phenomenological Research*, edited by Husserl, and also as a separate work.

Being and Time instantly attracted attention. Heidegger's reputation grew far beyond his former cult following; he suddenly attained international renown, and his professional worries were gone. In 1928, he was crowned with one of the greatest honors for which a phenomenologist could hope – he was invited back to Freiburg to occupy the chair in philosophy formerly held by the now-retired Husserl.

61. *The Concept of Time*, bilingual edn, tr. W. McNeill (Oxford: Blackwell, 1992).
62. Kisiel summarizes his account in *The Genesis of Heidegger's* Being and Time, pp. 311–14.
63. This draft was delivered as the lecture course *History of the Concept of Time.*
64. "Vorschläge für die Wiederbesetzung des Ordinariates für Philosophie", Hessisches Staatsarchiv Marburg, *Akten*, Accession 1966/10, 95; quoted in Kisiel, *The Genesis of Heidegger's* Being and Time, p. 480.

CHAPTER THREE

Being and Time:
Introduction and Division I

A few bibliographical notes are needed before we plunge into Heidegger's magnum opus. Two translations of *Being and Time* are available.[1] Both can be recommended, as both are faithful to the German and both include extensive, helpful indexes. It is often worth consulting both translations when one is reading a passage closely. The Macquarrie and Robinson translation is very well known, and usually very accurate and literal. It captures some subtle distinctions that the Stambaugh translation does not (for example, the difference between *Zeitlichkeit* and *Temporalität*, rendered by Macquarrie and Robinson as "temporality" and "Temporality"). Macquarrie and Robinson include many explanatory footnotes of their own, which are often quite helpful, and a German–English glossary; Stambaugh's version does not have these features. However, the Stambaugh translation is often more readable, improves the translations of some key words, corrects some errors, and includes the marginal notes that Heidegger made in his personal copy of the book (these notes are brief, and of limited use to beginners).[2] Below I will quote the Macquarrie and Robinson translation, but I will note Stambaugh's alternative translations of important terms. References to *Being and Time* in Chapters 3 and 4 will be parenthesized. They include, first, the Macquarrie and Robinson pages, and then, the pages of the later German editions of *Sein und Zeit*, published by Max Niemeyer.[3] The

1. *Being and Time*, tr. J. Macquarrie & E. Robinson (New York: Harper & Row, 1962); *Being and Time*, tr. J. Stambaugh (Albany, New York: State University of New York Press, 1996).
2. Only a few outright errors in the Macquarrie and Robinson translation are worth noting. Page 87 of the translation, lines 18–19, "the less one presupposes when one believes that one is making headway" should read, "the more one believes that one is proceeding without presuppositions". Page 247, line 35, "change and performance" should read "change and permanence". Page 256, line 1, "entities are of Dasein's kind of Being" should read, "there are entities with Dasein's kind of Being".
3. *Sein und Zeit* (Tübingen: Max Niemeyer Verlag). The seventh edition (1953) establishes the pagination for all later editions, which are essentially reprints of the seventh. The fourteenth edition (1977) is the first to include Heidegger's marginal notes.

Niemeyer page numbers are provided in the margins of both English translations and the *Gesamtausgabe* edition.

My commentary is designed to be read along with Heidegger's original text. When neither *Being and Time* nor this commentary sheds light on the issues, perhaps the reader's next recourse should be some of Heidegger's other writings. The lecture courses *History of the Concept of Time* and *The Basic Problems of Phenomenology* are closely related to *Being and Time*, and it is a good idea to consult them for their alternative formulations and added examples. Other secondary literature devoted specifically to *Being and Time* includes the works by Dreyfus, Gelven, Kaelin, Kockelmans, Mulhall and Schmitt listed in Part III of my bibliography.

The problem and the goal

In his Introduction, Heidegger wants to persuade us that the question of Being is meaningful and important, and he wants to get clear about how to ask and pursue such a difficult question in the right way. Since this opening part of the book is indispensable and especially challenging, we will review it more thoroughly than some of the subsequent chapters.

Being and Time begins with a quotation from Plato's *Sophist*: "For manifestly you have long been aware of what you mean when you use the expression *'being'*. We, however, who used to think we understood it, have now become perplexed" (19/1).[4] Heidegger's choice of this passage tells us, first, that he intends to bring an ancient question back to life. Secondly, the problem of Being seems at first to be no problem at all – but when we actually try to articulate what we mean by "be", we soon find ourselves at a loss for words. The challenge facing Plato, Heidegger and us is to overcome our natural sense that we already understand it all. Nothing could be more familiar than our phrases, "there *is* . . .", "there *are* . . .". But this familiarity with Being is no excuse to avoid philosophical thought – it is an *opportunity* for thought. Our familiarity with Being is itself mysterious, and calls for close scrutiny. In the course of this book, Heidegger will look very closely at our tendency to take things for granted, and at the rare moments when we resist this tendency. His first job is to snap us out of our tendency to take Being for granted, and wake us up to the *"question of the meaning of Being"* (19/1).

What does Heidegger mean by "meaning" (*Sinn*)? This question turns out to be difficult, and he will not be able to discuss "meaning" directly until §32 (192–4/151–2; see also 370–2/324–5). We can anticipate his discussion by

4. Macquarrie and Robinson's "being" translates Heidegger's *seiend*, which in turn translates the Greek *on*, the neuter present participle of *einai*, "to be". *On* is often ambiguous between "that which is" and "what it means to be". Heidegger tells us that Western metaphysics has suffered from failing to distinguish clearly between the two. Cf. Heidegger, *Plato's Sophist*, pp. 309–10.

saying that if something "has meaning" for us, we understand that thing. To ask "what is the meaning of x?" is to try to reveal x itself, to understand it. However, in order to understand something we must have the proper *context* for it. Heidegger refers to such a context as a "horizon". For instance, in a foreign country I may ask, "What is the meaning of that gesture?" A native explains that it means that some item is too expensive. Now I can place the gesture within the horizon of the activity of buying things, and the gesture is revealed to me – I understand it.

When things have meaning, they are somehow revealed as relevant to our lives, as playing a role in our world, as making a difference to us. This is particularly clear when we use the word "meaning" in an emphatic sense, as when I say that an unexpected visit from a long-lost friend was very meaningful; the visit stood out as prominent, it revealed itself intensely to me, because it touched on a dimension of my life that is important to who I am. But strictly speaking, *everything* we encounter is meaningful to us, to some degree. Even a piece of trash that I briefly spot out of the corner of my eye has meaning for me – otherwise I would not have noticed it at all.

When we ask, "What is the meaning of Being?" then, we are trying to enhance our understanding of Being itself (193/152). Being plays a role in our lives, but we understand it only darkly and vaguely. In order to reveal Being more clearly, we have to place it within the appropriate context, or horizon. Now Heidegger explains the title of his book: "Our provisional aim is the Interpretation of *time* as the possible horizon for any understanding whatever of Being" (19/1). That is, Heidegger is proposing that Being has to be grasped *in terms of time*: our sense of what it is to be must depend on temporality. Of course, at this point we do not know what the proper interpretation of time is, either – but at least Heidegger has given us a rough indication of his goal.

Does Heidegger reach this goal? Let us turn to the very last sentence of the book: "Does *time* itself manifest itself as the horizon of *Being*?" (488/437). After hundreds of pages, Heidegger sounds more tentative than he did at the start! The fact is that *Being and Time* is a fragment, a dead end, a "woodpath" that never makes it out of the woods. Heidegger will never show to his satisfaction that time is the horizon of Being. But some of us appreciate a good question at least as much as a good answer, and along the way to the dead end, there is so much to discover in the woods . . .

§1: The mystery of Being

And when I said that the proposition *I think, therefore I am* is the first and most certain of all to occur to anyone who philosophizes in an orderly way, I did not in saying that deny that one must first know what thought, existence and certainty are . . . But because these are very simple notions, and ones which on their own provide us with no knowledge of anything that exists, I did not think they needed to be listed. — Descartes[5]

The more the wise person thinks about the simple (that there can be any question of a longer preoccupation with it already shows that it is not so easy after all), the more difficult it becomes for him. — Kierkegaard[6]

Most of us are likely to agree with Descartes: what it means to be, to exist, is so obvious that it is hardly worth discussing. ("Exist" will have a technical sense in Heidegger's book, but for the moment we will use it as an everyday synonym for "be".) When we say something "has Being", it seems all we mean is that it exists, it is there, it is real, it is an actual thing instead of nothing. What else is there to say? Should we really waste our time studying the "meaning of Being"? Shouldn't we turn instead to questions about *beings*, concrete things that actually exist? Let's devote our energies to determining what there is and what we can know about it – one might insist.

This is the kind of prejudice that Heidegger combats in §1. Many details of his discussion will be clear only to readers who know something about Aristotelian and medieval metaphysics. Throughout the book, Heidegger writes for an audience that has received an education in the history of philosophy as thorough as his own. The good news for those of us who have not is that one can appreciate Heidegger's most important ideas without this kind of background knowledge. However, as one's knowledge of other philosophers grows, one's understanding of Heidegger will be enriched – and vice versa.

If we leave aside the references to traditional metaphysics, the most important lesson to be learned from §1 is that Heidegger agrees with Kant that "the 'self-evident' . . . is 'the business of the philosophers' " (23–24/4). One might suppose that the business of a philosopher is to begin with the obvious and build upon it, eventually reaching remote and unfamiliar territory. But for Heidegger, we have to begin with familiar territory and *stay* on it. The closer we look at it, the more we realize how surprising and difficult it is. Nothing could be more obvious than Being – and nothing could be harder to clarify. Heidegger wants to evoke a sense of surprise, or even shock, at what we take to be self-evident.

Section 1 is also a good place to begin observing the wide range of contexts in which the word "Being" can be used. For instance, "I *am* merry" seems to count as a case of our understanding of Being (23/4). In this sentence, "am" serves as a *copula*, connecting the subject "I" and the qualifier "merry". It is a commonplace in contemporary philosophy (and in symbolic logic) to distinguish this use of "be" from the *existential* use, as in the assertion "I am".

5. R. Descartes, *Principles of Philosophy*, in *Selected Philosophical Writings*, tr. J. Cottingham et al. (Cambridge: Cambridge University Press, 1988), p. 163 (translation modified).
6. S. Kierkegaard, *Concluding Unscientific Postscript to* Philosophical Fragments, vol. 1, tr. H. V. Hong & E. H. Hong (Princeton, New Jersey: Princeton University Press, 1992), p. 160.

The copula does not seem to imply any existential claims: for instance, if I say, "Unicorns *are* white", I certainly do not mean to imply that unicorns *are*, that is, exist. A third use of "be" is found in claims of *identity*, such as "The moon *is* Earth's natural satellite".

But it seems that Heidegger is not making any such distinctions. Is his project hopelessly confused from the start, then? Is the "question of Being" just a mystification based on the peculiarities of Indo-European languages? After all, many languages dispense with the luxury of a copula.

In response, Heidegger might say that these distinctions among senses of "be", which seem so self-evident, are worth rethinking. A complex history lies behind them. One way we can call these distinctions into question is by noticing that even an assertion about unicorns draws our attention to *something* that exists (not an animal, of course, but a myth, image or concept). Even a round square involves existence (the existence of a contradictory pair of concepts, not of a geometrical figure). Unicorns, round squares, the Last Judgment, Napoleon – all must involve existence, in *some* sense, in order for us to discuss them.[7] The sense of "be" as "exist" may be so fundamental that it is presupposed in any other sense of "be". Of course, at this point, all this is pure speculation – but it invites us to *ask* the question of the meaning of Being, and not to dismiss it out of hand.

It is also important to see that Heidegger is not just asking about the *word* "Being", or *Sein*. Language is important to Heidegger, especially in his later thought – but the question of Being is not just a question about language. Being is obscurely manifest to us not only when we utter words such as "is" and "am", but also "in any way of comporting oneself toward entities as entities" (23/4). A Chinese garment worker, in whose language subject and predicate can be connected without a copula, still understands Being in every sentence she uses, because her sentences are about entities, beings, things that *are*. "In each use of a verb we have already thought, and have always in some way understood, Being."[8] Even when the Chinese woman is not speaking at all, but just working at her sewing machine, she understands what it is for the machine, the garments and herself to *be*. These entities, and countless others, are available to her as entities, as things that matter to her, as items that are meaningful and real in her world. So although she does not have a word that precisely parallels the German *Sein*, and although she has never read Thomas Aquinas, she has an understanding of Being. For her, as for all of us, this understanding works perfectly well in the background of everyday life – but it slips away as soon as we try to look at it head-on.

7. For the history of philosophical thought on the copula see *The Basic Problems of Phenomenology*, Part I, Chapter 4. Heidegger makes the point I have just made when he argues against J. S. Mill on p. 204.

8. *The Basic Problems of Phenomenology*, p. 14. (In this citation and in some other citations throughout this book, I have slightly modified the translations in order to conform to the usage of the Macquarrie and Robinson translation of *Being and Time*.)

§2: Ourselves as the starting point

"How much is this typewriter?" I've spotted an antique typewriter at a flea market. I am *interrogating* the seller. I am asking *about* the typewriter. What I want to *find out* is its price. Before I could ask this question, I had to have some *familiarity* with typewriters, purchasing and flea markets.

"What is the meaning of Being?" A more daunting question! But perhaps it follows the pattern set by more ordinary ones. First, "every seeking gets guided beforehand by what is sought" (24/5). Before we can ask the question of Being, we must have some *familiarity* with Being. As we have seen, we do have what Heidegger calls a "vague average understanding of Being" (25/5–6). Rough and distorted though it may be, it allows us to ask our question.

Next, we must have something we are asking *about*. That is easy enough: *Being*. We must also have something we are trying to *find out*. That is easy too: the *meaning* of Being. Of course, as I pointed out above, to look for the meaning of Being is just to try to find the right context that will clarify Being itself. It seems that so far, we have not really made any progress. But at this point, Heidegger does make an important observation. Asking about Being is not like asking about a typewriter – because it is not a question about any *entity* at all. Being is "that which determines entities as entities, that on the basis of which entities are already understood . . . The Being of entities 'is' not itself an entity" (25–6/6). Heidegger sometimes refers to the difference between Being and entities as *the ontological difference.*[9] It is not an easy matter to grasp. But roughly, when we ask about Being we are not asking about any particular thing, nor even about the totality of things in the universe; we are asking why all these things count as *beings* in the first place. This makes our question unusual indeed. We are asking about a "thing" that is no thing at all. We must never make the mistake of confusing Being with a particular entity: not ourselves, not the universe, not even God.

But let's return to the formal structure of our question. We can expect our question to have one more element: we must *interrogate* something in order to get the answer. Very well, let's interrogate *entities* about their Being (what else *is* there?). But which entities? Planets? Atoms? Books? How can we possibly choose a particular entity to interrogate, when Being characterizes *every* entity whatsoever?

Heidegger now makes a crucial suggestion: we should begin by interrogating the entities who are capable of the act of interrogation – namely, *ourselves*. At this point Heidegger does not presume to have *proved* that this is the right way to begin (28/8); he will present a more complete argument in §4. But he does propose, reasonably enough, that in order to clarify the question we are asking, we ought to clarify our own Being as questioners (26–7/7). With this move, he embarks on the main project of the finished portion of *Being and Time*: the explication of our own way of Being.

9. E.g. *The Basic Problems of Phenomenology*, pp. 17, 319.

For some critics, this move makes *Being and Time* overly anthropocentric. Others are glad that Heidegger seemingly avoids the heights of ontological speculation to discuss our own, human lives. But it is important to see that Heidegger has not abandoned the general question of the meaning of Being; he just thinks that the question can best be understood if we understand ourselves as questioners. He is not confusing humans with Being itself – but he is interested in us *insofar as we have an understanding of Being* (and can thus raise the question of Being). This means that he is not concerned with producing a complete anthropology, an investigation of *all* aspects of the human species. Certain facets of our existence will be irrelevant to Heidegger's project (38/17, 170/131). For instance, he has nothing to say about our responsiveness to music. He would presumably claim that such things have little to do with our understanding of Being – although we may disagree.

We can now consider some central Heideggerian terminology. First, note that Heidegger speaks of investigating our own Being (27/7). It would be more conventional to speak of our *nature* or our *essence*, rather than our Being. In fact, we usually distinguish between the nature of something (its essence) and its Being (its existence). A dragon can be defined in its essence as a large, fire-breathing reptile; its existence is another matter altogether. But Heidegger treats both of these issues as issues about Being. Of course, he is well aware of the usual distinction, which he often calls the difference between "what-Being" (what something is) and "that-Being" (the fact that something is). But this is another traditional distinction that needs to be reconsidered and can be called into question.[10] Maybe the "that-Being" and the "what-Being" are not so distinct, after all. The particular difference it makes that there is an entity rather than nothing (the meaning of the entity's existence) may be linked to what *type* of entity it is (its essence). Maybe what it means to exist for an entity with the nature of a rock is very different from what it means to exist for an entity with the nature of a person. Rocks and humans may have different ways of being *present*, of being *there*.

This brings us to Heidegger's most important terminological innovation – the expression *Dasein*. This word is usually left untranslated. In everyday German it parallels our word "existence", but etymologically it means "Being-there". (Stambaugh, following Heidegger's instructions for future translations, hyphenates the word. The spelling "Da-sein" emphasizes the root meaning.) Heidegger uses this term to refer to us, the entities who have an understanding of Being.

Why not just use the word "man" or "human beings"? In general, Heidegger doubtlessly wants to avoid the tired old term "man" and invent a new usage, in order to get us to look at ourselves with fresh eyes. We are to conceive of ourselves in new ways, and challenge the prejudices of millennia of philosophy, psychology and anthropology. Why "Dasein" in particular, then? When he first introduces the word "Dasein" (27/7) Heidegger gives no explanation of why he has chosen it, but his reasons appear, directly or indirectly, as the text goes on:

10. For one extended discussion, see *The Basic Problems of Phenomenology*, pp. 77–121.

(a) We should notice that this noun Heidegger uses to designate us is the infinitive form of a *verb*. This suggests that what is distinctive about us is something more like an activity or process than like any sort of *thing*.

(b) It is not just *any* activity or process that characterizes us, but a way of *Being*. Our sort of Being, our mode of existing, is what marks us out. As I just suggested, our way of existing is qualitatively different from the way in which a rock exists. As Heidegger will shortly put it, the term Dasein is "purely an expression of [our way of] Being" (33/12). Dasein's "Being-what-it-is (*essentia*) must . . . be conceived in terms of its Being (*existentia*)" (67/42). Thus, Dasein is "a very specific expression of Being which is here chosen for an entity, whereas [normally we] name an entity in terms of its what-content and leave its specific Being undetermined, because we hold it to be self-evident".[11]

(c) *Which* way of Being distinguishes us? Being *there*. Of course, a rock is "there" in the sense that it has a spatial location. But we are "there" in a much richer sense: we inhabit a world, we are capably engaged in a meaningful context. It makes a difference to me that I am climbing this mountain, in this country, in this year – but to the mountain it makes no difference at all where or when it exists, because it is oblivious to all beings. We have a "there" as no other entity does, because for us, the world is *understandable*. Much of *Being and Time* will be devoted to exploring this phenomenon.

(d) Furthermore, we are "Being there" in the sense that Dasein "*is* in such a way as to be its 'there' " (171/133) – an odd assertion, and one that we will be prepared to absorb only when we have looked more closely at the concept of a world. But to anticipate the results of Heidegger's investigation, it is not just that we *happen* to be in a world, a "there" – rather, our "there" is so essential to us that we would be nothing at all without it. Conversely, it would be nothing without us. The world of Germany in 1927, for instance, as this particular world with all its meaning and structure, could not be what it was without the Germans of 1927; conversely, the Germans of 1927 would not have been who they were without that world. Our world is the context in terms of which we understand ourselves, and within which we become who we are. As José Ortega y Gasset puts it, "I am myself plus my circumstance".[12]

(e) There is one more sense of "Dasein", a sense that Heidegger stresses in his later work: we are the "there" *of* or *for* Being.[13] In other words, we are the site that Being requires in order (literally) to *take place*. Without Dasein, other entities could continue to be, but there would be no one to relate to them as entities. Their *Being* would have no meaning at all.

To review: in order to discover the meaning of Being in general, we are going to look at our own way of Being, Dasein's way of Being. We can

11. *History of the Concept of Time*, p. 153.
12. J. Ortega y Gasset, *Meditations on Quixote*, tr. E. Rugg & D. Marín (New York: W. W. Norton, 1961), p. 45.
13. "Letter on Humanism", in *Basic Writings*, pp. 229, 231.

tentatively say that what is distinctive about Dasein is the way it exists, the way it is enmeshed in its world, its "there". Our existence in a "there" somehow implies an understanding of Being – and allows us to raise questions about Being, as Heidegger is now doing.

At this point, Heidegger considers an objection that strikes at the heart of his method (27/7). We are trying to understand Being by examining Dasein – but how can we grasp Dasein's *particular* way of Being unless we *already* understand Being *in general?* Heidegger's entire project seems circular.

Throughout *Being and Time*, Heidegger is in dialogue with objections that he poses to himself. This particular objection is a persistent one; he will raise it again on 194–5/152–3 and 362–3/314–15. In fact, this type of objection is fundamental, because it can be raised against any philosophical quest. In Plato's *Meno*, for instance, the impatient Meno tires of trying to discover what virtue is. "How will you look for it, Socrates, when you do not know at all what it is? . . . If you should meet with it, how will you know that this is the thing that you did not know?"[14] The trouble is that in order to search for something, you must already be acquainted with that for which you are searching.

Socrates answers Meno with a myth: he tells him that we knew all things before we were born, and now we are just trying to remember them. The truth in this myth is that we can know something vaguely without knowing it clearly. When we philosophize, we try to get a clear understanding of something that is already vaguely familiar. This is exactly what Heidegger is doing when he asks the question of the meaning of Being. Thus, on the basis of a vague understanding of Being in general, we will clarify our understanding of our own Being and use this understanding, in turn, to clarify our understanding of Being in general.

Although in §2 Heidegger claims "there is no circle at all" in his approach (27/7), he is more accurate when he says that although there *is* a circle, it is not a vicious circle (194/153). The important thing "is not to get out of the circle but to come into it in the right way" (195/153), "to leap into the 'circle' " (363/315). The circle would be sterile and vicious if Heidegger began by setting down a definition of Being at large, or of our own Being, and then used the definition to prove dogmatic claims. Instead, he will begin with a general account of Dasein's Being which he will then *refine and reinterpret* in the course of his investigation. He constantly returns to his previous descriptions and reconceives them, trying to make them more accurate and nuanced. We can thus think of *Being and Time* as having a *spiral* structure: each turn around the "circle" reaches a deeper level.

Since the question of circular reasoning leads to the question of how human understanding in general works, we will revisit this issue when we have gone farther into Heidegger's account of Dasein.

14. Plato, *Meno*, tr. G. M. A. Grube, 2nd edn (Indianapolis, Indiana: Hackett, 1981), p. 13 (80d).

§3: Being and the sciences

There is a science that investigates being as being and what pertains intrinsically to it. It is not the same as any of the so-called special sciences. For none of those sciences examines being as being in general; instead, each of them separates out some part of it and investigates the attributes of that part. — Aristotle[15]

A course in philosophy will not satisfy the science requirements of any university. Ask scientists whether they use philosophy in their work, and you are very likely to get some variety of "no". But according to Aristotle – and Husserl, and Heidegger in *Being and Time* – philosophy is rightfully the queen of the sciences, if it correctly carries out the task of investigating Being.

What is supposed to give philosophy this prerogative? According to Heidegger, scientists who study a certain field have to presuppose certain things about the Being of the entities they are studying. (Here we are using the word "Being" where we might also use "nature" or "essence".) It falls to philosophy to develop the particular ontology of a field, an account of the Being of a particular class of entities, in the light of general ontology, or an account of Being as such.

A distinguished physicist once gave a lecture at the University of Chicago in which he claimed that physics had greatly refined its concept of time by measuring time in smaller and smaller increments. A listener objected that although physicists were measuring changes more accurately, this did not alter our *concept* of time, or shed light on the *nature* of time. "What is time itself?" the physicist was asked. He answered honestly: "Well, I'm not a philosopher." Physicists *take it for granted* that time, space, matter and energy exist, and have a certain way of Being. Physics as such does not try to clarify the Being of such entities – that task falls to philosophy. In this sense, philosophy is more fundamental than physics.

The same can be said of other sciences, sciences that study "for instance, history . . . life . . . language" (29/9). History takes it for granted that the past, in some sense, exists. It falls to philosophy to clarify the sense in which the past exists, in the light of the meaning of Being in general. Even if theology does not assume the existence of God, it takes it for granted that religious experience exists. Literary criticism assumes that literary texts exist – and so on. (Of course, literary critics *can* ask about the Being of what they study – but then they are doing philosophy, not literary criticism. The same can be said of other researchers.)

But why *bother* to raise the ontological question, the question of Being? Heidegger (like Husserl) holds that the sciences are experiencing a "crisis in [their] basic concepts" (29/9). He views the capacity to experience such a crisis as a sign of health in a field: it means that instead of just collecting data, researchers are beginning to wonder about their fundamental approaches to

---

15. *Metaphysics IV*, 1. I have translated *on* as "being", as Macquarrie and Robinson do in the passage from Plato's *Sophist* in *Being and Time*, p. 19/1. It is debatable whether Aristotle is asking about *Being* in Heidegger's sense, or about *beings* in general.

what they study. The only adequate basis for rethinking the Being of the entities studied by the various disciplines is a philosophical reflection on the question of Being in general. This means that the question of Being is much more than idle speculation.

One might object that scientific observation itself, not philosophizing, will give us the adequate concepts we need; all we have to do is gather more accurate information. But most historians of science and philosophers of science now recognize that the process of gathering information is always guided by certain presuppositions, and that those presuppositions will not be changed just by the accumulation of more facts. It takes a *revolution* to change them. As Heidegger remarks, scientists often prefer to ignore the conceptual foundations of what they do, because "it is too uncomfortable to sit on a powder keg, knowing that the basic concepts are just well-worn opinions".[16]

A philosophical inquiry into Being can have an impact not only on the concepts scientists use, but on the *method* they follow, for the proper method of a science depends on the Being of the entities it studies (30/10, cf. 350/303). Proper procedure in chemistry is not proper procedure in sociology, because the different things being investigated call for different approaches. It is wrong-headed to insist that there is a single scientific method or a single standard of accuracy for all the sciences (as Descartes does, and many fans of the "hard sciences" do today). Heidegger's aversion to rigid methodology is a constant in his writings.[17]

Of course, *Being and Time* was not completed, and Heidegger did not lay a new foundation for all the sciences. However, his work did eventually affect many people's understanding of the basic characteristics of certain domains of entities, including human beings, nature, art and the divine.

§4: Being and human existence

Most of us are not scientists, and not even all scientists care about the conceptual basis of science. But in §4 Heidegger claims that beyond the importance of the question of Being for science (its "ontological priority") it has an "ontical priority" for us: it is inescapably relevant to all human beings, given the kind of entities that we are. We simply *cannot help* being involved in the question of Being, like it or not. The philosophical inquiry into Being is just the "radicalization" of our prior engagement with Being (35/15). Since we are the entities who always have a special relation to Being, it is reasonable to begin our inquiry by interrogating ourselves (35/14), as Heidegger first proposed in §2.

16. *The Basic Problems of Phenomenology*, p. 54. In some respects, Heidegger's approach anticipates Thomas Kuhn's *The Structure of Scientific Revolutions* (Chicago, Illinois: University of Chicago Press, 1962). Kuhn argues that scientific revolutions are never brought on merely by new experimental data. They involve a crisis of confidence that precipitates a "paradigm shift", in which scientists start *thinking* and *researching* differently.
17. Heidegger's student Hans-Georg Gadamer was to develop this theme in *Truth and Method* (1960).

Heidegger's discussion in §4 is extremely important, but it is loaded with technical terms. We will first consider some facts about human life in everyday language, and then review the technical terms.

First of all, I am responsible for my own life. At every moment, I am following one possibility rather than a host of others – for instance, I go to the university today and teach my class, rather than joining the Army or shoplifting. Sometimes I choose carefully, but usually I just let myself fall into the most comfortable option. As I go on living, I build an identity. I become myself; I define myself as a professor, rather than a soldier or criminal. In this way, it matters to me who I am. Bugs and trees, in contrast, simply are what they are. They cannot have identity crises, because they do not need to determine their own existence.

As I live my life, I gain an understanding of who I am and what my possibilities are. Maybe I never put this understanding into words, but my life still makes sense to me. I am also necessarily aware of the world in which I operate. If I understand what it is to be a professor, I also understand what a university is, and how one gets to it, and what one can expect to find there. So I understand not only myself, but also the various kind of things and people I encounter around me in the process of being myself: students, colleagues, buildings, books, plants, roads. All these items have meaning for me.

Now let's review some terminology Heidegger uses in this section.

- *Ontology* is a philosophical investigation of Being.
- *Ontological* means pertaining to Being.
- *Ontical* means pertaining to particular facts about entities, without regard to their Being. For example, "How old is the sun?" is an ontical question, while "What is the way of Being of stars?" is an ontological question. Ontical questions stand a chance of being answered by experimental science, but ontological questions call for philosophy.
- *Existence* will be reserved from now on to denote Dasein's special way of Being, a way of Being in which *Dasein's own Being "is an issue" for it.* To anticipate somewhat, we can say that "existence" is appropriate as a name for our Being because we *ek-sist* in the etymological sense: we *stand out* into future possibilities, into a past heritage, and into a present world. Unlike rocks, we are not encapsulated in a present moment and position – we essentially reach out from ourselves. Because we do so, other beings matter to us, and our own Being matters to us as well.[18] Towards the end of Division I and in Division II, Heidegger will use "existence" and related terms primarily to designate the *futural* aspect of our Being (235/191, 274/231). This makes sense, because if we did not have the opportunity to choose future possible ways of Being, our Being could not be an issue for us.

18. On Dasein's temporality as "ecstatical", see *Being and Time*, p. 377/329. In *Being and Time*, ecstatical temporality is not explicitly linked to the term "existence". Heidegger discusses "ek-sistence" in "Letter on Humanism", in *Basic Writings*, pp. 229–34.

- *Existential* means pertaining to existence, that is, Dasein's way of Being. Existential analysis is a kind of ontology – it is an investigation of our Being. "How does Dasein relate to its future?" is an example of an existential question.
- *Existentiell* means pertaining to some individual Dasein's own existence. For instance, "Should I apply to medical school?" is an existentiell question. We all have an existentiell understanding of ourselves, which we gain simply by living. Often this existentiell understanding is defective, usually we are only partially aware of it, and it rarely turns into an *existential* understanding of human Being in general (in other words, it is *pre-ontological*). But having an existentiell understanding is a prerequisite for developing an ontology of Dasein.

To apply this terminology to the example presented above: since I *exist*, in Heidegger's sense, my Being is *an issue* for me. I have to determine my Being, I have to take a stance on who I am – and I do so by acting as a professor. In order to exist as a professor, I have to inhabit a world where I encounter all sorts of other entities (universities, books and much more). I thus have an understanding not only of my own Being, but of the Being of all the other entities in my world, because they, so to speak, are part of the game I am playing. I understand what it means for me and other entities to be. As Heidegger puts it,

> to Dasein, Being in a world is something that belongs essentially. Thus Dasein's understanding of Being pertains with equal primordiality both to an understanding of something like a 'world', and to the understanding of the Being of those entities which become accessible within the world (33/13).

Because we have to determine who we are by acting within a world, we are Dasein – the entity who "possesses – as constitutive for its understanding of existence – an understanding of the Being of all entities of a character other than its own" (34/13).

Of course, my understanding of myself and other entities is, to begin with, *existentiell*: I do not have any explicit theories about Being, but I simply am competent to exist and to deal with various kinds of entities. This competence involves an implicit understanding of Being. If I choose to make this understanding explicit, I can develop an *ontology*, a philosophical account of Being.

In §4, Heidegger is giving us a very condensed presentation of phenomena that he will have to revisit in much greater detail. This is his first time around the circle, and it will be deepened with each new turn. But by the end of this section, he has made at least one thing clear: the question of Being is built into our very existence.

§§5, 6 and 8: The plan of *Being and Time*

Sections 5 and 6 give the details of Heidegger's plan for *Being and Time*. Before reading these sections one should look at the brief §8 (63–4/39–40), where Heidegger summarizes his plan, breaking the work into Parts and Divisions.

Part One, Division I will explore how we *are in the world*, and it will do so primarily by analyzing Dasein in its "everydayness", as it exists "proximally and for the most part" (Stambaugh: "initially and for the most part") (37–8/16). Heidegger cannot explain these terms precisely until 421–2/370. But to put it roughly, he will be describing basic patterns of normal human existence, as it usually manifests itself.

Although he will describe our most normal, familiar way of Being, he warns us that he will not be relying on our normal, familiar interpretations of ourselves. "Dasein is ontically 'closest' to itself and ontologically farthest" (37/16) because what is most ordinary is what is hardest to grasp. (As Nietzsche puts it: "What is familiar is what we are used to; and what we are used to is most difficult to 'know' – that is, to see as a problem; that is, to see as strange, as distant, as 'outside us'."[19])

Two factors in particular lead us to misinterpret ourselves (36–7/15–16, 42/21): (a) Dasein understands its own Being "in terms of the 'world' ". That is, we assume that we are like the *things* that we encounter around us, when in fact, Dasein's existence is quite different from the way of Being of things. (This misunderstanding is the result of a tendency that Heidegger will call "falling".) (b) Dasein is blessed, but also burdened, with a large stock of prior self-interpretations. For instance, we have learned to interpret ourselves as rational animals, as sinful creatures, as egos in conflict with the id and the superego, or as evolving bearers of DNA. These accounts and concepts are unsatisfactory, since they are not based on an adequate interpretation of Being.

Heidegger's "analytic of everydayness", then, will try to break free from these sources of misinterpretation by taking an unusually intense look at our normal existence and developing fresh concepts to describe it, such as "Being-in-the-world" and "care". As we will see in a moment, problem (b) also requires a critical analysis of the history of philosophy.

Part One, Division II will *reinterpret* everyday existence in terms of "temporality" (38/17). Recall that *Being and Time* has a "spiral" structure: Heidegger keeps reinterpreting the phenomena in order to get a deeper understanding of them. Here he claims that temporality is the "meaning" of Dasein's Being. In other words, temporality is the key to understanding ourselves as we truly are.

The topics Heidegger discusses under the rubric of temporality are removed from the normal, familiar functions of everydayness. Here, he will examine rare moments of revelation in which we confront our own mortality and have the opportunity to make choices "authentically".

Part One, Division III was never published. This division was to take the crucial step from examining Dasein to determining the meaning of Being as a whole. Here, Heidegger wanted to show that time is the key to understanding not only our own Being, but Being in general. In other words, we can understand what it is to *be* only in terms of temporality.

19. F. Nietzsche, *The Gay Science*, tr. W. Kaufmann (New York: Vintage, 1974), p. 301.

We will probably never know how much of the unpublished portion of *Being and Time* Heidegger actually drafted, although it appears that he worked on it long and hard. Unfortunately, he decided that his account of time as the horizon of Being was completely inadequate, and he destroyed the manuscript.[20] But we will see at the end of our Chapter 4 that some hints of the content of Division III can be found in *Being and Time* and in the lecture course of 1927 *The Basic Problems of Phenomenology*.

Part Two was to "destroy" traditional ontology. The term "destruction" sounds rather crude, when in fact Heidegger intends to carry out a very meticulous analysis and criticism. The expressions "destructuring" (Stambaugh) or "deconstruction" (which Jacques Derrida made fashionable 40 years after *Being and Time*) are more apt. In fact, Heidegger himself sometimes uses the term *Abbau* ("de-construction" or "dismantling"). What he wants is "a critical process in which the traditional concepts, which at first must necessarily be employed, are de-constructed down to the sources from which they are drawn".[21]

Note that Heidegger plans to proceed in reverse chronological order, from Kant to Descartes to Aristotle. To borrow a term from another French thinker indebted to Heidegger, Michel Foucault, Heidegger wants to carry out an *archaeology* of the tradition. The late-modern soil on which we stand rests on the metaphysics of modernity, and this in turn is based on medieval and ancient thought. In the 1930s and 1940s, Heidegger will become fascinated by the earliest Greek thinkers, the pre-Socratic philosophers: he digs further and further down, in search of alternatives to the modes of thought that have been dominant in the West.

Although Part Two of *Being and Time* was never completed as such, Heidegger's other books and lecture courses carry out a very detailed critique of central texts in the history of philosophy, including the ones he singles out in §6.[22] We will look at some of the highlights of Heidegger's critique of Western thought in Chapter 5.

But why is this deconstruction necessary? In §6 Heidegger explains that Dasein "*is* its past" (41/20). Without our inherited interpretations of the world, we would not be Dasein at all – we would be an animal without a culture, language or norms. Our past is active in the present, making it possible for us to operate as Dasein. This applies to philosophy as well: "all philosophical discussion . . . is pervaded by traditional concepts and thus by traditional horizons and traditional angles of approach".[23] A philosophy can't be "built in mid-air".[24]

The problem, then, is not that we have a philosophical heritage, but that we normally take our inherited interpretations as self-evident. We assume that our

20. GA 66, pp. 413–14.   21. *The Basic Problems of Phenomenology*, p. 23.
22. The best source for Heidegger on Kant is *Kant and the Problem of Metaphysics*, tr. R. Taft, 4th edn (Bloomington, Indiana: Indiana University Press, 1996); on Descartes, *What is a Thing?* tr. W.B. Barton & V. Deutsch (Chicago, Illinois: Henry Regnery Company, 1967); on Aristotle and time, *The Basic Problems of Phenomenology*.
23. *The Basic Problems of Phenomenology*, p. 22.
24. *History of the Concept of Time*, p. 138.

own way of acting and thinking is the only way, and we suppress the fact that it has historical origins. In this way, the past gets petrified into a "tradition" in the narrow sense: a rigid, unquestioned conceptual structure (42–3/21).

In challenging this tradition, Heidegger is not trying to escape from the past altogether – after all, if he is right that Dasein is essentially historical (42/20), such an escape from the past is impossible. Neither is he examining the sources of our tradition merely in order to dismiss or reject them. Instead, his ambition is to make the past "our own" in a positive way (42/21). Instead of taking our tradition for granted, we have to rediscover the "primordial experiences" that gave rise to this tradition (44/22). These experiences have a rich content that can be quite illuminating as long as it is kept "within its *limits*" (44/22), that is, interpreted in the proper context.

Once we have explored some details of Heidegger's analysis of Dasein's Being, we will return to his reading of Western philosophy as a "metaphysics of presence".

§7: The method of *Being and Time*

In §7 Heidegger presents his understanding of philosophy as *transcendental, hermeneutical, phenomenological ontology*. In later years, he preferred to call what he did simply "thinking". While we might wish that he had kept things equally simple here, his jargon is not beyond clarification.

Instead of appealing to Husserl, Heidegger explains the term *phenomenology* by a laborious etymological route. First, he claims that the Greek word *phainomenon* means that which shows itself (51/28). This interpretation of the word is completely orthodox. However, we typically set up a dichotomy that Heidegger combats throughout his writings: we oppose the way things show themselves to the way things really are in themselves – we treat appearance and reality as radical opposites. This dualism is deeply entrenched in Western metaphysics. But for Heidegger, the "primordial signification" of *phainomenon* is not a deceptive, mere appearance, but the genuine self-display of a thing. (For instance, when termites *appear* in my basement, they are revealed as what they *are*: an all-too-real pest.) Certainly, some appearances are misleading, but misleading appearances are just special cases of self-display, cases in which a thing displays itself as what it is not (51/29). (When an insect that resembles a leaf appears in my basement, it really reveals itself to me, even though it reveals itself misleadingly, as a leaf.) The point is that when we examine *phenomena*, we are not just examining superficial illusions; we are trying to notice "the things themselves" as they reveal themselves to us (49–50/27). (Heidegger is fond of this Husserlian motto, although he abandons most of Husserl's technical terminology.)

When it comes to the "-logy" of "phenomenology", Heidegger's interpretation is less conventional. We usually translate *logos* in such contexts with the bland words "science" or "study". But he looks more closely at this fundamental Greek word, and arrives at the conclusion that *logos* essentially means *making something manifest* (56/33). To do "phenomeno-logy", then, is to make manifest that which manifests itself – "to let that which shows itself be seen from itself in the very way in which it shows itself from itself" (58/34).

This definition looks like an extremely elaborate tautology. After all this fuss, phenomenology turns out to be something very simple: revealing things. And this definition is also empty (one might say), since it says nothing about *how* we are supposed to reveal things. Heidegger is aware that his concept of phenomenology is, in a sense, simple and empty. The slogan "To the things themselves!" is "self-evident" because it is "the underlying principle of any scientific knowledge whatsoever" (50/28): *of course* we are trying to know things themselves. However, it is worth dedicating ourselves to this principle carefully, because it is so tempting to rely on ready-made techniques and concepts instead of letting the things themselves have the last word. Phenomenology is no "easy science, where one, as it were, lies on a sofa smoking a pipe and intuiting essences"[25] – it demands commitment and rigorous attention.

Even though there is no radical opposition between appearance and reality, there *is* a profound problem of illusion, falsehood and concealment. Being tends to lie hidden (59–60/35–6). We are normally so absorbed in *entities*, which display themselves obviously to us, that it takes a great effort to bring *Being* into focus, including our own Being. We tend to fall back into superficial and misguided interpretations. "It is therefore essential that Dasein should explicitly appropriate what has already been uncovered, defend it *against* semblance and disguise, and assure itself of its uncoveredness again and again" (265/222).

Although he calls phenomenology his "method", Heidegger has not specified any particular steps that must be followed by the phenomenologist. Like every thinker, he does have certain favorite approaches and turns of thought. But these are not codified techniques for thinking. In his view, the thing one is studying has to dictate one's approach. In this sense, "phenomenology" is an empty label – but its emptiness is a virtue, since it leaves us room for developing approaches that are appropriate to what we are examining.

What we *can* say about phenomenology is that it is fundamentally *descriptive* (59/35), not explanatory: Heidegger will be describing how Dasein and the world show themselves, rather than proving that they are this way or explaining why they are this way. His "existential analytic . . . does not do *any* proving *at all* by the rules of the 'logic of consistency'" (363/315). He is not "grounding" a proposition by constructing a deductive argument for it, but rather "laying bare" or "exhibiting" phenomena (28/8). If one looks for formalizable arguments in *Being and Time*, with identifiable premises and conclusions, one will find precious few.

For the English-speaking philosopher this can be disconcerting, as many of us have been trained to identify philosophy itself with the process of generating, analyzing and criticizing arguments. If there is no argument – we might

25. Heidegger, *Plato's* Sophist, p. 406.

39

ask – why should we accept Heidegger's "descriptions" as well-founded? What makes them any more than dogmatic assertions of opinion?

But Heidegger does not want to impose a dogma. His goal is to let Dasein *"put itself into words for the very first time, so that it may decide of its own accord whether, as the entity which it is, it has that state of Being"* which has been formally indicated in his interpretation (362/315). (For the concept of "formal indication", see pp. 17–18 above.) He wants to articulate aspects of existence that have never been articulated before. Until we have a vocabulary for discussing these phenomena, any proof or argument is premature. Heidegger's project thus demands a long process of forging new concepts and words (63/39), and his reader must have patience during this process. But he does not want us to suspend judgment forever – he wants us to decide for ourselves whether his descriptions are adequate. As we absorb *Being and Time*, we must constantly ask ourselves whether his account so far is thorough and illuminates our own lives. The grounds for a description given in a phenomenological text cannot ultimately be provided by the text itself – they are provided, if at all, by the *reader's* experience.

Now Heidegger is concerned not with just any phenomena, but with Being – in technical terms, his phenomenology is *ontology* (61/37). But what is Being? We have found several ways of conceiving of it initially, but of course, we do not have a precise answer to this question – after all, such an answer is the goal that *Being and Time* failed to reach. Still, in §7 Heidegger does give us some further indications of what it is that he is looking for.

Being is the hidden meaning and ground of entities, which show themselves obviously and overtly (59/35). Being is not completely hidden, however; it shows itself, but in an obscure way. For instance, describing a cat as an entity is a relatively easy challenge – we document its size, color, capacities, behavior and so on. But describing the *Being* of a cat is far more difficult. What does it mean that the cat *is* as a cat, or an animal? More generally, what does it mean that the cat *is* as an entity of any kind, as something rather than nothing? These ontological questions are bewildering. But in order for us to describe the cat that is there, we must already understand what it means for it to be there – we must already obscurely grasp the Being of the cat. Heidegger is trying to drag Being out from its everyday obscurity and get it to show itself "thematically" (55/31), in the clear light of phenomenological analysis.

Heidegger remarks somewhat cryptically that there can never be something further that is hidden behind Being and does not appear (60/35–6). In other words, our goal is simply to get Being to *show* itself to us clearly as a phenomenon – it makes no sense at all to wonder in addition, "What is Being like in itself, independently of how it shows itself to us?" For Heidegger holds that although most *entities* are independent of us, their *Being* is not. (This rather difficult point will be discussed further in §43c.) Being is necessarily linked to our understanding, because it is the difference that entities make *to us*. Being is what allows us to encounter every entity: thus, "the Being of the entity is found only in encounter"[26] – not in some hidden realm that is beyond our experience. For instance, in order to discover the Being of the cat, I need to examine the phenomenon of animal Being, a phenomenon that shows itself to me in advance and allows me to encounter the cat. If I can focus on this phenomenon and describe it, I will be doing a phenomenological ontology of cats.

Heidegger's phenomenological ontology is *hermeneutical*: that is, it *interprets* Being and Dasein, and it examines the process of interpretation itself (62/37–8). Interpretation (defined in §32) is the act of developing one's understanding of something and illuminating the thing. For example, when I learn that a gesture means that something is too expensive, I have interpreted the gesture.

Of course, my interpretation does not have to stop there – for instance, I can investigate what counts as "expensive". In fact, an interpretation is always subject to revision and elaboration. We have seen that Heidegger himself follows a "spiral" structure, in which he continually reinterprets the phenomena. There is no point at which we can safely conclude this process of interpretation and reach a perfect, definitive account of things. Early in *Being and Time*, Heidegger does imply that his investigation will eventuate in a clear "answer", a definite "concept" of the meaning of Being (22/3, 27/8, 40/19). But he also admits that we are "constantly compelled to face the possibility of disclosing an even more primordial and more universal horizon from which we may draw the answer to the question, 'What is *"Being"*?' " (49/26–7). We should never reduce our investigation to a "free-floating" assertion, a result (40/19, 60–61/36); for as soon as we do so, the activity of interpretation will cease and our insights will become bland truisms. This approach to thinking and writing is a constant in Heidegger.

Thanks largely to Heidegger, hermeneutics has gained wide acceptance as an approach to philosophy in general. Many thinkers now view knowledge not as a static set of correct propositions, but as a continuing search for better interpretations.

A check of the index will show the reader that Heidegger uses the term *transcendental* at several points in *Being and Time*. Notably, in §7 he claims, "Every disclosure of Being . . . is *transcendental* knowledge" (62/38). In §8 he describes time as "the transcendental horizon for the question of Being" (63/39). But he never explains the term very clearly. The words "transcendent" and "transcendental" are used in complex and elusive ways by the Scholastics, Kant, and Husserl. We cannot review the entire history of the words here, but we must touch on some points in order to shed light on Heidegger's usage.

"Transcendent" literally means "going beyond" or "lying beyond". In Scholastic metaphysics, which is based on Aristotle, Being is called "transcendent" because (for reasons we cannot go into here) Being is neither an entity nor a class of entities. In this sense, Being lies "beyond" all entities (22/3, 62/38). Heidegger adopts this usage because for him, too, there is a crucial distinction to be drawn between Being and beings. He seeks ontological, and not merely

26. *History of the Concept of Time*, p. 217.

ontical, knowledge. This knowledge of Being can be called "transcendental knowledge" (62/38).

The *world*, like Being, can be called "transcendent" (§69c). Heidegger also speaks of *Dasein's* "transcendence" (415/364). Roughly speaking, Dasein reaches *beyond* itself to a world that lies *beyond* it. But here we must be very careful not to picture Dasein as a thing in a box, and the world as the things outside the box. As we will see, Heidegger interprets Dasein as *essentially* "Being-in-the-world", where "world" means not a collection of objects, but a totality of meanings and purposes within which Dasein can act and can encounter other beings. Having a world is indispensable to existing as Dasein. "Dasein does not sort of exist and then occasionally achieve a crossing over outside itself, but existence originally means to cross over. Dasein is itself the passage across."[27] Dasein's transcendence depends on *time*: Heidegger will claim that by reaching into the present, the future, and the past, Dasein reaches *beyond* beings to their Being. A world thus opens up within which beings show themselves to Dasein. All this is involved in the Heideggerian notion of transcendence.

We must add a Kantian element to this mix, for when he wrote *Being and Time*, Heidegger took inspiration from the *Critique of Pure Reason*, where Kant uses the term "transcendental" in connection with his investigation of the "conditions of the possibility of experience". For instance, how is it possible for us to know that lying in the sun causes sunburn? For this, we need not only sensations, but also the category of causality. The category serves as a condition of the possibility of experience: the category must already be in place before we can make any judgments about particular causes and effects. An account of such categories and principles is what Kant calls transcendental knowledge.

Heidegger's project is similar to Kant's, for *Being* is a condition of the possibility of our experience of entities: whenever we encounter an entity in any way, we must *already* have an understanding of Being that makes this encounter possible. For example, before biologists can discuss the digestive system of the cat, they must already understand the Being of animals, and Being in general. By investigating Being, Heidegger is carrying out a transcendental project.

When we say that Heidegger's thinking is transcendental, then, we mean that he is investigating how Dasein, thanks to its temporality, reaches out to a world and to Being, thereby making possible its experience of beings. All this should become clearer as we proceed through *Being and Time*.

In later years, Heidegger will drop the expression "transcendental", because he wants to distance himself from certain Kantian connotations of the term. We will revisit this issue in Chapter 5 when we discuss the "turn" in his thinking after *Being and Time*.

27. *The Metaphysical Foundations of Logic*, p. 165. Dasein's transcendence is discussed at length in *The Basic Problems of Phenomenology*, *The Metaphysical Foundations of Logic*, and especially *The Essence of Reasons*, tr. T. Malick (Evanston, Illinois: Northwestern University Press, 1969).

I recommend that readers return to the details of §7 after familiarizing themselves with the entire book. But for now, we are ready to *do* phenomenology by focusing on the basic structures of Dasein that have been hinted at in Heidegger's introduction.

§§9–11: Existence and everydayness

Heidegger begins Division I with a summary (65/41). He takes care to sum up his progress at every such important juncture, and readers are well-advised to attend to these moments. Division I will present a "preparatory fundamental analysis of Dasein", and interpret Dasein's Being as "Being-in-the-world". The basis for this interpretation will be an examination of Dasein's everyday existence. In §§9–11, Heidegger explains why we have to begin with everydayness in order to grasp Dasein's Being.

We want to find the Being of Dasein – human nature, as it is usually called. But how do we start? We might want to begin with the facts we have uncovered about ourselves through psychology and biology (§10). We might want to look at "primitive" people, Dasein "in the raw", as supposedly revealed by cultural anthropology (§11). Today, we might be especially attracted to neurobiology, or to the interdisciplinary field called cognitive science.

But Heidegger warns us that the results obtained by these disciplines are no shortcut to Dasein. Every scientific standpoint rests on some ontological assumptions (§3). Any science of human beings must work with a prior understanding of human *Being* – and the data provided by the sciences will not, by themselves, clarify this prior understanding. We can pile up volumes of statistical and experimental results about ourselves without coming any closer to grasping what it is to be human.

Heidegger will not even consider a number of questions that the scientifically minded reader will want to ask. How did Dasein evolve? When does a fetus or newborn enter the condition of Dasein? What conditions are necessary in the brain in order for Dasein to take place? Can other species be Dasein? Can we create an artificial Dasein using computers? All these questions jump the gun: they cannot be asked intelligently until we understand the way in which Dasein *exists*. For Heidegger, the ontological question is more fundamental than these ontical questions.

Not only is scientific research unable to shed light on Dasein's Being, but it is all too likely that it operates with an *inadequate* interpretation of Being in general, inherited from Greek philosophy and Christianity (74–5/48–9). The sciences ultimately take Dasein as a *thing*, much as they may attempt to distinguish it from all other things (72/49). For Heidegger, Dasein is not a thing at all. Things are "whats"; their Being is "presence-at-hand" (Stambaugh: "objective presence"), and their ontological characteristics are "categories". Dasein is a "who" whose Being is "existence" and whose ontological characteristics Heidegger dubs *existentialia* (Stambaugh: "existentials") (67/42, 70–71/44–5).

What does this mean? Let us begin with things. Consider a piece of quartz under study by a geologist. The quartz is present-at-hand: it is given, it is actual here and now, and it presents several aspects to us. We can measure its size and mass (its quantity), inspect its color or taste (its qualities), and in general discern how it is. But the quartz itself, of course, has no relationship to its own Being: it cannot care about its own Being, choose it or interpret it. It simply is what it is, a sample of quartz.

The geologist, in contrast, is not simply what she is. She is not merely a certain type of object. If we ask her, "Who are you?" presumably she will not answer, "A sample of *homo sapiens*". She may tell us that she is a Canadian Jewish geologist and mother of two. These are not just properties of her, in the way hardness and a mass of two kilograms are properties of the quartz. Being Canadian, being a mother, and the other dimensions of her identity are not just facts given here and now. They are part of her past – and also part of her future, since they open up possible ways for her to be in her world. She is able to act, think and feel as a mother, a Jew and a geologist. Whenever she realizes one of these possibilities, she is choosing to be someone – she is interpreting who she is. The question of who she is, is always "an issue" for her (67/42); she is always assigned the task of being someone, like it or not. She may acknowledge this task and accept her existence as her own to take over, or she may exist "inauthentically", avoiding owning up to the task of Being (68/42–3). Yet either way, the task is *hers* as long as she lives. Heidegger thus speaks of the *Jemeinigkeit* of Dasein, its "in each case mineness" (Stambaugh: "mineness", "always-being-mine") (68/42). Because my Being is *mine*, it is always an issue for me – it is the special way of Being that Heidegger calls existence.

This means that we will never understand human beings adequately if we treat them as things. Rather than looking at the geologist in terms of quality and quantity, we should look at her in terms of her *existentialia* – the various dimensions of her existence as an entity who has to decide who she is. These would include her having possibilities, her being confronted with the alternatives of authenticity and inauthenticity, the "mineness" of her Being, and much more.

All these dimensions are features of the way in which Dasein *is*. In order to understand ourselves, we have to look at how we exist. This undercuts the traditional distinction between *what* something is and the fact *that* it is (see our discussion of §2 above). In the case of Dasein, in order to understand "what" Dasein is (if we are even allowed to use this terminology), we have to understand the special character of the *fact* that it is. As Heidegger puts it, Dasein is the "entity *whose what is precisely to be and nothing but to be*".[28] "*The 'essence' of Dasein lies in its existence*" (67/42). (In Chapter 5 we will ask whether this statement makes Heidegger an "existentialist".)

---

28. *History of the Concept of Time*, p. 110.

On 79/54 Heidegger appears to imply that every entity either exists (as does the geologist) or is present-at-hand (as is the quartz). But there are actually some other ways of Being. One very important way of Being is readiness-to-hand, the Being of things of use. Heidegger will examine readiness-to-hand in depth soon. It can be viewed as lying between existence and presence-at-hand, because although useful things are obviously not human beings, they form part of the human world and have meaning only in relation to human activity. Another important way of Being is that of non-human animals (75/49–50, 84–5/58). Heidegger investigates the Being of animals in depth in a lecture course of 1929–30 that we will discuss below. Artworks and gods may have their own ways of Being, too.

But the problem that faces us now is: how can we study the Being of Dasein in a way that does justice to its character as *existence*? Heidegger proposes that we must turn to what is "ontically closest" to us (69/43), and that is *everydayness*. We must, so to speak, catch ourselves in the act of everyday existence. This is a challenging assignment, since as soon as we look at ourselves, we tend to misinterpret ourselves.

One typical misinterpretation is to observe ourselves as if we were normally observers, to view ourselves as if we were essentially detached viewers. Heidegger's first job will be to disabuse us of this notion. In everyday existence, we are not spectators, but *engaged actors*. Once he has established this, he can proceed to show in the rest of Division I that as we do things in the world, our Being is an issue for us. We relate to our own Being, either authentically or inauthentically. This does not occur primarily through knowledge or self-consciousness, but through acting, through capably dealing with the beings around us.

Heidegger's claim that everydayness is "undifferentiated" (69/43) presents some difficulties. By "undifferentiated", he seems to mean a mode of existence that is neither authentic nor inauthentic (78/53). But he never clearly explains this concept, and he will almost always portray everydayness as *inauthentic*. This appears to conflict with his principle that "at the outset of our analysis it is particularly important that Dasein should not be Interpreted with the differentiated character of some definite way of existing" (69/43). He seems to have abandoned this principle as he developed his project, for as we will see, in §63 he claims that "ontological Interpretation [must] base itself on *ontical possibilities* – ways of potentiality-for-Being" (360/312). Inconsistencies such as this may reflect the fact that the text we know as *Being and Time* was finished in a rush, under the pressure of "publish or perish". Different interpreters have found different ways of resolving the problem.[29]

---

29. See e.g. M. Zimmerman, *Eclipse of the Self: The Development of Heidegger's Concept of Authenticity*, 2nd edn (Athens, Ohio: Ohio University Press, 1986), pp. 44–7; H. L. Dreyfus, *Being-in-the-World: A Commentary on Heidegger's* Being and Time, *Division I* (Cambridge, Massachusetts: MIT Press, 1991), pp. 26–7.

§§12–13: Being-in-the-world and knowing

By "intellectualism" as an indictment is meant the theory that all experiencing is a mode of knowing, and that all subject-matter, all nature, is, in principle, to be reduced and transformed till it is defined in terms identical with the characteristics presented by refined objects of science as such. The assumption of "intellectualism" goes contrary to the facts of what is primarily experienced. For things are objects to be treated, used, acted upon and with, enjoyed and endured, even more than things to be known. They are things *had* before they are things cognized. — John Dewey[30]

In Chapter 2 we saw that young Heidegger began as an "intellectualist" in Dewey's sense, and then realized that "theory" was secondary to "life". We are now ready to see how he articulates this insight in *Being and Time*. In the course of interpreting and reinterpreting our Being, he will christen this Being with a number of special terms. He has already used the word "existence". He now introduces one of his most important other expressions for Dasein's Being: "Being-in-the-world". This term indicates that we are essentially involved in a context – we have a place in a meaningful whole where we deal with other things and people. The particular content of this context will vary from person to person, and from culture to culture. But it can be said of Dásein in general that our relation to the world is not disinterested – it is active engagement. We are not, and never can be, radically detached from the world.

Heidegger begins to explain Being-in-the-world by contrasting it to presence-at-hand. For present-at-hand entities, such as the quartz, to be "in" a place just means to occur at some specifiable location in three-dimensional space (79/54). For Dasein, however, Being-in means *dwelling*, living *bei* the world (80/54). "Alongside" is a poor translation for the German preposition *bei*, which means "at" as in "at home" or "at my friend's house". Stambaugh renders it as "together with". "Amid" may be the best translation. When Heidegger writes that Dasein is *bei* the world and the entities in it, he means that, at least in everydayness, we are *at home amid* the things in our world.

For example, a Pakistani man drives a cab in New York City, and has a wife and child. His *world* is the entire set of issues around which his life revolves, including family, job and national identity. He is *in* this world because he lives in such a way that these issues matter to him; they give him possibilities for acting and for being who he is. Within this world, other entities can make a difference to him; he understands traffic, customers, schools and political events because his world gives him ways of dealing with them. Whether he likes it or not, his own existence is entangled in this context and bound up with the things that confront him here – this is his "facticity" (82/56). He necessarily has "concern" for the things in his world (*Besorgen*: "taking care" and "heedfulness",

---

30. J. Dewey, *Experience and Nature*, 2nd edn (La Salle, Illinois: Open Court, 1929), p. 21.

Stambaugh), and this is part of his way of Being as "care" (*Sorge*) (83–4/56–7; these concepts will be developed later).

Often, of course, we do not feel wrapped up in our surroundings: we are bored, or daydreaming, or relaxing. But for Heidegger, these are simply *"deficient* modes" of concern (83/57). The "deficient mode" is a typically Heideggerian concept that is all too easy to parody. (*"Being and Time* is crystal clear, but in a deficient mode", readers have been known to quip.) The idea is that cases such as daydreaming are the exceptions that prove the rule: even what appears to be disengagement is just a less intense form of engagement. If we look at our daydreams, after all, we find that they are about *things in the world* that *matter* to us somehow. Even the most jaded, blasé individuals have their own ways of being involved, their own issues about which they care. Someone who has truly reached absolute indifference is not Dasein anymore, but has entered another state of Being, either nirvana or vegetation, that is unintelligible to those of us who still dwell in the world.

However, there are some profound moments when we can become alienated from our world, and experience the whole world as uncomfortable and uncanny. At these moments we are not at home in the world, and there is even a sense in which *"the 'not-at-home'* [is] *the more primordial phenomenon"* (234/189). We will take a closer look at this claim when we reach Heidegger's account of "anxiety". For now it is enough to note that even at these moments, we still have to dwell in the world in order to *be* someone at all. We can become uncomfortable with our world, but we can never simply escape it.

Dasein is in its world, then, through engaged, concerned dwelling. This dwelling is not primarily *cognitive*; it is not built up out of observations, beliefs or knowledge. Rather, knowing is a specialized manifestation of Being-in-the-world that depends on a more basic, non-cognitive dwelling.

Now let us imagine Descartes reading *Being and Time*. When confronted with claims such as those in §12, he would probably object:

> But none of these claims have been proved yet! What are your *grounds* for saying that you are in the world? How do you even *know* that a world exists? After all, your belief that there is an external world is merely based on your sensations. Since those sensations have been unreliable in the past, you should begin by *doubting* whether there is an external world. (See the first of Descartes' *Meditations*.)

This Cartesian objection haunts Heidegger, and he will address it not only in §13 but also in §§19–21 and §43a. His basic reply is that "knowing is a mode of Dasein founded upon Being-in-the-world. Thus Being-in-the-world, as a basic state, must be Interpreted *beforehand*" (90/62). The question of Being is deeper than the question of knowing. Ontology precedes epistemology.

Before Descartes can ask whether he or the world exists, he must already understand what it *means* to exist. For Descartes, this is presumably a "very simple notion" that needs no explication. But according to Heidegger, if we do try to explicate the obvious, we find that what it means to exist, for a human being, is to "be-in-the-world" in his sense. Any human being is involved in a world, engaged in a sphere of concerns and issues. Belief and knowledge are *founded* upon this primordial Being-in-the-world.

Imagine our cab driver taking a passenger to a hotel through rush hour traffic. He is absorbed in the task of making his way through the stream of cars, buses and pedestrians. He is in his world, he dwells in it; his task and the things he encounters make sense to him in terms of a meaningful whole. This is not a matter of what he *believes* or *knows*; he is simply "fascinated" (88/61) by the process of being a cabbie. Suddenly, he runs into a massive traffic jam. It becomes clear that he can make no progress at all. His passenger gets out, exasperated. Now there is nothing for our cabbie to do but wait, and he "holds back from any kind of producing, manipulating, and the like" (88/61). He gives up on driving, and idly speculates on the causes of this traffic jam. He forms a *belief* that there is an accident ahead. He reviews the *grounds* for his belief in order to decide whether he really *knows* that there is an accident.

For Heidegger, this kind of example shows that knowing is an activity that is subsidiary to a more primordial Being-in-the-world. He even says that the very act of "objectively" trying to know something or staring at it presupposes "a *deficiency* in our having-to-do with the world concernfully" (88/61). For instance, the cabbie was *unable* to drive, and in this situation, questions of knowledge arose. When Heidegger revisits this issue in §69b, he will make it clear that the act of knowing involves not only a deficiency, but a deliberate "thematizing" or objectification (414–15/363). However this may be, concerned dwelling, rather than knowing, remains our basic way of existing. Normally "I do not perceive in order to perceive but in order to orient myself, to pave the way in dealing with something".[31] Even when I perceive solely in order to perceive, this has to be understood as a special mode of dwelling, not as complete detachment. If the cabbie were not engaged in his world at all, then the very concept of a traffic jam would be meaningless to him. Questions of knowledge always depend on Being-in-the-world.

One should not get the impression that Heidegger is *against* knowledge or science. His enemy is not the intellect – he is an intellectual himself, after all – but *intellectualism*. Intellectualists, such as Descartes, try to understand the self and the world primarily in terms of knowing. They fail to recognize that knowing presupposes dwelling.

Section 13 gives us Heidegger's basic response to Descartes, but this issue has not been settled yet, and we will have to return to it. Readers may want to keep in mind the following retort we can imagine Descartes making to Heidegger:

Of course I admit that I have to "be in the world", in *your* sense, before I can raise epistemological questions. I have to have some concerns.

31. *History of the Concept of Time*, p. 30.

But when *I* ask whether the world exists, I am asking whether my concerns relate to any really existing objects. "Being in the world" for you merely means acting *as if* there were an external world. My question is whether there actually *is* an external world, and you certainly haven't proved that there is one.

§§14–18: The world as a significant whole

This Cartesian retort helps us see that the meaning of "world" in Heidegger is quite different from the meaning of "world" in Descartes. Sections 14–18 explore the phenomenon that Heidegger calls "worldhood", or what it means to be a world. For many readers, these are among the most powerful analyses in *Being and Time*.

Section 14 establishes some terminology. *World* refers to "that '*wherein*' a factical Dasein as such can be said to 'live'" (93/65). For instance, our geologist's world is the whole sphere, or context, that organizes all her interests as a scientist, a Canadian, a mother and so on. A world, in this sense, is a significant whole in which one dwells. We use the term in a similar sense when we speak of "the Greek world" or "the world of sports". *Worldhood* (Stambaugh: "worldliness") refers to the Being of worlds, the essential structures that characterize every Dasein's world. "*World*", in quotation marks, refers to "the totality of those entities which can be present-at-hand" (93/64): stars, atoms, oceans and so on. Often enough, when we are theorizing, we think only in terms of the "*world*": we view reality as a collection of objects. We disregard the *world*, that is, our own involvement in a significant whole. Heidegger's ambition is to capture this phenomenon that is so familiar yet so difficult to grasp.

Heidegger begins to understand worldhood by analyzing the *environment*. (Stambaugh's translation of *Umwelt* reflects its root meaning: "the surrounding world".) The environment is the most ordinary, everyday kind of world (94/66). It is the world in which we *use and make things*. Although Heidegger is ultimately concerned with the environment itself rather than the things in it, he begins by examining these things, which he calls equipment (97/68) or ready-to-hand entities (98/69) (Stambaugh: "handy beings"). His first question, then, is: what is the Being of things as we encounter them in the context of using and making?

Before leaping into his analysis, we have to pause to consider what he is and is not doing. It might seem that by starting with the activity of using things, Heidegger is implying that *all* human activity can ultimately be reduced to some kind of productive manipulation of tools. This is not so, although his readers are often tempted into this misinterpretation. Soon after the publication of *Being and Time*, he had to protest, "It never occurred to me . . . to try and claim or prove . . . that the essence of man consists in the fact that he knows how to handle knives and forks or use the tram".[32] There are many

---

32. *The Fundamental Concepts of Metaphysics*, p. 177.

human activities that are not equivalent to using things in order to produce a useful result: for example, making a political decision, having a conversation with one's spouse, playing the cello, exploring a glacier, or studying calculus. These activities can all *involve* using things, but they cannot be *reduced* to utility. Despite some misleading formulations, Heidegger does not want to claim that everything we do is for the sake of a product, or that the Being of the environment, the instrumental world, is equivalent to worldhood in general.[33]

What Heidegger does want to do is take the environment as his main *clue* to worldhood. The activity of using and making is a better clue than the activity of studying and knowing, which is a more specialized and less "everyday" activity. The everyday environment provides an excellent opportunity to recognize ourselves as engaged actors who dwell in the world as a significant whole.

When we examine useful things, we may be tempted to describe them as if they were present-at-hand things. We might find ourselves describing an object in terms such as these: "'A continuous surface', he announced at last, 'infolded on itself. It appears to have' – he hesitated – 'five outpouchings, if this is the word.'" The speaker here is stating true facts about the object, but as long as he maintains a purely theoretical attitude, he does not really understand what it is. "Later, by accident, he got it on, and exclaimed, 'My God, it's a glove!'"

The person in question is "Dr P.", a patient of neurologist Oliver Sacks.[34] Dr P. has somehow lost the ability to connect what he *sees* to what he *does*. Without a link to normal human activity, his observations are correct, but completely misguided. It is only by *using* things that he can realize what they are. When we conceive of ready-to-hand things as if they were present-at-hand, we are putting ourselves into the lamentable position of Dr P. We are artificially disabling our sense of the practical world, and cutting ourselves off from the Being of equipment. Instead, we have to pay attention to equipment as it reveals itself *in use*. The only way to understand *ready-to-hand* entities is to *handle* them.

Heidegger's preferred example of equipment is a hammer, but let us illustrate his claims and terminology using the case of a pair of gloves worn on a winter evening.

(a) We understand the gloves – not primarily by observation, but by use, as we see in the case of Dr P. This is the special kind of "sight" that is proper to

33. In fact, it is a recurrent theme in Heidegger's writings that traditional ontology is unwittingly and inappropriately based on the activity of production (e.g. *The Basic Problems of Phenomenology*, p. 105). This is not necessarily inconsistent with his claim that traditional ontology is based on the activity of contemplation, since Heidegger suggests in *Being and Time* (p. 88/61) that contemplating the present-at-hand arises from a "deficiency" in using the ready-to-hand. Heidegger's own notion of Being-in-the-world or "care" as the Being of Dasein is supposed to be more fundamental than either contemplation or production (pp. 238/193, 415/364).
34. O. Sacks, *The Man Who Mistook His Wife for a Hat and Other Clinical Tales* (New York: Harper & Row, 1987), p. 14.

using things. Heidegger calls it *Umsicht*, the sight that occurs in the *Umwelt*, or environment (98/69). This "circumspection" is a know-how, or coping skill, that reveals the gloves to us as what they are.

(b) The gloves refer to "a totality of equipment" (97/68): they are part of a winter wardrobe, and we also rely on them when we grasp and manipulate other equipment. Our understanding of the totality of equipment is more fundamental than our understanding of this particular item, the gloves (98/68–9).

(c) The purpose of the gloves is to protect one's hands from the cold. They are usable; they have an "in-order-to" (97/68). They have a function, namely, providing warmth: they intrinsically refer to this "work" or "towards-which" (99/70).

(d) The gloves are made of natural materials (100/70). They refer to nature, in the form of natural resources. (Even if the gloves are made of a synthetic fabric, the fabric itself is ultimately fashioned from natural materials.) The gloves also refer to nature in that they are designed to protect our hands from certain natural conditions (100–101/71).

(e) The gloves refer to a user (100/70–71) – perhaps they are designed for someone with small hands.

Features (b)–(e) are all cases of *Verweisung*. This word is rendered as "assignment" and "reference" by Macquarrie and Robinson, and as "reference" by Stambaugh; I will translate it consistently as "*reference*", italicizing it and related words to emphasize that they are technical terms. The phenomenon of *reference* is crucial to understanding worldhood, but we are not ready to define it yet. For now, it is enough to see that it includes various types of relationships in which a thing points to something else.

We can use the diagram below as a reminder of a few things Heidegger has said. Here the ellipse represents the totality of equipment, and the arrows represent relations of *reference*. We will be expanding this diagram soon.

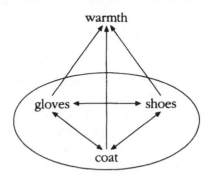

At certain moments, *reference* is brought directly to our attention (§16). These moments bring us closer to understanding not only things within the world, such as the gloves, but worldhood itself. I put on my glove and find that there are holes in the fingers; I'm annoyed at having to worry about this everyday item. Or I am looking for my gloves and cannot find them anywhere; I feel frustrated because my missing gloves are preventing me from going about my business outdoors. On another occasion, I am reaching for my keys in my coat pocket, but instead I feel a glove that stands in my way; I impatiently try to worm my way past it. At these uncomfortable moments, things take on a kind of presence-at-hand combined with readiness-to-hand (the ripped glove may start looking like a "continuous surface with five outpouchings"). This can mark the beginning of a theoretical attitude to entities.[35] But more importantly for our present purposes, I am forced to pay attention to *reference*. I cannot ignore the fact that gloves *refer* to a purpose, *refer* to me as their user, and *refer* to a totality of equipment – precisely because the gloves are not performing these *references* very well. (Often enough, we appreciate the importance of what we already have only when it is malfunctioning or threatened. This point will recur later in *Being and Time*.)

When the glove is missing or malfunctions, I become all too aware of how things are supposed to work in general; gloves are supposed to fit and function, along with the rest of my clothes, so that I can go about my business. In Heidegger's terms, "the whole 'workshop'", "the context of equipment" is displayed to me. And "with this totality . . . the world announces itself" (105/75). The world turns out to be a totality of *references* (107/76) or a context of *references* (121/87).

Of course, we still do not know exactly what *reference* is. Once again, Heidegger is using a concept before defining it. However, before readers get too annoyed with him, they should reflect that when it comes to *fundamental* concepts, this is the only way of going about things. A definition of a concept is effective only if we already understand the concepts we use in the definition. The *most basic* concepts have to be formed and communicated not by giving definitions, but by paying attention to phenomena and developing increasingly detailed descriptions. *Being and Time* is constantly forging such basic concepts.

To give a rough sense of what a *referential* totality might be, we can say that it is a web of meaning, a significant whole. It is the arena in which things make sense to us and fit into our lives. It is the overall scheme in which we can act, produce, think, and be.

It is tempting to interpret the *referential* totality purely in terms of utility, and view it as a set of functions of useful things. Heidegger's own examples encourage this interpretation. But this would be too narrow – it may account for the environment, which is the most familiar variety of world, but it does not cover worldhood in general. A world is not only an environment, but any context in which entities are available and meaningful to Dasein. Important features of the world for someone may include many *references* that go beyond mere utility – for instance, *references* that are structured around sin, beauty, or sincerity.

---

35. For a detailed interpretation of this portion of *Being and Time* in these terms, see Dreyfus, *Being-in-the-World*, pp. 69–83.

Signs (§17) are another opportunity for noticing the phenomenon of *refer-ence*. Signs are ready-to-hand things that function by giving us "an orientation within our environment" (110/79). They help us go about doing things be-cause they draw our attention to our place in the *referential* totality (114/82).

Let's take Heidegger's own example, a turn signal on a car (108–110/78–9). I am driving in the United States. As I approach an intersection, the left turn signal on the car ahead of me begins to flash. I understand that the car will have to wait for cross traffic before it can make its left turn, so I immediately slow down, look back to my right, turn on my own right turn signal, and move into the right lane to pass the car ahead of me.

I correctly interpreted the left turn signal – not by staring at the blinking light, not by analyzing it theoretically, but by responding capably (110/79). My competent reaction involved familiarity with the whole system of *references* that was at work here; I had to be comfortable with a complex set of traffic regulations and driving skills. If the system of *references* were different, the correct interpretation of the turn signal would differ too. For example, if I were in Britain, my behavior would have to take account of the convention of driving on the left side of the road. Signs always function within an overall environment, and alert us to our current place in that environment.

Section 18 is arduous and important. Here, Heidegger attempts a further clarification of worldhood and *reference*. In doing so, he introduces three new concepts: involvement (Stambaugh: "relevance"), the "for-the-sake-of-which", and significance.

Heidegger's example of hammering (116/84) gives us a concrete case we can use to explain these concepts. A carpenter is hammering while building a house. We already saw in §15 that there are several *references* involved here: the hammer is part of a totality of equipment; the act of hammering is for putting together the house; the house is for protection against the weather. These functions of the hammer are its *involvements*, and they are essential to its very Being as a hammer. *Reference* is the general term for the sort of connection that is found in every involvement (115/84).

We can now risk a rough definition of *reference*: a *reference* is a purpose or meaning that helps us make sense of an entity. However, defining the concept is less important than paying attention to the phenomenon that it is indicating. Our definition is just a provisional way of rephrasing some things that Heidegger has said. When we reach his discussion of the meaning of "meaning", we can revisit this definition of *reference*.

When we spelled out the chain of functions in which the hammer is in-volved, we eventually reached "a possibility of Dasein's Being", namely, being protected against the weather (116/84). Heidegger claims that all involvements ultimately depend on some possible way for Dasein to be. This possibility is the *raison d'être* of these involvements. Heidegger calls it the "for-the-sake-of-which". To take another example: a manager is typing on her computer keyboard. The keyboard is for typing, the activity of typing is for producing a memo, the memo is for increasing efficiency in the company, the efficiency is for profits, and the profits are *for the sake of* the manager's and other employ-ees' *being* successful. "Being successful" is one of those possible ways to exist that help us define our identities, help us determine our own Being, whether authentically or inauthentically (119/86).

Here we should note that when Heidegger says that all involvements are for the sake of a possibility of Dasein's Being, he does not mean that at bottom we are all *selfish*. The guiding possibility in one's life may be the possibility of existing generously and compassionately.

The carpenter and the manager understand what they are doing. They understand their own Being and the Being of the things they are using (not ontologically, of course, but practically). Heidegger's closer analysis of under-standing will come in §31, but for now it is enough to say that our understand-ing discloses *references*. In his terminology, we "signify" our own possibilities for Being and the involvements of the things we use. Worldhood can be described as the "relational totality of this signifying", or *significance* (120/87).

Frankly, Heidegger has probably introduced more terminology than he needs. The totality of *references*, the totality of involvements, and the totality of signi-fying are just subtly different perspectives on a single phenomenon, worldhood. In non-Heideggerian terminology, a world is *a system of purposes and mean-ings that organizes our activities and our identity, and within which entities can make sense to us.* It should be clear by now that our world is absolutely essential to *who we are*, so essential that Heidegger refers to our own way of Being as Being-in-the-world.

Let's expand our diagram now, putting it in general terms rather than in terms of an example, and adding the dimension of the "for-the-sake-of-which". This is, of course, only one possible way to represent Heidegger's ideas.

The world is the totality of *references*, which are represented by the arrows in this diagram. As we proceed, we will return to this diagram and supplement it once again.

I claimed that the environment, the world of using and producing, is just the most familiar world, not the only one. But Heidegger has made it hard to see this. His explanations of significance and involvement in §18 are put purely in terms of the ready-to-hand. Sometimes he even refers to ready-to-hand entities as "entities", pure and simple. It appears that the environment *is* the world.

However, several passages show that this is not so. For instance, on 113/82 Heidegger speculates that "the primitive world" may have nothing to do with readiness-to-hand and equipment (maybe non-literate cultures do not approach things in terms of our categories of usefulness and productivity). But then, worldhood is more than just environmentality. Heidegger has not given us much opportunity, however, to see other kinds of worlds, because he wants to emphasize that the most ordinary experiences, at least in modern Western cultures, involve using and making. Furthermore, his analysis of the activity of using things is certainly an effective way to show that we understand ourselves and our surroundings by operating skillfully within a complex system of significance – not by forming beliefs or knowledge-claims about objects.

§§19–21: The impoverished Cartesian "world"

We can now return to the Cartesian objection we considered at the end of our discussion of §§12–13. The objection ran: of course I "am in the world" in the sense that I have concerns and interests, but this does not answer the question of whether I am *really* in a world. Am I really surrounded by actual things? Do my perceptions correspond to reality, or are they illusions? Maybe nothing exists outside my mind.

Heidegger's answer will not come in full until §43a. But we are already prepared to raise some critical questions about the Cartesian standpoint. Descartes' skeptical arguments look very responsible and cautious – but in fact, they involve a whole set of uncritical assumptions about what it means to *be*, both for human beings and for other beings. Some of these assumptions are specific to Descartes' system, and I will not remark on them – readers who are versed in the details of Cartesianism should simply turn directly to §§19–21 of *Being and Time*, and they will not need further comment from me. Instead, I will focus on the elements of Cartesianism that have become so much a part of the modern outlook that for many people, they are simply "common sense".

Perhaps the most basic Cartesian assumption is that human life goes on "inside", not "outside". There is a special sphere in which human existence takes place, which we may call the mind, the subject, consciousness, the ego or the self. Outside this "subjective" sphere, there are (or may be) "external objects". These material, physical objects are alien to us; they have no consciousness or mind, they are just brute things situated in measurable space. Within my subjective sphere, I have perceptions or sense data that appear to represent external reality. However, I cannot immediately know whether these perceptions actually resemble external objects. Similarly, I assume that other minds – if there are any other minds – cannot directly know my true self or inner personality.

When we do make assertions about "external" objects, we tend to rely on what modern natural science tells us about them. The data we trust are quantitative facts, facts scientists obtain by measuring size, mass and motion. These "objective" facts can be systematized in general mathematical formulas, universal laws. We assume that what "really" exists "out there" then, is a set of objects moving through three-dimensional space – or if we are a bit more sophisticated, matter and energy distributed in space-time.

Of course, there are many other aspects of our experience that cannot be captured in quantitative terms: the poignancy of our family ties, the magnificence of a skyscraper, our patriotic or religious duties, and even the humble experiences of cooking, cleaning and moving about. But – so we assume – these have only a "subjective" reality. The world *in itself* consists only of particles and energy; the world *for us* includes subjective values that we project on to things. Judgments about good and bad, beautiful and ugly, are "value judgments" that merely reflect our own desires, instead of saying something about the world.

The result of these assumptions is a technological approach to the world. The right way to live, we suppose, is to clarify our own desires – or invent new ones – and then impose our will on the external world. Quantitative science gives us the key to forcing physical objects to obey our will. The following passage, which anticipates the use of nuclear fusion for energy, was published by Descartes in 1637. It is an extraordinarily prophetic vision of modernity.

> ... it is possible to arrive at knowledge that is very useful in life and ... in place of the speculative philosophy taught in the Schools, one can find a practical one, by which, knowing the force and the actions of fire, water, air, stars, the heavens, and all the other bodies that surround us, just as we understand the various skills of our craftsmen, we could, in the same way, use these objects for all the purposes for which they are appropriate, and thus make ourselves, as it were, masters and possessors of nature.[36]

The Cartesian assumptions I have just described are ingrained in our well-worn words "subjective", "objective", "value", "external" and "internal". Often enough, the common sense of today is the philosophy of three or four centuries ago.

Heidegger challenges these modern assumptions, first of all, by asking about the meaning of the "I am", a meaning that Descartes took for granted. For Heidegger, to be human is not to be a special kind of thing within a "subjective" sphere. Human existence is not inside a private precinct at all, but is "in

36. R. Descartes, *Discourse on Method and Meditations on First Philosophy*, tr. D. A. Cress, 3d edn (Indianapolis: Hackett, 1993), p. 35 (*Discourse on Method*, Part VI).

the world", so we have to jettison the crude dichotomy of inner and outer. We exist out in the open. It can even be said that we *are* the opening, or the clearing (171/133). Although it is hard to picture this, Heidegger would like us to think of ourselves as an event of opening, rather than as a thing inside a closed sphere. (And maybe it is best if we do not picture this, because *picturing*, re-presenting, may be appropriate only for present-at-hand objects, not for Dasein.)

One may object that, like it or not, the human brain is enclosed by the human skull. This is true, of course – and the brain should stay there. But the process of human *existence* does not take place merely inside the skull. It occurs when the human body interacts with the beings around it in such a way that those beings reveal themselves in their depths of meaning. If our connections to other beings were cut, we would not end up inside our mind – we would end up *without a mind at all.* (Experiments with sensory deprivation tanks show that after a time without any sensations, people lose themselves in hallucinations and disjointed thoughts; their ability to be Dasein is temporarily jeopardized.) The *mind* is dependent on *minding* – caring about other beings, which show up as mattering to us.

From a modern point of view, one may claim that if there were no human beings, there would be no religion, art, ethics or workshops – and that this shows that things such as purpose and beauty are subjective values, projected by our minds. One may argue that although, *chronologically* speaking, we encounter things as useful equipment before we encounter them as present-at-hand objects, this does not imply that utility is *ontologically* more basic than presence-at-hand. Isn't utility, and significance in general, a human creation?

But Heidegger insists that readiness-to-hand is how things of use are *in themselves* (101/71). Presumably he would grant that without Dasein, there can be no things of use (there may be a surface with outpouchings, but it is not a glove anymore). However, as long as Dasein does exist, the thing *really is* a glove. This is a fact about the thing, and the fact is not a creation of my will. Significance *is* Dasein-related, but it is not the *product* of Dasein's subjectivity, precisely because significance is so important to our Being: it is so fundamental that we cannot do or make anything unless a system of significance is already in place. We always depend on a pre-established network of purposes that draws on the established traditions of our community and shows us things, such as the gloves, as genuinely meaningful within our world. Certainly, we can be innovative and inventive within this world – but we can never create significance from scratch, by imposing "values" upon meaningless objects (131–2/98–9).

The simple distinction between subjectivity and objectivity is further undermined by one of Heidegger's favorite points: even the "objective" features of things, their present-at-hand attributes, reveal themselves only within a larger, significant context that cannot itself be explained in terms of what is present-at-hand. The geologist, for instance, measures the quartz and finds that it is 10 centimeters long. She is right: it *is* 10 centimeters long. But this fact would have no meaning for her, and she would never have bothered to find it in the first place, were it not for her larger world, the world in which she exists as a scientist, mother and Canadian. Astrophysicist John Trauger puts it well:

> Scientists do what fascinates them, and what fascinates them is not something you can discover with science. They're interested in investigating where planets come from, say, not because science tells them to do that, but because as human beings they find that interesting. They go after questions they consider worth the investment of a lifetime.[37]

To do justice to the *context* of science, we need to understand how things become fascinating and how we can build worthwhile lives within a meaningful whole. This whole includes all the richness of the realm of human experience – the "lifeworld" (as Husserl called it in his late work). We cannot reconstruct the lifeworld by taking quantitative, scientific facts and piling values on top of them. This procedure is simply backwards, because the lifeworld is what gives all facts their meaning (96/68, 131–2/98–9).

Heidegger's approach is holistic: in other words, he stresses that the experience of the meaningful world *as a whole* is more basic than the particular facts we discover about entities within it. The lifeworld, with all its significance, is what is fundamental for us. Our findings about the "world" of present-at-hand objects are just a narrow class of data that we can extract, under certain conditions, from what we experience. The Cartesian outlook suffers from intellectualist myopia: it examines a specialized class of entities within the world, present-at-hand objects, but it misses the world itself, the larger context in which these objects present themselves (122/89). In a sense, Cartesianism misses the forest for the trees. This is natural enough, because the background that allows things to present themselves tends to *remain* in the background; it is easy to overlook it. It can also be *unsettling* to come to grips with our lifeworld – as we will see later in *Being and Time*.

Heidegger challenges our modern assumptions, then, about our own Being and the Being of other entities. We can expect that he will challenge our technological attitude to life, as well. This aspect of his thought is not very clear in *Being and Time*, but it becomes quite important in his later work. And even in *Being and Time* he never describes our relation to tools in terms of imposing our will on things – although this is the vocabulary most of us would tend to use. Instead, he speaks in terms of "freeing" the ready-to-hand (114/83) and "letting something be involved" (117/84–5). At the deepest level, our way of Being *allows* the everyday world to happen – our will does not *make* it happen. This position foreshadows his later concept of *Gelassenheit*, or "releasement", which we will encounter in our Chapter 5.

We have not refuted Cartesian skepticism. But we can begin to suspect that Descartes' concerns seem proper only if one has a narrow, impoverished view

37. Quoted in D. Sobel, "Among Planets", *The New Yorker*, December 9, 1996, p. 90.

of the world – a view that unworlds the world, a view that tries to drain things of all the meaning they have for us as engaged actors and reduce them to their calculable aspects.

§§22–24: Quantitative space and the space of appropriateness

When we hear the word "space", we may think of outer space, a void dotted with stars that glide past us as in a science-fiction movie. Or we may think of analytic geometry, with its x, y and z axes of three-dimensional space. But is space just an empty framework in which objects can occur, or a system of assigning Cartesian coordinates to things? These concepts of space cannot capture the experience of being in an unfamiliar, threatening neighborhood, or finding the scissors just where we expected to find them, or feeling that a room is spacious, or putting one's glove on the wrong hand. These are spatial experiences that call for a richer, non-quantitative vocabulary.

In these sections, Heidegger tries to develop such a vocabulary. He will do the same for time in Division II. He tries to move us away from thinking of the world purely in mathematical terms, and towards an understanding of the world in terms of *appropriateness and inappropriateness* (115/83, 467/414). Full-fledged space consists not of points where objects are located, but of *places* where things and people *belong* or *do not belong* (136/102, 145/110–111). Full-fledged time consists not of instants when objects are present, but of *right and wrong moments* (467/414). In full-fledged time and space, things *matter* to us (141/106).

This takes us right back to the contrast between the Heideggerian and the Cartesian concepts of the world. From the Cartesian standpoint, questions of appropriateness and inappropriateness are just subjective; the objective facts about the world are quantitative. But Heidegger would reply that in order to describe the world in which we live, we have to use more than numbers – and even numbers are meaningful to us only in terms of the world of appropriateness and inappropriateness. The astronomer determines that a certain star is millions of kilometers away from the sun. This is correct, but it *means* something to the astronomer and to the rest of us only if we can relate it back to the lifeworld in which three kilometers are a gentle afternoon stroll, and thirty kilometers are a good day's hike.

As technology progresses, our sense of space and time is mutating, even eroding. Heidegger's comment on radio on 140/105 indicates his fears about this process. Macquarrie and Robinson omit an interesting phrase included by Stambaugh: radio is "expanding and destroying the everyday surrounding world". In a lecture course, Heidegger elaborates: "In the radio Dasein today realizes . . . a peculiar extension of the process of bringing the world nearer. . . . This frenzy for nearness is nothing but reduction in the loss of time. But reduction in the loss of time is the flight of time from itself."[38] In Division II we

38. *History of the Concept of Time*, p. 227.

will see that genuinely accepting our own temporality requires us to stop understanding time merely in terms of efficiency. If Heidegger had lived to experience fax machines, cellular phones and the Internet, he would shudder.

§§25–27: Being-with and the "they"

So far, Heidegger has described the everyday world inhabited by Dasein – that is, the entity who has an understanding of Being. This world consists of a network of *references* that reveal where things belong and how they fit into our lives. We also know from §4 and §9 that Dasein is distinctive thanks to its way of Being: "existence", a way of Being in which Dasein is responsible for *who it is*. So it is natural now to turn from the things we use to ourselves as users, and ask, with Heidegger, "*who* it is that Dasein is in its everydayness" (149/114).

If we are Cartesians – and so many of us moderns are, whether we know it or not – we are likely to try to answer this question through self-conscious introspection. "Who am I?" I ask myself. I look inward, and find some version of my true self: the real me, the inner child, the ego, or the self-conscious subject. However I may describe myself, I picture myself as some sort of subjective thing that is isolated from other subjectivities and from the "outside" world. Then I answer the question: *I am myself.*

But for Heidegger, this statement does not shed much light on my way of Being. And it can be all too misguided if it involves Cartesian assumptions, such as the assumption that I am an "internal" thing isolated from "external" things. For Heidegger, Dasein is not a thing at all. Furthermore, Dasein is not normally self-conscious and introspective – so my experience of introspection can mislead me about who I normally am. I have to reflect on who I was *before* I began to reflect, while I was still absorbed in the everyday world. I then discover that, first, my own existence essentially involves relationships to other Dasein. Secondly, I do *not* normally exist as myself – I exist as just anyone, as no one in particular.

In §26, Heidegger points out that in the everyday environment, I always experience things in relation to other people (153–4/117–18). The glove is not only my glove; it is the glove I bought from the *clerk* at the shop owned by *So-and-so*, and *fashion authorities* this year recommend this design. If I rub two sticks together to make fire, I am imitating what I once watched *another* do. In short, there is a social context for all the equipment we use. So even when no other people happen to be around, I acknowledge their importance simply by using something. My ways of using the thing, and the thing itself as a tool, *refer* to my human community.

Heidegger's name for this communal dimension of my own Being-in-the-world is *Being-with*. He calls the Being of other people, insofar as I encounter them as belonging to my world, their *Dasein-with* (Stambaugh: *Mitda-sein*)

(155/118). We now need to expand our diagram of Being-in-the-world to take account of Being-with as a feature of my existence:

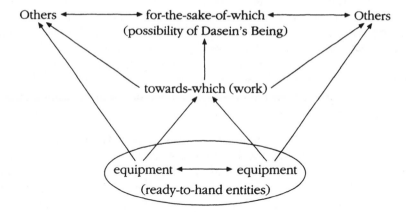

When he claims that Being-with is part of Dasein's Being, Heidegger is not trying to prove that others actually exist "outside" me (156/120). He is not trying to refute solipsism or solve the "problem of other minds" – he is really not concerned with this problem. He is more interested in undermining the prejudices that lead us to conceive of our own existence in terms of "inside" and "outside" in the first place.

If he is right, one can never get to know oneself through isolated introspection, through some attempt to slip out of one's own culture and community. We are inescapably social beings. Even the categories "inner child" or "noble savage" are *cultural* categories, concepts that make sense only within the particular ways of Being-with that are predominant within some community.

On 158–9/122, Heidegger gives us some promising hints of a phenomenology of human relationships – only to abandon the project as soon as it has begun. Here he distinguishes between two forms of Being-with, "leaping in" and "leaping ahead". Leaping in is a very common phenomenon: one does something for someone else, relieving the other of the need to do it. This is the case whenever anyone is hired to do a job, so our entire economy is based on leaping in. But leaping ahead is a more unusual phenomenon; it is authentic (159/122, 344/298) because it is directed not towards the things with which another is concerned, but towards the other's own way of existing. Leaping in can be illustrated by a teacher who provides students with ready-made answers, while leaping ahead can be illustrated by a teacher who (like Heidegger) provides his students with questions and encourages them to seek the answers for themselves. This passage suggests that Heidegger's notion of authenticity may have some ethical import (to put it in Kantian terms, it appears that he is urging us to treat others not only as means, but as ends in themselves). We will consider the question of "Heideggerian ethics" more closely in Chapters 4 and 5.

Section 26 offers excellent illustrations of the Heideggerian concepts of "deficient and indifferent modes". Being hostile to others, being shy before them or ignoring them are just permutations of Being-with. For Heidegger, these less-than-complete human relations are typical of everyday life (158/121, 162/125). Even being alone is a mode of Being-with (156–7/120). This may sound highly paradoxical, but we should remember that solitude always has some sort of social significance. If one lives alone, one has to interpret oneself as a hermit, a loner, friendless or independent – and these ways of understanding one's existence make no sense except in reference to the cultural standards of some *community*.

Section 27 is known for its powerful writing. Here Heidegger claims that usually, one does not exist authentically: one does not truly own up to one's own existence. Instead, one exists as *das Man*. The German pronoun *man* means "one", as in "One simply doesn't do such things". Maybe "the Anyone" would be a better translation of *das Man* than "the 'they'". I normally behave and understand my world just as anyone would. For example, in selecting my clothes, I take care not to look unfashionable – I consult my own sense of style and propriety. But this sense of style is really not "my own". It is simply how *one* dresses, how *they* dress in my community – and I *am* the "they".

Can I escape the "they" by dressing *against* prevailing fashion, then? No – the "they" is much more insidious than that. If I rebel by adopting a counter-cultural hairstyle, body markings and clothes, I am still basing my personal look on the "they" – I still depend on the "they" as a guideline (a negative guideline) for how I should behave. Furthermore, I am embracing a new "they" – the countercultural "they". Often enough, "nonconformists" are rigid conformists within their own subculture. It takes hard work to devise a truly individual way of dressing – such as Heidegger's "existential outfit", which Karl Löwith perceived as an attempt to shock the "they".[39]

Many other cases of existing as the "they" are less obvious than choosing one's clothes, and are not deliberate or conscious at all. For instance, the "they" dictates the polite distance that should be maintained between two strangers. We behave in accordance with this basic form of "distantiality" (164/126), although we are usually unaware of it until we travel to a foreign country, where we perceive people as "cold" or "pushy" because their sense of polite distance is different from ours.

In everydayness, the "they" dominates our perceptions and interpretations to such an extent that "we do not say what we see, but rather the reverse, we see what *one says* about the matter".[40]

The "they" tends to "level down" all possibilities (165/127). For the "they", a potentially groundbreaking work of art or a fresh political idea gets reduced to the status of a minor news item – something to engage our curiosity for a minute, until we get bored and move on to the next item.

39. Löwith, *My Life in Germany Before and After 1933*, p. 45.
40. *History of the Concept of Time*, p. 56.

It may look as if Heidegger is demonizing the "they" and is hostile to public life altogether. But if Dasein's Being essentially involves Being-with, then it is ontologically *impossible* to exist as Dasein without depending on some shared, communal norms. Why does Heidegger speak as if there were a better alternative to the "they"?

The fact is that much of §27 blurs the distinction between two phenomena: (a) the "they" as an *existentiale*, a basic and necessary feature of our Being, and (b) the *existentiell* condition in which one relates inauthentically to the "they" in sense (a). On 167/129, Heidegger finally makes this distinction: he calls (a) the *"they"* and (b) the *they-self*. The *"they"* is a constant: I am *always* familiar with a range of social expectations and interpretations that mark me as belonging to a culture. When I exist as the *they-self* – as I do, most of the time – I simply accept these expectations and interpretations, and let my world be structured by them. But it is also possible for me to exist as an *authentic* Self (167/129). In this case, I work with my culture in order to work out *for myself* who I am.

It is important to note that even *"authentic Being-one's-Self* [is] *an existentiell modification of the 'they' – of the 'they' as an essential existentiale"* (168/130, compare 312/267). The most authentic and original artwork, political decision or personal choice is dependent on the range of possibilities available in one's culture. Heidegger's outfit, for instance, did not come from Mars – it expresses his own appropriation of some German traditions. We can never simply *extricate* ourselves from the "they" of our community (213/169, 224/179, 345–6/299, 435/383). Authenticity does not involve jettisoning one's own tradition – which is impossible – but *clear-sightedly* and *resolutely* pursuing a possibility that is opened up by this tradition.

For Heidegger, the self – whether it is inauthentic or authentic – is not a *thing* of any kind. It is not some hard core of our Being, some existential peachpit that remains untouched and unchanged throughout our lives. Instead, it is an existentiell possibility, a *way of existing* (152–3/117, 365/317–18). If our language allowed it, it would be best to turn "I" into an adverb rather than a pronoun. Instead of saying, "I'm dressing", one could then say, "dressing minely" – or "dressing unminely", which according to Heidegger is the norm.

It seems, then, that both the they-self and the authentic Self are existentiell modifications of the "they" as an *existentiale*. But Heidegger makes a statement later in the book that casts doubt on this interpretation: "the they-self . . . is an existentiell modification of the authentic Self" (365/317). Perhaps this is just a minor inconsistency that we can resolve by systematizing Heidegger's somewhat erratic terminology. (For instance, there may be a distinction to be drawn more clearly than Heidegger does between "the authentic Self" and "authentic Being-one's-Self", where the former is some sort of *existentiale* and the latter is an existentiell possibility.) But perhaps this problem points to an instability in the very distinction between necessary *existentialia* and existentiell possibilities. This distinction is strongly reminiscent of the traditional metaphysical distinction between essential predicates (which are necessary) and accidental predicates (which are only possible). For instance, a flower's planthood is essential to it, but its redness is accidental: it can continue being a flower if it stops being red, but not if it stops being a plant. Similarly, Dasein can still be Dasein if it stops existing authentically, but not if it stops Being-with. But is this traditional (and commonsensical) distinction between necessary features and merely possible features really appropriate to Dasein, if "those characteristics which can be exhibited in [Dasein] are in each case *possible* ways for it to be, and *no more than that*" (67/42, my emphasis)? Whether or not *Being and Time* is inconsistent on this point, we will see that in Heidegger's later work we find far fewer references to necessary or essential characteristics of Dasein's Being. Dasein itself becomes a *possibility* for human beings, and Heidegger tries to develop a non-traditional concept of essence as "essential unfolding" (*wesen* as a verb).

Aside from these conceptual problems, readers may object that Heidegger's portrayal of everyday selfhood is very restricted. He seems to ignore various factors that contribute to who we are: talents, character, family history, sexuality and so on. Although Heidegger will have much to say about authentic selfhood, he never fills out his portrayal of everyday selfhood with these elements of individual psychology. He might claim that these factors are not relevant to Dasein, that is, to our status as the entities who understand Being – but this claim is debatable. Most likely, Heidegger ignores many such established psychological categories because he is wary of the metaphysical assumptions they may involve. In particular, he wants to steer clear of the assumption that human life goes on primarily inside a private, "mental" space, a psyche that can be considered in isolation from its surrounding culture. For Heidegger, all human possibilities, and all our vocabulary for describing these possibilities, are made available to us by our culture – our "they".

§28: The basic features of Being-in

We saw in §12 that Dasein is "in" the world not merely by being located in it as a thing would be, but by dwelling in it. The world is not just a place where Dasein happens to be – it is an inseparable part of Dasein's Being. If someone is a lighthearted, provincial Chinese swineherd, this means that his *world* is a world whose amusing and pleasing features stand out for him, a world organized around the concerns of a Chinese province, a world in which many important *references* involve caring for pigs. He *is* how things show themselves to him. Thus Heidegger can say, "*Dasein is its disclosedness*" – it *is* its own world, or "there", or "clearing" (171/133; "clearing" will become one of Heidegger's favorite words in his later period). It is now time to look more closely at how we dwell in our world, how we are the "there".

Division I, Chapter 5 carries out this task. Heidegger will distinguish the following structural features of Being-in:

• *Attunement.* The term *Befindlichkeit* designates our moods as ways of *finding ourselves in the world*. There is no ideal English equivalent, but we can use "attunement" to approximate what Heidegger means.[41] One's attunement discloses one's *thrownness*: attunement is our way of finding ourselves thrust into the world. Having an attunement thus involves having a *past*, for I always find myself *already* attuned to the world in a certain way. Heidegger will focus on fear (§30) and later on anxiety (§40) as particularly interesting cases of attunement.

- *Understanding*. This is our fundamental ability to be someone, to do things, to get around in the world. It is the basic "know-how" that allows us to deal with beings. Understanding involves *projection* into the *future*; it opens up possibilities for us. Heidegger will show that understanding, in this sense, is more primordial than theoretical assertions about things (§§32–33).

- *Discourse*. This is the articulation of the world into recognizable, communicable patterns of meaning. It is involved in both attunement and understanding (172/133). The world that is opened up by moods and grasped by understanding gets organized by discourse. Discourse makes language possible.

- *Falling* (Stambaugh: "entanglement", "falling prey"). This is a tendency to get absorbed in the entities that we encounter in the *present* world. It is typical of everydayness. Falling is the usual way in which thrownness gets manifested. It includes its own, superficial forms of understanding and discourse.

All these features of Being-in fit into the overall scheme of having a past, having a present and having a future. We are thrown from the *past*, which attunes us to the world; we understand this world in terms of possibilities that we project into the *future*; we fall into the world and become fascinated by the entities *present* in it. Heidegger will conceive of this overall structure in terms of "care", "temporality", and "historicity". We can begin to see why his book is titled *Being and Time*.

My brief explanations so far are only preliminary sketches that need to be filled out with convincing detail. Heidegger will provide much more conceptual detail and some telling examples; my main concern will be to provide added examples.

§§29–30: Attunement

Some of us are more sensitive to the meanings of moods than others. Those who are less sensitive will tend to assume that moods separate us from reality. A cheerful mood pleasantly distorts reality by viewing it through "rose-colored

---

41. This is Stambaugh's translation. "Disposition" would be another good way to render *Befindlichkeit*, because it helps us think of our mood as what "positions" us in the world, giving us an orientation. Others have tried "situatedness", "disposedness", "affectedness", "so-foundness", "attuned self-finding", and even "where-you're-at-ness". Macquarrie and Robinson's rendition of the word as "state-of-mind" is inappropriate. After all, Heidegger consistently tries to avoid giving the impression that Dasein exists inside a subjective sphere, such as a mind.

glasses". Jealousy is a pair of green glasses that skews the world in a less agreeable way. But the *objective* thinker – one might suppose – will take off the subjective mental "spectacles" and look at things as they really are: neither good nor bad, neither ugly nor beautiful, but simply a set of hard facts.

For Heidegger, however, moods are *disclosive*. They show us things in a more fundamental way than theoretical propositions ever can. For example, fear (§30) does not cut us off from things – to the contrary, it *reveals* something as a threat. Similarly, "We are in the habit of saying that 'love is blind' [but] love really gives us sight".[42]

If we may indulge in the language of the 1960s, a situation gives off its own, distinctive vibrations, and through our moods, we can tune into them. Someone who gets "bad vibes" from a room full of people will be in that room in a special way, will notice things that others would not, and may understand the situation quite well (he might recognize that the crowd is in a shared mood of anger). Another person, who is in the wrong mood, may not "pick up the vibes" and may completely miss the meaning of the situation, even if she can list hundreds of facts about the people who are there.

Thus, not all moods are *equally* disclosive. Someone may be trapped in an inauthentic or inappropriate mood. In this case, the mood still shows things, but it shows them in an overly restricted way. This is why we need to gain some control over our moods (175/136). Our goal should not be to escape from moods altogether, but to find the *right* moods. (One wishes Heidegger had said more about how to do this.)

Some other ways of talking about moods can shed still more light on attunement. My friend asks me, "How's it going?" I answer, "Not so great". – What is the "it" here? It is nothing in particular: things in general, life, or as Heidegger calls it, *"Being-in-the-world as a whole"* (176/137). I am always attuned in some way to my *overall* situation. This is how I am there – or, better, how I am my "there" (178/139).

Of course, sometimes the "it" is more specific: for instance, I may reply that I am angry or sad about particular events. These moods (or emotions, as we are more likely to call them) are about individual features of my life. Heidegger claims that the moods that open up Being-in-the-world as a whole (such as anxiety, as we will see) are more important and more revealing than moods that are about specifics (such as fear).

I may also answer my friend, "Oh, I got up on the wrong side of bed this morning". This phrase is also revealing, because it points to the fact that attunement involves having a *past*. I find that I have been *thrown* into the world in a particular way (a wrong way, in this case). My having gotten up on the wrong side of bed is not just a bygone occurrence that is here no more; it is an ongoing burden that I am carrying with me (173/134). In Heidegger's terms, our thrownness is not just "factuality", but "facticity" (174/135). A factical entity is faced every day with the task of being what it has already been and

42. *History of the Concept of Time*, p. 296.

choosing what it can be. (This task is especially apparent in that unusual mood in which it seems strange that we have to be who we are. "Why am I *this* particular person?" we ask. "Why do I exist *here*? Why *now*?")

Since it is hard to carry the burden of existing, it is no wonder that most moods are inauthentic, evasive. My mood of depressed irritability, for instance, probably "veils" my environment more than it discloses it (175/136): instead of taking clear-sighted action in response to my situation, I ineffectually resent it. Even my remark about "getting up on the wrong side of bed" is as misleading as it is revealing. I tend to dismiss my mood as something random and meaningless, and thus I make the mood even less disclosive.

Since we are always thrown into the world in some way, we can never become *moodless*. The "cool" teenager wearing sunglasses on his expressionless face is in a mood of bored indifference (or he is in the mood of *wanting* to be bored, since he believes boredom is a sign of maturity). The "objective" scientist recording the trails of subatomic particles may be in a mood of fascination, or of leisurely wonder (177/138). Someone with no attunement at all would be nobody at all, because such an entity would have no way of being enmeshed in the world. We can never simply get rid of our thrownness, our past. Hence the peculiarly Heideggerian double adverb that appears throughout *Being and Time*: "always already".

Often enough, Western philosophers have tried to escape from "subjective" emotion and mood, and have sought "objective" clarity and certainty through the intellect alone. If Heidegger is right, this is really an inauthentic attempt to evade one's thrownness and facticity – it is a desire to have no past. Descartes, for instance, at a moment when he has "no worries or passions", retreats by himself to "a small stove-heated room", where he reflects on how much better it is to produce everything according to one's own plan, rather than relying on tradition.[43] He concludes that "it is almost impossible for our judgments to be as pure or solid as they would have been had we the full use of our reason from the moment of our birth and had we never been led by anything but our reason".[44] When he emerges from his artificial womb, he is determined to build his own system of truths through reason alone. Heidegger would point out, however, that every system has to rely on the past – both on one's own pre-rational familiarity with the world and on the millennia of cultural and philosophical tradition. There is no way to build truth from scratch. The very idea of being born with the full use of reason is absurd, because reasoning presupposes a prior revelation of the world, a revelation that is largely achieved through attunement.

There is a price to be paid for accepting Heidegger's analyses. Although he rehabilitates moods, restoring their meaning and disclosive force, he cuts us off from the possibility of *absolute* or *total* knowledge: since Dasein is thrown and factical, we always experience the world from a particular perspective, and we can never guarantee that we have found a final and best perspective.

43. Descartes, *Discourse on Method*, pp. 6–7.   44. *Ibid.*, p. 8.

We will have to ask whether this leaves us in a state of radical skepticism and relativism – the fate that Descartes feared above all.

§§31–33: Understanding, interpretation and assertion

Thanks to our attunement, we find ourselves disposed in the world, positioned in it. Within this world, entities display themselves to us in countless ways. We are aware that this is an excellent restaurant, that winter evenings are cold, that stray dogs can be dangerous, that the Earth orbits the sun. How does the universe, in all its variety, become clear to us? How is it that we *understand* ourselves and the things around us?

We might be tempted to begin by examining assertions: for instance, "The Earth orbits the sun". We can investigate how this statement fits with others into a system (such as an astronomical theory). We can formulate and reflect on the scientific method which we follow to establish and validate this statement. We can even abstract from the content of the assertion and look at it formally, just as a proposition that claims something about something. We can produce a system of formal logic, which specifies how to derive a proposition from other propositions. These general goals encompass many of the questions discussed by today's philosophers.

Of course, *Being and Time* does not develop any such "theory of theory". It is not that logic is incorrect, or that there is no value in philosophy of science – but there are more fundamental questions to be asked, in Heidegger's view. Propositions are not a good clue to the essence of understanding, because we must already understand things *before* we formulate propositions about them. Our involvement in the world cannot be reduced to a set of claims. (An extreme example of such a reduction is Wittgenstein's *Tractatus Logico-Philosophicus*, where the world is defined as "all that is the case", and what "is the case" is understood as what can be expressed in a proposition. Wittgenstein's later views are much closer to Heidegger's.)

More fundamental than any assertions we may make is our ability to *do things* in the world in the first place. We under*stand* by taking a *stand*, so to speak – by seizing upon some way of existing and acting. In order to do so, we have to be fit to *stand up* to what we are doing – we have to be capable and competent. Heidegger tells us that his term *Verstehen* (understanding) "is intended to go back to" *Vorstehen* (etymologically, fore-standing), which means skilled management.[45] According to Heidegger's previous analysis of worldhood, this means that we disclose things by letting them be involved in a possibility of our own Being (116/84). For the sake of *being* a well-dressed winter pedestrian, I concern myself with protecting my body from the cold, and I put on my gloves in order to do so. As I put my gloves on, I disclose them; they are clearly revealed to me as these particular ready-to-hand things. I disclose

45. *The Basic Problems of Phenomenology*, p. 276.

other beings, too, in terms of possibilities in fields where I have competence. I understand that I *can* get a good meal at this restaurant, and that I *can* be bitten by a stray dog. Heidegger proposes that we disclose present-at-hand objects, too, in terms of possibilities – although he does not explain this very clearly (184/144–5).

Once I have disclosed the gloves, I can form an assertion about them if I wish, such as "The gloves are warm", but normally there is no call to do so. We need not assume that I have to have such assertions stored in my mind before I can relate to the gloves, any more than a bird has to form beliefs about aerodynamics before it can fly. We are not databases stocked with trillions of propositions that orient us in life. Oriented living comes first; it gives rise to propositions on special occasions. (For instance, I may say "The gloves are warm" to my wife in order to thank her for giving them to me on my birthday.)

In §§31–33, then, Heidegger focuses on "understanding" as *having possibilities*, "projecting" available ways to be. (Heidegger has already discussed our thrownness, and now he is discussing the other side of the coin – our throwing, our projecting. To borrow a phrase from his later *Contributions to Philosophy*, Dasein is a "thrown thrower" – someone with both a past and a future.)

Thanks to our projection of possibilities, we understand things. When we pursue a possibility intensively and use it to reveal beings further, we are *interpreting*. Interpretation can give rise to *assertions*.

Let us look more closely now at understanding as a relation to possibility. If having possibilities is so crucial to our existence, we cannot be reduced to what we actually are at any given moment – our present characteristics. I am not just what I am – I am who I am not yet (185–6/145). This sounds quite paradoxical. But consider our everyday experience of getting to know someone by asking what she does. She answers, "I'm a sculptor". What does this mean? At this moment, she is not sculpting, so the statement does not refer to her present characteristics. She has sculpted in the past, but she has also done millions of other things that she may or may not do again. The statement "I'm a sculptor" means (if it is truly a revealing statement) that the *possibility* of sculpting is an important possibility for her. She understands herself and her world largely in terms of it. She approaches things as someone who *can sculpt*. This is more fundamental than any particular plans she may make or pictures she may form of her future self (185/145). Such plans and pictures are just particular manifestations of her basic "sculptorly" approach to existing. Her very identity is formed by her ability to sculpt. And in general, our Being is an "ability to be" or "can-be" (183/143–4) (*Seinkönnen*, translated by Macquarrie and Robinson as "potentiality-for-Being" and by Stambaugh as "potentiality of being"). "The Dasein which I myself am in each instance is defined in its Being by my being able to say of it, *I am, that is, I can*."[46]

Heidegger briefly mentions the difference between authentic and inauthentic understanding on 186/146. We will stay with our sculptor as an illustration.

46. *History of the Concept of Time*, p. 298.

She may be inauthentically absorbed in her world and understand herself in terms of it: she may be wrapped up in her sculptures, and understand herself only as the means for producing them. But if she understands herself *authentically*, she approaches the world in the opposite way: she sculpts in order to *exist creatively*. (Of course, this does not mean that she does not care about her sculptures: to the contrary, she explicitly *chooses* to involve herself in sculpting.)

As we project possibilities for ourselves – whether authentically or not – we simultaneously disclose other entities in their own possibilities (184/144–5), and *we even understand Being itself* (187–8/147) (this crucial claim is never fully explained in *Being and Time*, but we will investigate it further at the end of our Chapter 4). We "see" Being and beings, in a broad sense. Heidegger opposes this "sight" to "pure intuition" (187/147). In the philosophical ideal of pure intuition (which Husserl called "adequate evidence") one is presented with something in its sheer presence: a phenomenon is fully revealed, fully given. For many thinkers, the model for pure intuition is a distinct sensation (such as a direct vision of the brightness of the sun) or a lucid recognition of a truth (such as a moment of insight into the Pythagorean theorem). Heidegger's claim is that such intuitions can never take place outside the context of thrownness and projection. To put it in temporal terms, presence is made possible by having a past and having a future. If I did not project the possibility of being someone, and if I were not attuned, thrown somehow into the world, I could never have an intuition of the sun or the Pythagorean theorem. I would be utterly closed off; nothing could be there for me, because I would have no "there" at all.

Heidegger's remark on intuition hints at his critique of Western thought in general. Since ancient Greece, our ideal of knowledge has been context-free intuition – a sort of disengaged staring (88/61, 177/138, 215/171, 410/358). Along with this ideal comes a concept of beings in general as having the sort of Being that is accessible in intuition: presence-at-hand (187/147). Heidegger fights against this metaphysics of presence by asking us to recognize that intuiting present-at-hand objects is only a limited, derivative mode of understanding. This recognition comes at the price of giving up our hopes for total, perfect understanding – pure presence. We will never escape the restrictions of our moods and the limitations of our particular possibilities, even if some ways of existing are more revealing than others.

What we *can* do is pursue an available possibility, using it to unfold our understanding into a developed *interpretation* (§32). Again, Heidegger focuses on practical life, since this is the most ordinary kind of existence. In everyday life, we may interpret something by improving it (189/148–9). For example, I spend an afternoon gardening. My backyard garden fits into the possibility of gardening as a possibility that I understand, and this is why I am able to treat the garden *as* a garden. I now work with my prior understanding; I approach the garden with certain expectations and goals and set about improving it. I notice that there are weeds in the garden, and I treat them *as* weeds: I uproot them. I treat some vegetables *as* ripe by harvesting them. I treat some plants *as* needing water by irrigating them. On the basis of my prior understanding of gardening, I am interpreting the components of the garden *as* items to be dealt with in various ways. The entirety of these *as*-es "constitutes the interpretation" (189/149).

Without my prior understanding of gardening, I would be incapable of interpreting the garden this way; I must already be projecting possibilities in regards to a situation in order to interpret it. Thus, an "interpretation is never a presuppositionless apprehending of something presented to us" (191–2/150). An interpretation is always guided by fore-having, fore-sight, and fore-conception (191/150). The meaning of these expressions is rather vague, but the main point is that, in various ways, we must already have a "take" on something, as we say, before we can interpret it.

Heidegger stresses that we never experience anything that is free of all *as*-es. One of his favorite examples is noise (207/163–4). We always take a noise *as* the sound of something; we always take a hue *as* the color of something. We simply do not experience raw, uninterpreted sense-data – these are the inventions of philosophers who are still obsessed with the possibility of pure intuition. Contrary to the usual story, modern natural science is based not on presuppositionless observations, but on a distinctive set of presuppositions (413–414/362). There is no knowledge or experience free of prejudices, that is, prejudgments.

Is Heidegger, then, a skeptic who claims that we cannot know anything because we are locked into our particular prejudices? Or a radical relativist who says that any interpretation is as true as any other? In fact, he is neither. After all, it would make no sense for a radical relativist or skeptic to write a book that tries to persuade us that his interpretation of Dasein is a sound one. He writes, "the way in which the entity we are interpreting is to be conceived can be drawn from the entity itself, or the interpretation can force the entity into concepts to which it is opposed in its manner of Being" (191/150). We must never allow our presuppositions "to be presented to us by fancies and popular conceptions, but rather [we must work out] these fore-structures in terms of the things themselves" (195/153). Heidegger believes in objectivity – but objectivity does not mean the complete absence of prejudice and points of view. Instead, true objectivity involves a willingness to revise one's point of view in the light of what one discovers. Responsible interpreters approach things with presuppositions, but also adjust their presuppositions to the things. As we have seen before, interpretation is a circular process – but this hermeneutic circle is not a vicious circle that gets us nowhere (194–5/152–3). It can clarify and deepen our understanding.

However, no understanding is absolute, that is, independent of prejudices and projections – so "relativism and skepticism spring from a partially justified opposition to an absurd absolutism and dogmatism of the concept of truth".[47]

47. *The Basic Problems of Phenomenology*, p. 222.

Absolutists and dogmatists view interpretation merely as the means of constructing some perfect, accurate system of assertions. But in fact, interpretation is an open-ended, ongoing process which, as long as it continues, provides more insight than any static system ever can. When interpretation comes to a halt, it becomes no more than a petrified set of concepts, a way of thinking that is no longer willing to revise its presuppositions.

We are now ready to explore the phenomenon of *meaning* (192–4/151–2). When a thing is accessible to us, the thing "has meaning". Meaning is the context that gives us access to the thing. Since this context comes from *our* own ability to project possibilities, we can say that meaning "is an *existentiale* of Dasein" (193/151). For example, my familiarity with gardening as a possibility provides a sphere of meaning within which I can go about tending my garden. The plants and soil then "have meaning" for me: that is, I understand them and can interpret them. They reveal themselves to me as relevant to my own possibilities for existing.

In our discussion of §§14–18, we provisionally defined a *reference* as a purpose or meaning that helps us make sense of an entity. Heidegger's explanation of "meaning" lets us improve this definition: a *reference* is a possibility that we can project and that lets us encounter an entity *as* something or other. For instance, if I say that a plant in my garden *refers* to the work of feeding me, this is equivalent to saying that I am capable of approaching it and encountering it as a possibly edible thing.

If the world is a totality of *references* (107/76), then the world is a totality of possibilities – a complex of options with which we are familiar, and which allows us to approach beings in a competent way. The world is a sphere of meaning within which we can go about existing. Entities in general, and Being itself, then "have meaning" for us: we understand entities and Being, and we can even begin to work out an interpretation in which we ask explicitly about the meaning of Being.

One should not get the impression that we create the world, as a totality of possibilities, through some act of will. Instead, Heidegger would presumably say that we are initiated into the world in early childhood, as we become full-fledged Dasein by learning how to participate in a community. This community presents us with a field of opportunities, and we learn to dwell in the world by projecting particular possibilities. No individual Dasein can create the entire network of significance, and most of the choices we make are not deliberate acts of will, but nonreflective exercises of skill.

Section 33 explores the special occasions on which interpretations give rise to assertions. Heidegger uses his favorite example, the heavy hammer; I have already given an example with gloves; here is one more example, with gardening. As I am weeding in my garden, I may have no assertions whatsoever floating through my head; I may simply be pulling out the dandelions by their roots, and this in itself constitutes an *interpretation* of them as weeds. But I may have occasion to formulate an assertion. A child asks me, "Why did you pull out that pretty flower?" I answer, "Because it's a weed". I am now *sharing* with the child my *view* of the flower as having the *definite character* of harming the plants that I am cultivating (see Heidegger's three characteristics of assertion on 196–7/154–5).

If I like, I can now write down the sentence, "Dandelions are weeds". I can even formalize it in symbolic logic: $(\forall x) (D(x) \rightarrow W(x))$ (translated back into English: it is true of any object that if it belongs to the class of dandelions, then it also belongs to the class of weeds). I begin to think of the flower as a thing, and dandelionness and weediness as its properties. I am now considering the flower as a present-at-hand entity. But I should not lose sight of the fact that the dandelion made sense to me well before I objectified it and formulated an assertion about it. Heidegger complains that traditional metaphysics and logic *begin* with assertions or propositions (*logos* in a narrow sense) and view them as the home of meaning and truth (196/154, 209/165). They treat assertion as if it were "free-floating" (199/156) rather than recognizing its roots in Being-in-the-world (the expression "free-floating" is always pejorative in Heidegger). This critique applies to Heidegger's own early views – for he himself once subscribed to the theory of "validity" that he now denounces so vigorously on 198/155–6 (see pp. 11–12 above). Any theory that begins with propositions, including symbolic logic (202/159), is utterly incapable of grasping the nature of meaning.

Heidegger's critique of logic is a frequent theme in his work, and is the starting point for several of his lecture courses.[48] He does not deny the correctness of any theories within logic itself. Rather, he holds that the discipline of logic, as a theory about *logos* in the narrow sense of propositions, cannot shed light on the most fundamental problems of philosophy: what is meaning, what is truth, what is Being? Such questions can be approached only by investigating *logos* in a more primary sense – *logos* as the process by which the world opens up and entities are revealed to us.

Heidegger does not feel free to commit logical fallacies, but he does think that the rules of logic have little to tell us about how to speak, read or write in an illuminating way. Although it is possible to analyze his own texts as sets of assertions, he often stresses that it is more important to pay attention to the questions and the sequences of thoughts in his work – the *context* of his assertions. "The point is not to listen to a series of propositions, but rather to follow the movement of showing."[49] If we attend to where a text has been and where it is going, we can take part in the process of developing concepts that are appropriate to the things under discussion; if we merely boil the text down to some propositions, our own preconceptions are likely to remain undisturbed.

---

48. See GA 21, *The Metaphysical Foundations of Logic*, and *Basic Questions of Philosophy: Selected "Problems" of "Logic"*, tr. R. Rojcewicz & A. Schuwer (Bloomington, Indiana: Indiana University Press, 1994).
49. "Time and Being", in *On Time and Being*, p. 2.

Every phenomenological proposition, though drawn from original sources, is subject to the possibility of concealment when it is communicated as an assertion. Transmitted in an empty and preattuned way of understanding it, it loses its roots in its native soil and becomes a free-floating naming.[50]

§34: Discourse

Some philosophers begin to reflect on language by considering assertions, such as "Dandelions are weeds". Heidegger, of course, does not. First of all, asserting is only one of many uses of language, or as analytic philosophers often call them, speech acts (204/161): for instance, one could also command, "Destroy that weed!" or ask, "Is that a weed?" More importantly, speech acts and vocabularies and grammars – all the elements of *language* – are based on an essential trait of *Dasein's Being*, a trait that Heidegger calls *discourse*. Unless we grasp how we ourselves exist as discursive entities, we will never understand the nature of particular manifestations of this discursiveness, such as words, sentences and languages.

Attunement and understanding are always working together to reveal the world, granting it intelligibility. Heidegger describes discourse (rather vaguely) as the articulation and expression of this intelligibility (203–4/161). It does not seem that he intends to identify discourse with speaking; rather, discourse is the fundamental way in which patterns of meaning are manifested to us. This is the ontological precondition for language, and it naturally leads to language: "to significations, words accrue" (204/161). As an entity with discourse, I am capable of noticing how the world is articulated – that is, how it involves *articulations*, joints, that differentiate and unite it in patterns of meaning. For instance, I may be in a nervous mood (attunement) as I approach my garden, which is intelligible to me because I am capable of gardening (understanding). The garden now shows up for me, is manifest to me, as a set of annoying, urgent tasks – and these tasks fall into meaningful patterns (discourse). Discourse makes it possible for me to share my situation with others in language. I can say, "My garden is getting overrun by weeds!" and the garden will be manifest to others. I can reveal the garden to others because as Dasein, I am characterized by discourse; I am able to deal with patterns of meaning.

It should be no surprise that Heidegger does not understand language as a bridge between private, subjective spheres (205/162). We are already "outside", already enmeshed in a meaningfully patterned world along with other people. Communication simply makes our shared experience more explicit.

Heidegger's discussion of hearing and keeping silent (206–8/163–5) is meant to shed more light on discourse as part of Dasein's existence. Because I have discourse, I can pay attention to what someone is telling me about my garden,

---

50. *History of the Concept of Time*, p. 87. Cf. *Being and Time*, pp. 60–61/36.

or I can refuse to tell someone what I am doing there. Like speaking, listening and silence depend on discourse as an ability to deal with patterns of meaning. Heidegger's notion of "keeping silent authentically" (208/165) – a telling silence – will prove to be important in his interpretation of conscience in Division II.

Language is an occasional theme throughout *Being and Time*, and it becomes a primary theme in Heidegger's later work. In his "Letter on Humanism" (1947), he will even write that "language is the house of Being". We will investigate this sentence in Chapter 5.

§§35–38: Falling

Yet who can tell how many times each day our curiosity is tempted by the most trivial and insignificant matters? Who can tell how often we give way? . . . It is true that the sight of them inspires me to praise you for the wonders of your creation and the order in which you have disposed all things, but I am not intent upon your praises when I first begin to watch. It is one thing to rise quickly from a fall, another not to fall at all. — St. Augustine, *Confessions*, X, 35[51]

Much as Heidegger takes pains to de-theologize his work, the concept and the name "falling" certainly owe much to his Christian background. This is not necessarily a defect, of course – it may be that a Christian upbringing helps to focus one's attention on a very real and universally human condition.

Falling is the movement or direction of everyday Being-in-the-world. Everyday Dasein exists as a they-self, and is wrapped up in what it is doing, which it understands in a superficial and conventional manner. Heidegger's analysis of falling shows how the basic structures of Being-in – attunement, understanding and discourse – play themselves out in everyday situations.

Falling can be illustrated by a common experience: I find myself in front of a magazine rack in a bookstore. Hundreds of colorful publications on every topic draw my attention. I flip through a magazine about celebrity gossip, then skim a computer journal, then wonder what today's newspaper has to say and devour the headlines there. I am fascinated by all this material, absorbed in it, but in a superficial way – I do not pay much attention to any particular item, since I am already flitting on to the next. Perhaps I stand there for an hour. Afterwards, I am a little dazed. I snap back to myself, remember why I was here, and get on with my business. Although I have been "brought up to date" on what people are talking about, I have the nagging, irritating feeling of having wasted my time, and I cannot say that I have learned anything of consequence.

For Heidegger, all everyday behavior is much like my behavior at the magazine rack. We are guided by what people ordinarily do, say and believe. In our

51. St. Augustine, *Confessions*, tr. R. S. Pine-Coffin (Harmondsworth: Penguin, 1961), p. 243.

eagerness to keep up to date, we do not take the time to explore anything thoroughly for ourselves. We use routines and passing interests to avoid committing ourselves to clear choices about who we are and what we are doing.

Much as in his discussion of the "they", Heidegger appears to be condemning everydayness in these sections, even though he claims he is making no moral judgments (211/167, 220/176). Such claims are very controversial. Some readers take Heidegger at his word, but according to others, this is simply his way of wrapping his personal moral opinions in the mantle of sober ontological facts. This problem is a good opportunity to reconsider our usual dichotomy between judgments of fact and value judgments. It may be a *fact* that everyday existence is superficial, ambiguous and evasive. These words may do more than just express disapproval; they may describe reality. If we react to this reality with disapproval, that may be because of the pull of a different style of existence, authentic existence, which Heidegger will describe in Division II.

In any case, he would insist that although we sometimes resist and overcome falling, falling is a permanent tendency in the human condition. Furthermore, any authentic grasp of things that temporarily overcomes falling must develop *from* everyday superficiality and ambiguity – it cannot simply step outside of everydayness and reach a pure state of consciousness, completely unpolluted by our everyday attitudes and judgments (213/169, 224/179).

Falling is so pervasive because it is a direct result of thrownness (223/179). As Heidegger claimed on 213/169, "In no case is a Dasein, untouched and unseduced by this way in which things have been interpreted, set before the open country of a 'world-in-itself' so that it just beholds what it encounters". If we could face reality head-on, without the baggage of a past, then we would not constantly be sucked back into convention, comfort and conformity. But we are always *thrown* into the world from a past that provides us with conventions and with the "they". A person without a past is a person without a world – and is in fact no person at all. Our established, comfortable ways of existing are the basis on which we interpret everything. Usually, we simply accept this basis as given, and are absorbed in life's immediate concerns – in short, we are falling. And this must be so – for if we were constantly challenging our conventions, we would be paralyzed. Without any enduring basis for our interpretations, we would forever be teetering on the brink of what Heidegger earlier called "the abyss of meaninglessness" (194/152).

§§39–42: Anxiety and care

Falling is necessarily our normal, everyday mode of existing. But not all moments are normal and everyday. A case in point is the mood of anxiety (*Angst*). Heidegger's analysis of anxiety shows just how disturbing it is to face up to the human condition, which he now baptizes with the new name "care".

The theme of anxiety is a departure from the focus on everydayness in Division I so far. Anxiety is rare, and the everyday perspective tends to dismiss it as a moment of meaningless confusion. But if everyday falling promotes superficial interpretations of the world and ourselves, then any deeply illuminating experience must be unusual and jarring. In fact, we will tend to avoid such uncomfortable experiences by clinging to the numbing attractions of everydayness. In this sense, falling is tempting (221/177). Not only is falling necessary for our routine functioning, but we tend to indulge in falling even when we have an opportunity for a non-routine, profound, but disconcerting experience.

Anxiety is not the *only* deeply illuminating mood. In "What is Metaphysics?" (1929), Heidegger mentions delight in the existence of someone we love.[52] In the opening of *Introduction to Metaphysics* (1935), he speaks of profound joy and profound ennui.[53] *The Fundamental Concepts of Metaphysics* (1928–29) even includes 100 pages of lectures on boredom. (Was Heidegger trying to evoke this mood in his hapless students?) All of these experiences have the potential to wake us up to the difference it makes that there is something rather than nothing.

Still, it is *Angst* that Heidegger is most famous for describing, and this is the mood that he chooses to elucidate in *Being and Time*. (Kierkegaard was the first thinker to examine this phenomenon at length, in *The Concept of Anxiety* [1844]. Some prefer to translate *Angst* as "dread". Since the existentialist boom of the 1950s, the German word has become so well-known that it is now almost an English word. Stambaugh leaves it untranslated.) But what *is Angst*? Unlike fear, anxiety is not about anything in particular (231/186). It is a generalized mood that is about my Being-in-the-world as a whole (233/188). In anxiety, specific entities and their meanings seem irrelevant, inconsequential, insignificant (231/186). As Heidegger puts it in "What is Metaphysics?", beings "slip away" in anxiety.[54] This mood may come over me at any time. Perhaps when I am busy weeding in my garden, my activity suddenly seems meaningless. I know that I am weeding in order to maintain the garden, and that I maintain the garden for pleasure and food, and that pleasure and food form part of my normal life – but this life as a whole seems pointless. I wonder, "What's the meaning of all this, anyway?" "What am I doing here?" "Who am I?" The security of everyday existence, in which the meaning of life seems well-grounded and obvious, has been shattered. Anxiety *is* a moment of meaningless confusion, as the everyday perspective has it – but it is "meaningless" not in the sense that it is trivial, but in the sense that it involves a deep *crisis* of meaning.

I am ordinarily at home amid the things in my world; as we saw in §12, Heidegger even conceives of Being-in in terms of dwelling (80/54). But in anxiety I feel alienated, homeless, unsettled (*unheimlich*, literally "not at home") (233/188–9). Heidegger even tells us that in comparison to ordinary, everyday

52. "What is Metaphysics?" in *Basic Writings*, p. 99.
53. *An Introduction to Metaphysics*, tr. R. Manheim (New Haven, Connecticut: Yale University Press, 1959), p. 1.
54. "What is Metaphysics?" p. 101.

dwelling, "*the 'not-at-home' must be conceived as the more primordial phenomenon*" (234/189). What are we to make of this?

First, we must note that when one feels homeless, one does not revert to present-at-hand entities' way of being "in" a place merely by being located at a particular point. Neither does one stop being in the world altogether. Anxiety is a particular *way* of being in the world, and only Dasein can experience it.

Secondly, in anxiety the meanings and functions that are so familiar in everyday dwelling do not simply disappear. In fact, by becoming a problem, they strike one with unusual force. By putting the familiar in an unfamiliar light, anxiety gives one the opportunity to come to grips with one's life, to dwell in the world clear-sightedly and resolutely. Anxiety illustrates a principle that we also saw in the case of non-functioning ready-to-hand entities (§16): when things fail us, we appreciate their importance.

But why is homelessness more primordial than being at home? When Heidegger makes this claim, he seems to be saying that we can never depend on an unshakeable foundation for our world. The world is a tissue of meanings that are fragile, contingent and subject to reinterpretation. No matter how solid our faith may seem, or how comfortable we may be with our lives, we are exposed to the possibility of anxiety. In fact, this possibility sets us apart from mere animals. A bird is incapable of alienation because its goals and needs are fixed for it by its nature. Even when it is in an unfamiliar or frightening environment, it always resorts to an immediately available way of trying to cope with this environment. The bird cannot step back from its instinctive understanding of things and call it into question. This means that animals are tied to their "home" more tightly than we can ever be.

But, paradoxically enough, we are also capable of dwelling more intensely than any animal can. We are capable of challenging our own interpretations, reaffirming them or revising them; in this way we build ourselves a home for the future out of our past. Dasein dwells *historically*. In Division II of *Being and Time* and in his later writings, it becomes clear that Heidegger is intent on awakening us to our own historicity. If we are authentically historical, we will not settle dully into the comfort of our world; we will welcome the homelessness of anxiety as an opportunity to reconfigure and reclaim our home.

What else can the unnerving experience of anxiety tell us about our Being? In §41, Heidegger takes anxiety as an indicator of three interrelated aspects of Dasein that belong together in "care".

First, as he already claimed in §9, my own existence is an issue for me: I am assigned the task of being someone, and the way in which I deal with the possibilities open to me will determine who I am. Much as I might like to, I cannot base my identity on the things I deal with from day to day. My garden, job, or social status cannot define the purpose of my life; I have to find that purpose myself by choosing some possible way of existing (232/188, 393/343). Dasein "is always only that which it has chosen itself to be".[55] Since anxiety

---

55. *The Basic Problems of Phenomenology*, p. 278.

reveals this task of choosing who I am, it can inspire a change of course. I may soon shrug off anxiety and return to normal, but this experience may also develop into a crisis that serves as a turning point in my life story; instead of tending my garden, I may decide to become a social worker, poet or entrepreneur. I may also choose to remain who I am – but in such a way that I truly *choose* this identity, instead of just letting it happen. Heidegger refers to our need to determine our own identity as Dasein's existentiality (235/191, compare 274/231) or its Being-ahead-of-itself (236/192). To anticipate Division II, we can think of this dimension as our having a *future*.

Secondly, I am not *pure* possibility; I already have a life. I am already familiar with an established identity and world – the very world that anxiety is calling into question. Whatever I make of myself, I cannot radically disengage myself from the world – so I will have to exist on the basis of what I already am. This feature of my Being is my facticity, thrownness, or Being-already-in-the-world (236/192). Again anticipating Division II, we can view this dimension as our having a *past*.

Thirdly, anxiety can help me realize that I am normally absorbed in my daily tasks, oblivious to both my existentiality and my facticity. From my anxious state of alienation, I can recognize that I am normally at home in a world that I take for granted. Being at-home-amid (*bei*) entities is our usual way of having a *present*.

The three dimensions of our existence are not unfamiliar to us from Heidegger's previous analyses. However, he hopes that the experience of anxiety will help us see how these dimensions fit together into a single structure: "ahead-of-itself-Being-already-in-(the-world) as Being-at-home-amid (entities encountered within-the-world)" (237/192, translation modified).

Why does Heidegger use the word "care" to describe this structure? "Care", like the German *Sorge* and Latin *cura* (§42), usually refers either to managing and looking after things, or to troubles and worries. But since "Being-in-the-world is essentially care" (237/193), care is manifested even in moments that we would ordinarily describe as "carefree" or "careless": I am ahead of myself, already in the world, and at home amid entities, even when I am daydreaming, having fun, driving recklessly or calmly meditating. This makes Heidegger's choice of words a little puzzling. However, in describing Being-in-the-world, we have already used the word "care" to point to some essential features of our Being: most importantly, we cannot help caring about our own Being and the Being of other entities, because we are such that beings *matter* to us, they make a difference to us. As we have seen, even anxiety does not *separate* us from the world – in fact, it makes the world an urgent problem for us. Although Heidegger does not directly say so, his language of "care" is an implicit criticism of all philosophies of detachment. He holds that there is no way to avoid being rooted in a past and faced with a future. Human beings can never become timeless, placeless and radically indifferent. Although there is nothing necessarily wrong with "carefree" moments of enjoyment and relaxation, or moments of sober, scientific objectivity, we are deluding ourselves if we suppose that such moments extricate us from the web of temporality into which we are woven by our very Being.

§§43–44: Reality and Truth

Having given us a description of everyday existence and interpreted existence as care, Heidegger uses the last two sections of Division I to address some fundamental problems about the relation of Dasein to reality and truth.

In §43a, Heidegger directly confronts a problem that has been dogging him from the start: the so-called problem of the external world. When we last considered Cartesianism, in §§19–21, we raised the suspicion that this problem appears compelling only if one accepts certain presuppositions. If one presupposes that the subject is a special kind of thing that exists within a private sphere, and that other things are merely objects to be measured and manipulated, then it seems legitimate to raise the question of whether we have access to these "external" objects. But as Heidegger insists, if it turns out that these Cartesian presuppositions distort our very Being, then Cartesian skepticism about the external world will also turn out to be distorted. Before we ask what we *know*, we have to ask how we *are*. Since I *am* before I *think* (254/211), ontology precedes epistemology.

At this point, Heidegger has provided enough of an ontology of Dasein to make it quite clear that he rejects the presuppositions of Cartesianism. Dasein has a special way of Being, care, by virtue of which it finds itself enmeshed in a world – that is, a system of meanings and purposes. Thus, "the world is disclosed essentially *along with the* Being of Dasein" (247/203). If I understand myself as a factory worker, then I understand the world of factory work: I am able to deal with issues such as productivity and pay. My own identity simply cannot be separated from the sphere of concerns and issues in which I operate.

Heidegger now adds a crucial claim: "with the disclosedness of the world, the 'world' has in each case been discovered too" (247/203). Recall that "world", in quotation marks, refers to "the totality of those entities which can be present-at-hand" (93/64). This is just what Descartes means by "world". Heidegger's claim, then, is that as I go about living my life, things are revealed to me. If I exist as a factory worker, the factory building itself must be available to me, along with many other entities, such as machines, raw materials and my co-workers. (All of these beings "can be present-at-hand": they can manifest themselves as mere objects under certain special circumstances, although normally, of course, they are much more than that.) In short, it is essential to my own way of Being that I have access to beings other than myself. "Along with Dasein as Being-in-the-world, entities within-the-world have in each case already been disclosed" (251/207).

Readers must decide for themselves whether these claims are legitimate, or whether they are simply naked assertions. Is it still compelling to wonder whether I may be dreaming the factory, or whether I am insane, or deceived by an evil demon? In any case, Heidegger has not *proved* that entities are uncovered to us – he sees the very request for a proof as misguided (249–50/ 205–6). He responds to the skeptic's demand for a proof of the external world not by offering a proof, but by refusing to play the skeptic's game and trying to cure us of the misguided attitudes that make the game compelling in the first place. He writes (in a sentence that sounds thoroughly Wittgensteinian), "Perhaps it is precisely the task of a philosophical investigation ultimately to deprive many problems of their sham existence".[56] Heidegger ascribes philosophical pseudo-problems to falling (250/206), to the everyday tendency to evade the *truly* pressing issues: who am I, and what am I to do?

Heidegger holds that the discoveredness of beings is so fundamental to human existence that it is prior to anything that can be proved or disproved. As he will explain further in §44, to deny discoveredness is in effect to deny one's own Being – to commit an act of "suicide" (271/229).

In §43b and §43c, Heidegger discusses the ontology of the real. We usually use "reality" as a synonym for beings in general, but for Heidegger, "real" beings are a particular kind of entity: present-at-hand things (254/211). The Being of these things is their "reality". (Etymologically, *realitas* means precisely "thinghood".) Present-at-hand things *are* not merely in relation to us, but in themselves: they have properties that are independent of us. Thus, an investigation of reality has to investigate independence and in-itself-ness.

Heidegger argues that in order to understand these features of reality, we have to begin by interpreting our own way of Being, care (255/211). This may sound highly paradoxical. If real entities are independent of us, how can we understand their Being by turning to ourselves?

Heidegger's answer is worth reading carefully: "Being (not entities) is dependent upon the understanding of Being; that is to say, Reality (not the Real) is dependent upon care" (255/212). If Dasein disappeared from the planet, other things would continue to be. Ready-to-hand entities might no longer be – it can be argued that a tool without a user is no longer a tool. But other animals could live on, rocks would still be present-at-hand, and so on. However, *Being* would no longer be given. This statement may sound less strange if we recall that Being is "that on the basis of which entities are already understood. . . . The Being of entities 'is' not itself an entity" (25–26/6). Being can be described as what it means for entities to be – or as the background against which entities can show up as entities – or as the difference it makes that there are entities, rather than nothing. But entities can mean something, or show up, or make a difference, only *to someone*. If there is no one to whom entities can make a difference, then Being cannot take place, or be given to anyone.

Note that this works both ways: Being depends on Dasein, but Dasein also depends on Being, because Dasein is essentially the entity who understands Being. As Heidegger puts it, "Being 'is' only in the understanding of those

56. *History of the Concept of Time*, p. 162.

entities to whose Being something like an understanding of Being belongs" (228/183).

In regards to the question of reality, this means that reality, as a kind of Being, depends on human understanding. Real *things* are independent of us, but what it *means* to be real depends on us. One should not misinterpret Heidegger as saying that we can arbitrarily *decide* what it means to be real. Instead, he is claiming that in order to understand what it means to be real, we have to look at how things present themselves as real *in the context of human life*.

For example, our geologist is studying a piece of quartz that is undeniably, solidly real. It was real before she studied it, and it will continue to be real once she is done with it. Now, how does this mineral come to have the *meaning* "real" for the geologist? How does it *reveal* itself as real in her life? How does it make a difference to her that the quartz is real, rather than unreal? According to Heidegger, we cannot answer these questions unless we investigate how the geologist's existence is rooted in a past, projects towards a future, and falls into the present. Thanks to this care structure, she is in a world – a world of many concerns, including her family, religion and profession. Within her world, some things *present* themselves to her in such a way that she can study certain aspects of them with the methods of geology. Reality is the kind of presence that characterizes such aspects of things. Now, neither the quartz nor anything else could present itself to the geologist in any way without the context in which things can present themselves to us in the first place – and that context is care. Although we are getting ahead of ourselves a little, we can say that care, which is thoroughly *temporal*, provides the context that gives meaning to reality. This is a special case of the general thesis towards which Heidegger is working in *Being and Time*: time provides the context that gives meaning to all modes of Being.

In §44 Heidegger continues to explore what is relative to Dasein, and what is not. The theme here is truth, which is traditionally associated with Being and is traditionally understood as some sort of "correspondence" or "agreement", either between things and statements, or between things and mental judgments.

Section 44a reviews a number of positions (including the theory of "validity" that young Heidegger himself had adopted) and comes to the conclusion that "agreement" is a most unclear concept. The concept of "uncovering" is more helpful (261/218) – as is suggested by the Greek word for truth, *aletheia*, which etymologically means "unconcealment". To use Heidegger's own example: I say that a painting is hanging askew. I then look at the painting, and confirm that this statement is true. The usual interpretation of this event would be that I found a correspondence between my mental representation of the painting and the painting itself. Heidegger prefers to think of it this way: when I confirm that my statement is true, I am confirming that it *uncovers* the painting. In other words, my statement helps the painting show itself as crooked. This approach helps us avoid the Cartesian contrast between the inner subject and outer objects, and it helps us focus on what Heidegger takes to be essential: the fact that things *display themselves* to us.[57]

One advantage of focusing on the fact that things show themselves is that it naturally leads to the question of how it is *possible* for things to show themselves. As we know, Heidegger's answer is that our own Being, care, makes this possible. Things can be "discovered" only because Dasein is primordially "disclosed", opened up, by care. Dasein is "in the truth" (263/221) thanks to the dimensions of care that Heidegger reviews on 264/221–2.

But Dasein is also "in untruth" (264/222), because falling generates hackneyed, superficial interpretations of the world. As we fall, we get wrapped up in the particular beings with which we are dealing, while the meaning of these beings becomes shallow and dull. For instance, I may be so absorbed in cleaning house that as I straighten out my Degas, I automatically treat it as just another pretty decoration, without suspecting its real artistic power. My everyday understanding of the Being of this work of art does uncover the entity, but only in an impoverished way. In other words, the entity shows itself to me, but in an overly restricted and misleading manner. The unconcealment that forms part of our existence is accompanied by concealment. In Division II we will see that authentic existence can refresh our understanding and "defend [unconcealment] *against* semblance and disguise" (265/222). However, the battle for truth can never be won once and for all; falling is a permanent tendency in our Being.

If it seems strange to claim that we are both in the truth and in untruth, consider that this claim can apply even to assertions. A statement can be illuminating, yet at the same time misleading. "My Degas is pigment and cloth, just like the upholstery on my old sofa." This statement illuminates a real parallel between the painting and the piece of furniture, but what it primarily expresses is a refusal to acknowledge what is unique to the painting as a work of art. The statement both uncovers and conceals. Dr P.'s description of a glove as "a continuous surface with five outpouchings" is another case in point: it is accurate, but it misses what is essential. In his later writings, Heidegger is fond of saying that such statements are "correct, but not true": that is, they do reveal something, but they shed no light on what is *most* important – they may even promote an attitude that *covers up* what matters most. If we extend this principle from the narrow domain of statements to all human practices, we can see that although beings are always manifest to us as we do things, they are usually manifest in superficial ways.

Pages 266–8/223–5 explain the origin of the conventional understanding of truth as correspondence. Once care has revealed things for us, we are capable of making illuminating statements that share these revelations with others. We can then be misled into thinking that the illumination, the truth, is somehow

57. A note on translation: Heidegger never speaks of "what one has in mind" when one makes an assertion (260/217, 261/218). The phrase *was gemeint wird* should be translated "what is meant". Heidegger always avoids suggesting that meaning is confined to a private subjective domain, such as a mind.

contained in the statements, when instead, the basic illumination precedes and makes possible the statements. Truth then gets conceived as a present-at-hand relation between a present-at-hand assertion and a present-at-hand state of affairs. It is probably right, in some sense, to say that true statements "correspond" to things, or are in harmony with them – but we will never understand this harmony until we consider the source of the original illumination that makes it possible.

Many philosophers contrast the correspondence theory of truth with the coherence theory: the more our beliefs form a consistent system, the truer they are as a whole. Heidegger would object that this theory still focuses on beliefs as the bearers of truth. Beliefs and assertions are founded on a more fundamental phenomenon: care.

If truth is illumination, then truth is relative to Dasein (270/227). Heidegger's claim here is very similar to his earlier claim that Being is relative to Dasein. If we keep in mind that truth means unconcealment, then what he says will seem closer to common sense. Heidegger uses Newton as an example (269/226–7); we will use Einstein. If Einstein was right to claim that $E = mc^2$, then the relation of energy, mass and the speed of light expressed in this equation is a relation that predated Einstein, and will continue as long as the universe continues. Einstein did not create this relation; he recognized it, and tried to do justice to it in his statements (cf. 270/227). However, the *formula $E = mc^2$ was* created by Einstein, and it was not *true*, that is, illuminating, until Einstein formulated and explained it. If there were no human beings who could interpret this formula, then it would no longer be illuminating. An assertion can be enlightening (or misleading) only if there is someone who can be enlightened (or misled). To sum up: there can be *beings* without Dasein, but *truth* and *Being* cannot occur without Dasein.

There is much to say about truth as unconcealment, and this is one of Heidegger's favorite themes in his later writings. The simple fact that things show themselves to us turns out to be an inexhaustible source of wonder and puzzlement.

We have reached the end of Division I. What has Heidegger achieved so far? By focusing on our everyday practices, he has developed a rich interpretation of Dasein's way of Being. Dasein is always enmeshed in a field of interconnected possibilities – a world. Dasein is always attuned to the world in a certain way, and capably pursues various opportunities within it. Dasein is also a member of a community with shared norms and expectations. By participating in its community and its world, Dasein establishes what matters to it. In this way, we explore the beings around us at the same time as we establish who we are. This interpretation of human existence is strikingly different from the Cartesian picture that still dominates much of science and common sense. For Descartes, I am a conscious thing, connected (perhaps) to material things by my perceptions and judgments. For Heidegger, I am not a thing at all, but an engaged participant in the world. Perceptions and judgments are less fundamental to this process than *practices* – ways of doing things.

CHAPTER FOUR

Being and Time:
Division II and Beyond

It may seem that by the end of Division I, Heidegger has given a thorough interpretation of our Being. He has conceived of Dasein in terms of existence, Being-in-the-world, and care; he has described the elements of care and their interconnections; he has described various kinds of entities we encounter. However, in §45 he points out that he has not yet examined *authentic* existence – and this means that the depths of Dasein itself lie unexplored. The intimations of authenticity in Division I have indicated that it is a way of Being in which Dasein is truly itself, in which we are not simply absorbed in falling and the they-self, but live with clarity and integrity. We need to consider authenticity in order to understand the deep character of our Being, in particular our *temporality*.

Division II, then, will investigate a number of phenomena that are bound up with authenticity, such as death, conscience and resoluteness. Authentic existence will illuminate our temporality, and Heidegger will then reinterpret everydayness in terms of temporality. We need to describe these crucial aspects of Dasein if we are ever to answer the question of how Dasein can understand Being in general.

My analysis of *Being and Time* from now on will be more concise than it has been so far, because I assume the reader has gained some facility with Heidegger's language and concepts, and because my explanations of Division I have already anticipated some major ideas in Division II.

§§46–53: Facing up to mortality

If you knew that this was the last day of your life, what would you do? Look for pleasures? Rob your neighbor's house? Spend time with your family? Pray? Write poetry? Read Heidegger?

The answer to this question says a lot about who you are – what you care about the most and how you really want to live. The certainty of death is liberating, in a sense: it frees us from trivialities. If we lived each day as if it were our last, we would not waste time on empty gestures; we would focus, each of us, on the task of being ourselves. The sense of impending death is known for making one's life flash before one's eyes: in this moment one reviews one's life story as a whole, and sums up its successes and failures, judging who one has been in the light of who one chooses to be. When we sense the fragility of life, we also sense its significance. Death brings one face to face with oneself.

Of course, we do *not* live each day as if it were our last. If we knew we were going to die in the next few hours, we would probably feel an over-whelming sense of unfinished business, and wish that we had been more serious about living our lives. In everyday existence, we generally ignore the possibility of death; we tell ourselves that brooding on death is "morbid". Still, each moment really *could* be our last, and our everyday consciousness prevents us from reaping the benefits of facing up to this fact.

As long as readers keep in mind this phenomenon of facing up to mortality, they will be able to follow Heidegger's meticulous analyses in §§46–53. He begins with a puzzle (§46): if Dasein has future possibilities open to it as long as it exists, then how can we ever grasp it as a whole? To say that someone is essentially a sculptor, *and nothing else*, would be to eliminate her freedom to choose what she is going to make of herself. Even if she continues to choose to be a sculptor, she is not *just* a sculptor – she is, more importantly, a chooser. It seems that, since she is a chooser, she can never be grasped as a whole, finished thing. In general, it appears that we can never specify what Dasein is as a whole without eliminating its freedom. Death, of course, appears to be the end of Dasein and its possibilities. Do we become a whole, then, when we die? But it would be strange to say that we are complete only when we no longer exist.

Clearly, these puzzles require us to analyze what we *mean* by "whole". It turns out that different kinds of entities have different ways of being a whole and reaching an end (§48). Dasein's way of being a whole is unique. It involves neither the elimination of possibilities nor their realization – it is a certain way of *having* possibilities in which these possibilities are *limited*. Dasein's possibilities are always limited by *the possibility of the impossibility of existing* – and this is what Heidegger means by "death" (294/250, 307/262).

The word "death" makes it difficult to distinguish the phenomenon Heidegger is discussing from what he calls "demise" – the actual event in which a human body ceases to function (291/247). The word "mortality" would probably have been more helpful, if slightly less dramatic, than "death" – in fact, in some later writings he prefers to call us "mortals".[1] Mortality is an ongoing condition of

---

1. See e.g. "Building Dwelling Thinking" and "The Thing", both in *Poetry, Language, Thought.*

human beings, not a one-time event; it is a possibility that essentially belongs to us, not an actual happening. This is Heidegger's theme.[2]

Strange as it may sound, Heidegger claims that my mortality is my "ownmost" possibility (294/250): in other words, what makes my life my own is ultimately the sheer fact that it is mine to live, mine to make something of, in the face of my possible non-existence. Every other possibility is something that I may be free not to do, and that someone else may be able to do just as well as I can. But my death is a possibility that necessarily faces me alone: no one can face it for me (284/240).

Heidegger says that his claims about death do not deny the possibility of an afterlife (292/247–8). "As long as I have not asked about Dasein in its structure and as long as I have not defined death in what it is, I cannot even rightly ask what could come after Dasein in connection with its death."[3] If pressed on this point, he might explain himself as follows. If there is an afterlife for us, and if we continue to be Dasein in the afterlife, then we will continue to be faced with death as a possibility, and the Beyond will be a *world*, in the Heideggerian sense. On the other hand, if we become truly immortal in the afterlife, and death is no longer a possibility for us at all, then we will have entered a radically different state of Being and will no longer be Dasein. An entity whose possibilities always have to remain open, who is guaranteed a future and is essentially impervious to death, is not Dasein. Such an entity would have a fundamentally different way of acting and understanding.

Heidegger claims that death is "certain" (300–2/256–8). "This certainty, that 'I myself am in that I will die', is *the basic certainty of Dasein itself*. It is a genuine statement of Dasein, while *cogito sum* [Descartes' 'I think, I am'] is only the semblance of such a statement."[4] Even this claim does not deny an afterlife. Recall that "death" means *mortality* – a *possibility*. The claim that death is certain, then, means that our nonexistence is certainly *possible*. This statement is less sophistical than it looks: death is not just a remote possibility that cannot quite be ruled out, but a possibility that necessarily hangs over everything we do, at every moment (302/258).

Once Heidegger has made it clear that death must be understood as a possibility that belongs to all human life, he sketches an authentic response to death (§53), which he calls *Vorlaufen* (306/262). The word literally means "running forwards"; perhaps "facing up" would be a better translation than "anticipation". Authentic existence involves facing up to mortality – not by worrying about when demise will come, but by accepting the finitude of one's possibilities and choosing in the light of this finitude. As we saw, the realization

---

2. Readers may want to consult the following vigorous critiques of Heidegger's views on death, and decide for themselves whether these critiques are based on a confusion of death with demise: J-P. Sartre, *Being and Nothingness*, tr. H. E. Barnes (New York: Washington Square Press, 1966), Part IV, Chapter 1, II (E); P. Edwards, *Heidegger on Death: A Critical Evaluation* (La Salle, Illinois: Hegeler Institute, 1979).
3. *History of the Concept of Time*, p. 314.   4. *Ibid.*, pp. 316–17.

that each moment could be one's last liberates one from the everyday trivialities and distractions of the "they".

Heidegger claims that anxiety is about death (295/251, 310–11/266). Let's return to our description of a moment of anxiety in order to understand how death is involved in it. I am weeding in my garden when my activity suddenly seems pointless. "What is the meaning of all this?" "Who am I?" I ask. I am alienated from myself as a gardener and from the garden as part of my world. In fact, I am uncomfortable with *every* role I can play in the world, and indifferent to everything around me: all this seems meaningless. What is left over? Simply the naked truth that I find myself in a situation where I am forced to make something of myself. But this is precisely what I realize when I face up to mortality: when I accept the fact that my possibilities are neither unlimited nor guaranteed, I realize the importance of choosing a possibility and defining myself by it. When I feel that this could be the last moment of my life, I necessarily ask myself what my life adds up to and who I am. Do I really want to live and die as a gardener (a sculptor, a politician, a priest)? In anxiety, I face up to mortality because I feel the fragility of my life and the necessity of deciding what it all means.

§§54–60: Owning up to indebtedness and responsibility

Heidegger is not easily satisfied: he claims that as yet, he has presented no evidence that we can actually achieve authenticity. The phenomenon of *conscience* provides the further "testimony" he is requiring (311/267). (In these sections, he exploits a lot of legal terminology.)

As always, readers must approach Heidegger's analyses with their own experiences fresh in their mind. They must focus on the peculiar sensation of what he terms the call of conscience. Let's say that a tax lawyer is working late at night on the details of a case, trying to minimize the taxes that his client must pay. He becomes increasingly uneasy; he begins to have a feeling of wrongness. His conscience is bothering him.

Now, there are many possible interpretations of this feeling. Is he doing something illegal, and is he afraid of the law? Maybe so, but certainly one's conscience can be troubled by legal actions, too. Is he breaking some moral code, then? If so, how does he know what this code is? Is God alerting him to the golden rule, as a Christian might say? Is his own reason alerting him to the categorical imperative, as a Kantian would claim? Or, as a sociobiologist would have us believe, is his instinct telling him that his actions are evolutionarily unfit?

What is common to all these interpretations is that they assume that the call of conscience is a response to some particular violation of what is right; conscience tells me that I am guilty *on this occasion*. But Heidegger views such moral judgments as relatively superficial (328–9/283, 332/286, 334/288). According to him, conscience can speak out at *any* moment, and it is always justified in doing so – because "entities whose Being is care . . . *are* guilty in the very basis of their Being" (332/286). We are always essentially guilty, for guilt is not about what we have or have not done, but about two inescapable features of care. We have already encountered them, but Heidegger now puts them in a fresh perspective.

We ordinarily associate guilt with *causing* something that we should *not* have caused, or with *not* causing something that we *should* have caused. From this everyday notion, Heidegger extracts the formal concept of "Being-the-basis of a nullity" (329/283). In other words, guilt involves both some sort of *foundation* and some sort of negativity, or *not*-ness. Guilt, in this general sense, can be found both in our having a past (a dimension of guilt I will call indebtedness) and in our having a future (a dimension of guilt I will call responsibility).

I am *indebted* because I have a past which must serve as a *foundation* for my existence, but which I *cannot* control (329–330/284). I did not bring myself into the world, and I cannot now change what I have been, but I have to work with what I have been in order to be someone. In the case of our lawyer, he has to live with the fact that he finds himself in this time and place, with the experience and habits of being a tax lawyer. Whatever he becomes in the future must somehow be based on his past. It would be inauthentic to pretend that he can create himself anew, and have complete control over his entire existence.

I am *responsible* because on the *foundation* of my past, I project possibilities that are *not* other possibilities (331/285). That is, I cannot be everything at once, but am forced to choose an approach to the world that excludes other approaches. If the tax lawyer continues to be a lawyer, he is excluding other career and life possibilities. It would be inauthentic to pretend either that he has no other options, or that he can afford the luxury of not choosing at all.

Heidegger's concept of guilt, then, offers us a new way of looking at the past and future dimensions of our Being. At this point it may be useful to summarize the various concepts that we have applied to these two dimensions.

Past	*Future*
thrownness	projection
attunement	understanding
facticity	existentiality
Being-already-in-(the-world)	Being-ahead-of-itself
indebtedness	responsibility
	potentiality-for-Being

Heidegger claims that we need a special moment of insight, the call of conscience, to alert us to these aspects of our existence, because everyday existence is absorbed in the present and avoids owning up to guilt. In the call of conscience, then, Dasein as care is silently calling Dasein as the fallen they-self, alerting inauthentic Dasein to the indebtedness and responsibility that are part of care itself (322/277).

Of course, we must not think of these two Daseins as two different persons or things – say, a little angel and a little devil. The authentic and the inauthentic self are not separate entities at all, but different ways of Being for a single entity (152–3/117, 365/317–18). The call of conscience is a conflict between two styles of existence. One should also be careful not to interpret conscience as a retreat from the "external" world into one's own "inner" self. For Heidegger, the self has no Being apart from its Being-in-the-world. Authentic existence is not an escape from the world, but a way of existing in it (318/273, 344/298).

The authentic style of existence involves "choosing to choose" (313/268, 314/270). We are always choosing, in a sense, because we are always projecting possibilities. But we do not always choose to choose; often enough, we shrug off the burden of responsibility by acting as if our choices were mandated by our social status, fate, law, race or some other force. The lawyer may tell himself, for instance, that he has to help his client pay lower taxes because that is his job. This attitude obscures the fact that his career is a possibility of existing that he has chosen, and that he is continuing to choose. Conscience asks us to *own up* to our guilt. It asks us to make our actions our *own* (*eigen*, in German) and thus to exist *authentically* (*eigentlich*).

Owning up to guilt, like facing up to mortality, is connected to anxiety (322/277). The world feels perfectly comfortable and secure as long as we deny indebtedness by supposing that we have complete control over who we are – or if we deny responsibility by supposing that our life is all laid out for us in advance, and there is no need for us to make difficult choices. When we recognize guilt – the fact that we exist "as an entity which has to be as it is and as it can be" (321/276) – the meaning of our lives can seem all too fragile. This is exactly what one feels in anxiety.

When one owns up to guilt, one becomes *resolute* (§60). Resoluteness (*Entschlossenheit*) is a particularly illuminating form of disclosedness (*Erschlossenheit*) (343/297). It opens up the world clearly, and even allows authentic relationships to others – although Heidegger has frustratingly little to say about this (344–5/298).

Why is resoluteness so illuminating? Recall that the *world* is structured as a field of *reference*-relations. In particular, we understand ready-to-hand entities in terms of the network of purposes into which they fit, purposes which are ultimately for the sake of a possibility of Dasein's Being (116/84). Naturally, then, when we get clear about the possibility that is guiding our lives by resolutely choosing it, the world at large becomes clearer (344/298). What Heidegger calls "the Situation" opens up to us (346/299). The Situation is the authentic way of being "there", of inhabiting the present. In the Situation, one no longer exists as a falling they-self, but seizes one's thrownness and interprets it in terms of an explicit choice.

The tax lawyer, for instance, may ordinarily be absorbed in the daily routine of his work. He understands his life superficially, merely in terms of "what must be done" to succeed as a lawyer. Conscience can remind him that it is his responsibility to make something of himself on the basis of who he already is.

Now he may choose a very different course for his life – or he may choose to remain a lawyer. In either case, he has gained a clearer understanding of who he is, what is truly important to him, and what he needs to do in the world; he has entered the Situation.

We should not overestimate the power of resoluteness. Resoluteness cannot "resolve" anything in the sense of guaranteeing authenticity in the future. Resolutions have to be reaffirmed and defended against our constant tendency to drift back into irresoluteness (345/299). (As we all know, it is not enough to be resolute only on New Year's Day.)

Heidegger also cautions us that "even resolutions remain dependent upon the 'they' and its world" (345–6/299). I can never create an utterly new set of meanings for my life; I have to draw on the available stock of interpretations of life, which have all been filtered through the "they" (cf. 168/130, 213/169, 435/383). Whether I choose to be a lawyer, a mystic or a chemist, it is the common sense of my culture – the "they" – that provides me with my initial understanding of what these options mean. Authentic existence seizes a possibility furnished by the "they" and makes this possibility its own.

One final clarification: resoluteness is not rigid stubbornness (355/307–8). An authentic person is free to change her mind – but she will do so because she lucidly grasps her Situation in relation to who she chooses to be, and not because of whim, cowardice or social pressures.

There is no doubt that Heidegger's interpretation of conscience and guilt is unusual. I leave it to the reader to decide whether he succeeds in showing that ordinary views of conscience can be explained as superficial manifestations of conscience in his sense (§59). The broader question is whether his concept of authenticity is too formal and empty. Some critics object that the notion of authenticity gives us no guidance at all. The joke among Heidegger's students ran: "I am resolved, only towards what I don't know."[5] Heideggerian conscience speaks by remaining silent (318/273, 342–3/296), and Heideggerian ethics, if there is such a thing, seems to give us no standards whatsoever. The tax lawyer who feels the pangs of conscience may resolutely decide to remain a tax lawyer, or resolutely decide to give all his money to the poor, or resolutely decide to embezzle a pile of money and fly off to the Bahamas. The paramount rule that Heidegger gives us is simply: choose! But if there are no guidelines for choosing, don't we end up with an arbitrary irrationalism?

Heidegger's retort is that the very demand for such guidelines is an attempt to turn life into a neat, calculable business venture with a money-back guarantee. If our conscience provided us with tidy, unambiguous rules, it "would deny to existence nothing less than the very *possibility of taking action*" (340/294). In other words, genuine decisions involve taking a risk in the context of a unique situation. For Heidegger, rules have no authority for "a free existing". Instead, we can take inspiration from heroes or role models: we can revere

5. Löwith, *My Life in Germany Before and After 1933*, p. 30.

"the repeatable possibilities of existence" (443/391). But to try to set up some particular possibility of existence as the universal, objective purpose of life is, he suggests, "*the* misunderstanding of human existence in general".[6]

At some points Heidegger does imply that some types of existentiell possibilities are more authentic than others, and he seems to be gesturing towards an ethics. We saw that in §26 he distinguishes between authentic "leaping ahead" and inauthentic "leaping in". Elsewhere he distinguishes between types of friendship:

> a friendship may no longer and not primarily consist in a resolute and thus mutually generous way of siding with one another in the world, but in a constant and prior watching out for how the other sets out to deal with what is meant by friendship, in a constant check on whether he turns out to be one or not.[7]

Of course, whenever Heidegger makes remarks such as this he is quick to add that he does not intend them as moral or religious preaching. It is a pity that his fear of appearing to dictate individual choices discouraged him from pursuing his phenomenology of human relationships.

The question of Heidegger's ethics, or lack thereof, is a difficult question that deserves to be considered by all his readers – especially, many would insist, given his own political decisions in the 1930s. We will consider the question of his politics in our next chapter.

§63: Existentiell truth as the basis of existential truth

Division II, Chapter 3 is rather complex. Heidegger begins by combining his analyses of death and guilt to explore the possibility of "anticipatory resoluteness" – in other words, a kind of owning up to guilt that faces up to mortality (§62). He then provides some important reflections on his general method (§63). In §64 he explores the nature of selfhood, and in §§65–66 he introduces the concept of temporality. To sum up this chapter, Heidegger is establishing the fundamentally temporal nature of the self by examining the most authentic way in which the self can possibly exist; §63 justifies this procedure. We will depart slightly from the text by beginning with the methodological issues.

Section 63 addresses a suspicion that most readers cannot help feeling by now: Heidegger seems to be basing his account of Dasein on his own, personal ideal of "authentic" existence. It appears that he was already working towards this ideal from the first page of *Being and Time*. Is the whole book just a way of promoting his own preferences and passing them off as valid for all human beings?

6. *The Metaphysical Foundations of Logic*, p. 185.
7. *History of the Concept of Time*, p. 280.

In part, this objection is based on the idea that one should begin a scientific investigation free of all presuppositions and prejudices. But we have already seen that for Heidegger, this is a very wrong-headed idea. All understanding depends on projecting certain possibilities in advance (191–2/150). This is not a vicious circle, but a fruitful one (194–5/152–3, 363/315). If we "presuppose" as little as possible about Dasein, we will just end up with an artificially vacuous concept of Dasein. Instead, we should begin with the rich understanding of Dasein that we already possess, and use this understanding as a guide to our further research.

But there is a further dimension to the problem that Heidegger has not fully addressed before now. If he is trying to grasp the Being of Dasein as such – human nature, to use old-fashioned language – why is he giving such priority to "authentic" existence, which is only *one* possible mode of human Being? After all, if we wanted to grasp the nature of water, it would be wrong to take ice as our primary model. Instead, we should find what is common to water in *all* its forms, frozen, liquid and vapor, without giving preference to any one of these.

However, Heidegger would reply, water is a present-at-hand entity, while Dasein is an *existing* entity: its Being is an issue for it, and it has always decided for itself who it is by adopting some specific way of Being. This means that we always understand existence on the basis of a *particular* possibility of existing. I can never begin by understanding myself as a case of Humanity as such. I begin by understanding myself as this son, this husband, this teacher, this American – and this is not a theoretical understanding, but a way of approaching the world, of living. This way of life gives me a certain insight into myself, others and things around me. If I ever philosophize about human nature, I have to do so on the basis of this insight. "The ontological 'truth' of the existential analysis is developed on the ground of the primordial existentiell truth" (364/316).

What does this mean, and what does it not mean? Heidegger is certainly not saying that we can never discover broadly applicable truths about Dasein: one can challenge and deepen one's own self-understanding until it sheds light on basic structures of human existence. He would not agree with the belief one finds today in some academic circles that we can speak *only* as mouthpieces for our particular corner of facticity (say, as lesbians of color). Heidegger is not implying, either, that any existentiell starting point is as good as any other. Some forms of existentiell understanding are relatively superficial, and people who understand themselves and their lives superficially will be handicapped in their interpretations of Dasein. What he *is* saying is that philosophers cannot do otherwise than *begin* with the understanding they possess as particular, living human beings – limited and defective though this understanding may be. Ontology has to start with "*ontical possibilities*" (360/312). This is why Heidegger has taken a possibility with which he is familiar on the existentiell level, the possibility of existing authentically, as his main clue to the Being of Dasein.

Heidegger's claims in this section appear to contradict his claim in §9 that Dasein should not be "construed in terms of some concrete possible idea of existence" (69/43). It seems clear that from the start of Division I, he has tended to interpret everydayness as inauthentic – that is, he has construed it in terms of the existentiell possibility of authenticity.

Is Heidegger calling on *us*, then, to live authentically? Does he think that a personal transformation is a prerequisite to understanding *Being and Time*? Commentators differ on this question.[8] In my own view, the answer is yes. Since some ways of life are more insightful than others, it seems clear that a philosopher must live as insightfully as possible. Heidegger claimed as early as 1919 that "genuine insights" require "the genuineness of a personal life".[9] He consistently holds that the correctness of theories depends on a more basic unconcealment that pertains to our Being-in-the-world. It follows that seekers of truth, such as writers and readers of philosophical texts, must not only construct the right theories, but also *live* in the right way.

But what if Heidegger is wrong, and what he calls authenticity is *not* the right way to live? What if other styles of existing are more insightful? One may worry that he is imposing a false ideal on his readers. But fortunately, he is not dogmatic about his findings. He does not claim to have proved anything beyond a doubt, but to have articulated certain phenomena for the first time. We may then "*decide of* [our] *own accord*" how illuminating his interpretation is (362/315). As he puts it near the end of the book, his way is "only *one way* which we may take" – but whether "this is the *only* way or even the *right* one can be decided only *after one has gone along it*" (487/437, translation modified). In addition, he claims to make no "authoritarian pronouncement" about how we should choose to live (360/312). Of course, Heidegger obviously views authentic existence as deeper and less deluded than everyday existence – but we are free to delude ourselves if we wish! Furthermore, he has not specified any particular course of action that we should choose. In fact, some critics, as we just saw, object to the very indefiniteness of his concept of resoluteness. Heidegger's notion of authenticity is too rich for some, too thin for others.

§§62, 64–65: Temporality as the key to the Being of Dasein

Now that we understand why Heidegger is using a particular possibility, authentic existence, as the clue to Dasein's Being in general, we can see how

---

8. Zimmerman, in *Eclipse of the Self*, argues that Heidegger demands an existentiell transformation in his readers; M. Gelven, in *A Commentary on Heidegger's* Being and Time, 2nd edn (DeKalb, Illinois: Northern Illinois University Press, 1989), takes the opposite point of view.
9. Notes by Oskar Becker from Heidegger's lecture course "Die Idee der Philosophie und das Weltanschauungsproblem", quoted in Kisiel, *The Genesis of Heidegger's* Being and Time, p. 17. These words from the end of the course are not included in the *Gesamtausgabe* version (in GA 56/57).

he uses "anticipatory resoluteness" as the clue to temporality, which he calls the "ultimate" basis for understanding Dasein (351/304).

In §62 Heidegger rounds out his portrayal of authenticity by showing how resoluteness is connected to death. (This is not his final treatment of authenticity; his fullest presentation of it will come in §74.) He argues that since resoluteness is a recognition of guilt, and since the future dimension of guilt involves Being-towards-death, resoluteness in its most developed form must involve anticipation (facing up to mortality) (353–4/305–6). For example, one may resolutely choose to be a lawyer – one may project the possibility of being a lawyer as a guiding possibility in one's life. But this possibility is one that others can share, one that cannot *ultimately* define one as an individual. My "ownmost" possibility, as we have seen, is the possibility of having no more possibilities: death. No one can take over or share my own mortality. One's mortality is one's own as "one's occupation, one's social status, or one's age" (283/239) can never be. Complete resoluteness, then, does not merely choose a publicly available option such as being a lawyer, but chooses one's own fundamental capacity for existing in the face of death.

Anticipatory resoluteness should not be confused with any sort of cult of death or some suicidal attitude. It simply means that one accepts our basic condition as human beings: we have to make something (or someone) of ourselves, and this project of living is subject to some important limitations. First, the life one builds must be based on one's facticity, on who one already is. Secondly, one's life will exclude an infinity of other possible lives that one could have led. Thirdly, a human life is susceptible to termination at any moment. When we make our choices in full recognition of these limitations, we take authentic, clear-sighted stances. This way of life is not morbid, but soberly joyful (358/310). For a fine example of anticipatory resoluteness one can consider the *Phaedo*, Plato's portrait of the last day of Socrates' life. Socrates – who illustrates many aspects of authenticity – dies as he lived, thinking and provoking others to think, courageously, serenely and steadfastly.

As Heidegger explains in §64, taking a steadfast stance is the only sort of constancy that we can achieve (369/322). We do not possess an underlying, enduring soul or self: there is nothing about Dasein that is present-at-hand throughout its life, simply because Dasein's way of Being is not presence-at-hand. Dasein's Being is care, and the kind of steadiness that care admits is anticipatory resoluteness, or steadfastness. We tend to think of ourselves as having an unchanging, thinglike self because falling leads us to treat ourselves as if we had the same sort of Being as the things we encounter in our world (368/321–2).

Some philosophers are fond of asking what, if anything, remains the same about a person who undergoes various changes. If my brain were transplanted into another body, would I be the same person? What if I suffered from amnesia? But Heidegger never asks such questions. He would claim that these so-called problems of personal identity cannot properly be explored without a thorough ontology of our way of Being. Until we carry out such an ontology, we are too likely to assume that sameness, or identity, means the continued presence of something that remains unchanged. For human beings, however, identity can only mean taking a stance – authentically choosing one possible way of existing.

Other philosophers, such as Kant, and religions, such as Buddhism, have questioned or denied the existence of a thinglike self. But Heidegger emphasizes that in addition to recognizing that we are not present-at-hand entities, we have to analyze the Being that *is* ours, namely, care.

When we do, we find that the "meaning" of care is temporality; in other words, temporality is the context that makes care possible and intelligible (§65). We can even say, "*Dasein itself . . .* is *time*".[10] We have now reached one of the key points in Heidegger's book.

We have already been anticipating Heidegger by using temporal terms to describe Dasein's Being: having a future, having a past and so on. But now we must ask what these terms really mean. We ordinarily think of time as a timeline – a sequence of instants or points on the line. We exist at one moment, the present, but we are constantly moving on to the next moment; before us there stretches an infinity of past moments, and ahead of us stretches an infinity of future moments. However, Heidegger will soon denounce this ordinary understanding of time as yet another manifestation of fallenness. What, then, is the meaning of "future", "past" and "present" as they apply to Dasein's own Being?

Future means "the coming in which Dasein, in its ownmost potentiality-for-Being, comes towards itself" (373/325). This is the most important dimension of our temporality. It is the condition of having to choose to be who I am. We have explored various aspects of this condition, including its finitude: the future is finite, because it is bounded by mortality.

Past means being thrown – already being in a world. Heidegger claims that the future is, in a way, the source of the past (373/326). This claim makes no sense in terms of the ordinary understanding of time as a timeline, but it does make sense within Dasein's existence. My potentiality-for-Being is not unencumbered by a past; I am already someone, and I can never eliminate my past. But in turn, my past gets its *meaning* for me only from my projection of a future. Let's say that a woman was born into a poor family. This fact is part of her life, part of who she is, only insofar as it enters into her future. She may pursue the possibility of being a stockbroker, and she may then interpret her past as a life of deprivation from which she is emerging. She may, instead, pursue the possibility of being a novelist; her past is then revealed as a source of stories. Our lives are always a process of taking over who we have been in the service of who we will be. As Heidegger puts it elsewhere, "we are [what] we were, and we will be what we receive and appropriate from what we were, and here the most important factor will be *how* we do so".[11] "The actuality of what has been resides in its possibility. The possibility becomes in each case manifest as

10. *History of the Concept of Time*, p. 197.   11. *Plato's Sophist*, p. 158.

the answer to a living question that sets before itself a futural present in the sense of 'what can we do?'."[12]

Present means "making [entities] present" (374/326); it is the process that allows things around us to present themselves to us, to unconceal themselves to us. This presence of entities happens only within a world, and the world opens up only thanks to the past and the future. For the woman who pursues the project of being a novelist and appropriates her past as a source of stories, the world opens up as a place filled with fellow artists, audiences, publishers and so on. Her future and her past give rise to her present.

Heidegger calls our temporality "ecstatical", standing-out (377/329). This term provides a useful contrast to the temporality of present-at-hand entities. A piece of quartz has a past, but it does not stand out of its present into its past in the way we do: the mineral's past is not something it has to decide what to do with. It does not stand out into its future, either: its future is irrelevant to what it is at this moment. It does not need to make any choices – its Being is not an issue for it. Even its present is not present *to* it in the way our present is present to us: nothing unconceals itself for the piece of quartz. Present-at-hand entities are locked into a state in which past, future and present make no difference to them at all. We, on the other hand, project into a future, are thrown out of a past, and are consequently in a present world where things can make a difference to us.

We might also contrast our ecstatical way of Being to the Being of animals. For Heidegger, the analysis of Dasein must come first; we can then understand lower animals, living things other than Dasein (75/49–50, 291/247). In *The Fundamental Concepts of Metaphysics*, a lecture course of 1929–30, he argues that although animals are not wholly worldless, their world is impoverished. Instead of standing out into past, future and present, animals are merely caught in an instinctive "ring".[13] The impoverished world of a cat, for instance, is a closed set of opportunities for eating, hunting, mating and so on. Since the cat's Being is not an issue for it in the way ours is for us, the cat cannot struggle with the meaning of its environment, make free choices within this environment, or decide who it is going to be on the basis of who it already is. Thus, a cat cannot transcend its own instincts and be exposed to the difference it makes that there is something rather than nothing. It can encounter beings as alluring or threatening, but cannot really encounter beings as beings. Heidegger offers us no clue to how Dasein might have evolved from lower life forms, and some critics find that he exaggerates the distance that separates us from other living things. However, there is no denying that his analysis of animal Being in this lecture course is rich and intriguing. These lectures are also notable for their extensive use of scientific findings about animal behavior; elsewhere, Heidegger can be rather cavalier in his claims that scientific data are irrelevant to philosophy.

12. *The Metaphysical Foundations of Logic*, p. 72.
13. *The Fundamental Concepts of Metaphysics*, p. 255.

When Heidegger calls temporality ecstatical, he does not mean to say that it literally carries us out of ourselves, or makes us stand out from ourselves – because that would imply that in principle, we could stay *inside* ourselves. "The whole of these three ways of being-carried-away does not center in a kind of thing which would of itself lack any being-carried-away, something present-at-hand unecstatically which would be the common center for initiating and unfolding the ecstases."[14] Dasein is *essentially* "outside". This makes it much harder to picture than a present-at-hand thing and much harder to fit into our traditional concepts.

§66–71: Reinterpreting everydayness in terms of temporality

Heidegger's next move in *Being and Time* is a perfect illustration of his circular, or spiral, theory of interpretation. Recall that an interpretation must begin with a preliminary, general view of something; this general view can guide us to insights, which then lead – or should lead – to a revised general view, and so on (194–5/152–3). This implies that the early stages of an interpretation are always rough-and-ready approximations that need to be reinterpreted later on. Naturally, then, Heidegger returns to the themes of Division I and painstakingly reinterprets them in terms of temporality. He even warns us that once we have gained "an idea of Being in general" (382/333) – in the projected Division III – we will need to revise our previous analyses once again. One begins to wonder whether interpretations can ever come to an end.

Is Heidegger just making things difficult? In a sense, yes. He wants to wipe away the lingering traces of obviousness from what he has been saying, and awaken us to the mysterious, questionable character of our everyday experience (380/332, 382/333, 423/371). We have to wean ourselves away from the habit of reducing experience to common-sense platitudes, and train ourselves to be surprised by the ordinary. We then enter the unfamiliar territory that lies within the familiar.

Sections 66–71 repay close reading: they provide a helpful review of Division I, cast its findings in a new light, and in doing so clarify the notion of temporality. However, I will not provide a complete summary here, since most of the themes of these sections are not new and I assume that readers are by now somewhat used to Heidegger's language. (The new concept of the "horizonal schema" in §69c will be discussed at the end of this chapter.) In lieu of a detailed guide, I will present a concrete case and then analyze it using some of the more important concepts from these sections.

Suppose that an auto mechanic is repairing a transmission. His attention is consumed with performing this familiar job. He is what he does, as Heidegger likes to put it (155/119, 163/126); he defines himself as a mechanic. This is not to say that he thinks, "I am a mechanic", but simply that he acts as a mechanic

---

14. *The Metaphysical Foundations of Logic*, p. 207.

acts, without questioning this role or explicitly choosing it. He is wrapped up in his job, and is concerned only with whether he will succeed in fixing this transmission.

Suddenly, the man feels a sharp pain in his chest. It is gone in a minute, but he is alarmed. This frightening experience becomes the occasion for an episode of anxiety; he is not merely afraid of dying, but feels anxiety in the face of his own mortality. He remembers that his life is his own, and that at each moment, it is up to him to make something of himself. He remembers that his job does not define him. Instead, *he* defines what his job will mean to him: it is a source of income that supports his family, and this support matters to him because he chooses to exist as a good family man. In this moment, he recalls "what it's all about" and reaffirms it. When he returns to working on the car, he does so as a choice and not as a mere routine.

Now let's analyze these events using the following temporal vocabulary from Division II, Chapter 4. (The vocabulary is introduced on 386-9/336-9 and conveniently summarized on 401/350.)

	Past	*Present*	*Future*
Inauthentic:	forgetting	making-present	awaiting
Authentic:	repetition (Stambaugh: retrieve)	moment of vision	anticipation

When the mechanic is inauthentically absorbed in his job, he has *forgotten* his thrownness. The fact that he happens to have been thrust into this situation, along with his particular past, is not remarkable to him – he pays no attention to it, and simply acts as if he had always been a mechanic by nature. He has fallen into the present environment, and is concerned merely with *making present* the things he is dealing with. He reaches for tools and parts, manipulates them and brings about results. He keeps track of these ready-to-hand entities, maintaining them ready for work; he remembers just as much as he needs to in order to do the job (Heidegger calls this *retaining*: 389/339). He *awaits* the results of his work. His relationship to the future is just a matter of seeing what will come of his efforts. He is so wrapped up in what he is doing that he is almost behaving like a cat that is absorbed in pouncing on a bird. (Of course, he can hardly be *blamed* for this. All our everyday tasks go more smoothly when we simply take them for granted than when we question them. Everydayness could not function without inauthenticity. We can be blamed only if we stubbornly resist anxiety when it does come.)

When the man experiences anxiety, he gets in touch with the deeper modes of the ecstases of temporality. He now *anticipates* his mortality: that is, he experiences his possibilities as limited. He is now capable of *repeating* his choices, that is, taking up his previous life, reinterpreting it and reaffirming it. (He need not affirm his choice to be a mechanic; he could also choose to "repeat" some other possibility that is available to him in his culture, but which he has neglected up to now. We will soon explore this notion of repetition more thoroughly.) In an authentic *moment of vision*, he sees his current situation and understands how it forms part of his life. The repair shop is not just his place of work; it is the stage on which he is improvising the drama of his life story.

Our example does not illustrate the *theoretical* attitude to the world, which is the topic of §69b. A theoretical thinker is dedicated to comprehending how present-at-hand entities present themselves (414/363). If this dedication is genuine, then it involves a resolute choice to exist scientifically, so we can say that "science has its source in authentic existence" (415/363). But the danger of the theoretical attitude is that we may come to identify Being in general with presence-at-hand. This metaphysics of presence then prevents us from understanding other ways of Being, including our own relation to our future and our past.

One should not get the impression that the three ecstases of temporality are independent of each other. In both authentic and inauthentic existence, all three ecstases are always at work together (401/350). They open up a world, or clear the "there" (402/351), by carrying us away to their "horizons" (416/365). But in inauthenticity, the past and future are *subordinated* to the present, whereas in authenticity, the present gains a fresh and deeper meaning from the past and, especially, from the future. As we are about to see, the "there" opens up most radically for us when repetition carries us to the past as our *heritage* and anticipation carries us to the future as our *fate*.

§§72–77: History, heritage and fate

Heidegger has said little about history so far, but he views it as absolutely crucial to our Being. In fact, that is precisely why he has not introduced the theme earlier; in order to understand it, we first need detailed interpretations of many less profound phenomena. In Division II, Chapter 5, he is ready to present us with his vision of the historical character of our existence – and his most passionate descriptions of authentic existence.[15]

Heidegger is not primarily concerned with history as the academic study of battles, treaties, political movements and so forth. In fact, he is not primarily concerned with the battles and other historical events themselves. His main focus is the fundamentally historical nature of human existence as such. Heidegger calls it *Geschichtlichkeit*, historicity.[16] It is thanks to our historicity

15. This chapter is clearly indebted to Dilthey, as Heidegger says at the beginning of §77 (one of the earliest sections of the book in order of composition).
16. Stambaugh's "historicity" is more mellifluous than Macquarrie and Robinson's "historicality", and since "historicity" has become the usual word for this phenomenon in English, I will use it too. The less frequent word translated as "historicity" by Macquarrie and Robinson is *Historizität* – the state of being interested *scientifically* in the past. *Geschehen*, translated by

that past events and things can be meaningful to us in such a way that we can study them scientifically. Furthermore, we can be authentically historical even if we are not historians (448/396).

Historicity can be called the way in which "Dasein *stretches along between* birth and death" (425/373, 427/375). We might say that because of our historicity, our lives form *stories*, dramas that unfold from birth to death. (Other animals have the sort of life that is studied by *biology*, but human life also calls for *biography*.) We can also describe historicity in terms of what Heidegger has already said about temporality; in fact, the interpretation of historicity is "just a more concrete working out of temporality" (434/382).

We have seen that we are thrown out of the past and into the present as we project a future. Heidegger now specifies that the possibilities that we project have to be drawn from the past as a *heritage* (435/383). I cannot simply invent a life project that I have dreamed up completely on my own. My source for possible projects is the heritage that I share with others in my community, the wealth of possible self-interpretations that my culture has accumulated over millennia. Thanks to my heritage, I have the option of guiding my life according to the possibility of being, for instance, a conservative or a revolutionary. These lives, among others, are made available to me by people who serve as possible role models in my culture. Authentic existence always "repeats" some inherited possibility (437/385). Thus, the past is a storehouse of opportunities to exist authentically: "everything 'good' is a heritage, and the character of 'goodness' lies in making authentic existence possible" (435/383). Past objects and events. can have meaning for us, and can be studied by historians, only because the past is still with us, serving as our heritage. Thus, strange as it sounds, *possibilities* are the things that properly concern historians (446–7/ 394–5).

Heidegger does not mean that I have to do exactly what someone else did in the past – in fact, this would be impossible. His notion of "repetition" (*Wiederholung* – Stambaugh's "retrieve" is better) does not mean aping the past, but appropriating it freely and creatively (437/383). For instance, if I choose Picasso as my "hero", that does not mean that I will go through a blue period, a pink period and a Cubist period. Instead, I take Picasso's way of existing as a model and point of reference for my own life. Again, Christians who speak of "imitating Christ" do not mean that one should go around proclaiming oneself the son of God, but that the life of Jesus should serve as an inspiration that can be adapted to one's own circumstances. Heidegger would claim that caring intensely about one's own past and wrestling deeply with it does not necessarily make one a conservative; in fact, it makes genuine revolutions possible. This is exactly what he himself is trying to do in his "destruction" of Western metaphysics.

Macquarrie and Robinson as "historizing", is the ordinary German word for "happen". Hence Stambaugh's translation: "occurrence". *Historie* – the scientific study of the past – is rendered by Macquarrie and Robinson as "historiology" and by Stambaugh as "historiography".

What, one might ask, if we want to appropriate a tradition other than our own? A Westerner might want to become a Zen Buddhist, or an African shaman – and why not? Heidegger might retort that if these possibilities are open to the Westerner at all, it is because they *are* somehow connected to his or her own culture; there must be something in the Western heritage that opens the way, at least initially, to participating in a Japanese or African tradition. He would see today's "multiculturalism" as superficial and inauthentic:

> the opinion may now arise that understanding the most alien cultures and 'synthesizing' them with one's own may lead to Dasein's becoming for the first time thoroughly and genuinely enlightened about itself. Versatile curiosity and restlessly "knowing it all" masquerade as a universal understanding of Dasein. [222/178]

Heidegger would probably insist that Europeans are necessarily Eurocentric, since their choices have to be made on the basis of European culture, at least to begin with. (When a Westerner espouses anti-Eurocentric views, for instance, this project is usually unwittingly in the service of Western conceptions of justice and equality.) Heidegger himself concentrated throughout his life on retrieving the hidden possibilities of Western thought by deconstructing the dominant Western intellectual tradition. This is not to suggest, however, that he dismissed Eastern thought; to the contrary, he approached it with cautious, interested respect.[17]

Heidegger's notion of a heritage makes many critics uncomfortable; they find this notion chauvinistic and ominous, especially in the light of his nationalist politics of the thirties. Others, however, claim that it is only Heidegger's thought that makes it possible to deconstruct all chauvinisms. In our next chapter we will revisit these strikingly different interpretations of the political implications of Heidegger's philosophy.

Aside from heritage, the other two important concepts introduced in §74 are *fate* and *destiny*. Often enough, we use these words to suggest that something is beyond our control ("it was just fate"). But Heidegger does not intend to eliminate freedom. On the other hand, he does not believe we are so free as to

17. See Heidegger, "A Dialogue on Language between a Japanese and an Inquirer", in *On the Way to Language*, tr. P. D. Hertz & J. Stambaugh (New York: Harper & Row, 1971); *Heidegger and Asian Thought*, G. Parkes (ed.), (Honolulu, Hawaii: University of Hawaii Press, 1987); H. W. Petzet, *Encounters and Dialogues with Martin Heidegger, 1929–1976*, tr. P. Emad & K. Maly (Chicago, Illinois: University of Chicago Press, 1993), Chapter 7; and R. May, *Heidegger's Hidden Sources: East Asian Influences on His Work*, tr. with a complementary essay by G. Parkes (London: Routledge, 1996). May demonstrates that Heidegger was familiar with Chinese and Japanese thought through translations and secondary sources, and that there are some close parallels between passages in these sources and some passages in Heidegger's own writings, especially his later essays. May concludes that East Asian thought had a decisive influence on Heidegger's philosophy, and that Heidegger tried to conceal this influence. However, it is safer to say that he found many provocative similarities to his own ideas in Eastern thinking, but was reluctant to make claims about a tradition that he did not know deeply and whose texts he could not read in the original languages.

be able to invent ourselves from scratch and create a completely new meaning for our lives. The words "fate" and "destiny" suggest the burdens that our freedom must carry, and the finitude of our choices. "Fate" is another name for authentic resoluteness, "in which Dasein *hands* itself *down* to itself, free for death, in a possibility which it has inherited and yet has chosen" (435/384). We are free, but our freedom is necessarily limited; our possibilities have to be drawn from our own heritage, and we are always faced with the possibility of having no more possibilities. If readers understand this "finite freedom" (436/ 384), they will be able to follow Heidegger's discussion of fate.

Destiny is the shared "historizing" of a community (436/384) – the way in which a group draws on a shared heritage and works out a shared fate. A community is not a collection of wholly independent individuals. We share moods, concerns and decisions, and our history tends to follow the movements of "generations" (a concept Heidegger borrows from Dilthey). For instance, the generation of the 1960s shared a certain set of possibilities and issues, although they held varying opinions and made varying choices. For Heidegger, destiny comes to light through "communicating" and "struggling". When we articulate the issues that face us and wrestle with competing interpretations of these issues, a shared decision and direction can emerge. Although Heidegger has little to say about destiny in *Being and Time*, it is a very important phenomenon that continues to occupy him in his later thought.

Why do we think of history not in terms of heritage and fate, but as a sequence of events – "one damn thing after another"? Predictably enough, Heidegger blames this common conception on falling (§75). Absorbed in the world, we watch the things that are reported in the news, and place them in a timeline that we call history. The meaning of this sequence of events is shallow or utterly absent – it is a tale told by an idiot, signifying nothing, or else we subject it to a clichéd, easy interpretation dictated by the current common sense of the "they". Heidegger wants us to pay attention to how the world is originally opened up for us by our relationship to our future and our past. This interaction between past and future, birth and death, is the real origin of history. Once we recognize this, instead of falling into the present, we are able to discover deeper meanings in events by making resolute choices.

Heidegger's notion of historicity raises a number of delicate questions about historicism and historical relativism. He rarely addresses these questions directly, but they are well worth considering. Heidegger is sometimes described as a "historicist". The value of this label depends on exactly what one means by it.[18] If one means that for Heidegger, there is no truth that is not relative to a historical period, the label is correct. The "there" opens up differently for different people and nations in different ages, because they are making different choices on the basis of different heritages: things reveal themselves

18. On the complex relation of Heidegger to the German historicist tradition, see Bambach, *Heidegger, Dilthey, and the Crisis of Historicism* and J. A. Barash, *Martin Heidegger and the Problem of Historical Meaning* (Dordrecht: Martinus Nijhoff, 1985).

to Dasein in various ways at various times. "Because Dasein is historical in its own existence, possibilities of access and modes of interpretation of beings are themselves diverse, varying in different historical circumstances."[19] Even science is "in the grip of . . . historizing" (444/392).

However, if one means that for Heidegger, all views, at all times in history, are *equally* true, then the label "historicist" is wrong. He always makes it clear that an authentic stance is more revealing than an inauthentic one: it shows us entities in greater depth. Furthermore, some ages are more prone to authenticity than others (167/129). So even though no unconcealment lasts forever or is independent of history, unconcealment does happen, and some practices unconceal better than others.

One may object: what about "2 + 2 = 4"? Isn't this proposition absolutely and eternally true, and can't it be understood by anyone, regardless of the historical period? Heidegger would probably answer: the phenomenon that this formula indicates is *not* historical, and it can be noticed by any entity who can be presented with other entities and is capable of counting them. But in order to be presented with entities, one must be related essentially to one's own past and one's own future: in other words, one must exist historically. Furthermore, the nature of one's particular relationships to the past and future will determine the depth of one's *interpretation* of the phenomenon indicated by "2 + 2 = 4", and in this way, this interpretation will be relative to one's position in history. For even the meaning of simple arithmetical truths is subject to interpretation. The correct statement "2 + 2 = 4" implies some prior understanding of what and how numbers *are*. No sane person would believe that two and two are five, but the question of the Being of numbers is open to dispute. Are numbers invisible, eternal entities? Are they structures of our mind? In different times and places, people will unconceal the Being of numbers in different ways, some more illuminating than others.

One may also raise the following argument. "Heidegger claims that all truth is historical – but this claim is itself supposed to apply *universally*. Since Heidegger himself lays claim to an ahistorical truth, he contradicts himself." However, it is not inconsistent for Heidegger to point out some universal structures common to all Dasein (such as historicity itself) while holding that his *way of interpreting* these structures is historically situated. We just saw that although mathematical relationships are ahistorical, our ways of unconcealing these relations are historical. Similarly, Heidegger can unconceal universal aspects of Dasein in a *manner* that springs from his experience as a twentieth-century European. There is nothing self-contradictory about this project. However, it does leave open the possibility that Heidegger is wrong; other thinkers, with the resources of other ages and places, may unconceal Dasein more effectively.

It may be very difficult to decide whether one particular historical epoch is more enlightened than another. Sometimes, two different ages are *both* enlightened in different ways, in that they illuminate different aspects of beings.

19. *The Basic Problems of Phenomenology*, p. 22.

It would be inappropriate, then, to judge one age by the standards of the other. Thus Heidegger writes:

> [We cannot] say that the Galilean doctrine of freely falling bodies is true and that Aristotle's teaching, that light bodies strive upward, is false; for the Greek understanding of the essence of body and place and of the relation between the two rests upon a different interpretation of beings and hence conditions a correspondingly different kind of seeing and questioning of natural events. No one would presume to maintain that Shakespeare's poetry is more advanced than that of Aeschylus. It is still more impossible to say that the modern understanding of whatever is, is more correct than that of the Greeks.[20]

This is one of the most relativistic-sounding passages in Heidegger's writings. It may seem that he is saying that any interpretation is as good as any other – but that reading goes against the grain of his thought. It makes more sense to read him as saying that ancient and modern physics are both illuminating: they unconceal different sides of experience.[21] But such claims presume that we moderns can somehow take part in the ancient understanding of the world, and decide whether it is illuminating. How is this possible? How can we transcend our own epoch or place to understand and assess some other culture's ways of unconcealing? Heidegger clearly thinks that this can be done, since he devotes a great deal of energy to interpreting the Greeks and deciding what is true and untrue in their thought. But this cannot involve rising *above* history. Instead, it involves a confrontation and dialogue with the other.[22] Through this confrontation, we can learn from other ways of understanding the world. As Heidegger's student Gadamer puts it, our interpretations always have a historical boundary, or "horizon", but it is possible to carry out a "fusion of horizons" with others' interpretations. We are finite, but flexible. And once we have been initiated into a new interpretation, we can decide to what extent it helps us uncover the phenomena.[23]

Entities, then, are unconcealed in various ways to Dasein at various times. And Being is the difference that entities make to Dasein. We might ask, then:

20. "The Age of the World Picture" (1938), in *The Question Concerning Technology and Other Essays*, tr. W. Lovitt (New York: Harper & Row, 1977), p. 117.
21. As Hubert Dreyfus puts it, "one can reject the claim that there is *a* [single] correct description of reality and still hold that there can be *many* correct descriptions" (*Being-in-the-World*, p. 265). For Dreyfus' persuasive interpretation of Heidegger as a "hermeneutic realist" or "plural realist", see *Being-in-the-World*, pp. 251–65.
22. One of Heidegger's most important short reflections on this theme is "Wege zur Aussprache" (1937), in *Aus der Erfahrung des Denkens (1910–1976)*, GA 13, where Heidegger discusses the relation between France and Germany.
23. In his 1925 lectures on Plato's *Sophist*, Heidegger forcefully affirms that a keen appreciation of our historicity is compatible with a dedication to uncovering "the things themselves". See R. Polt, "Heidegger's Topical Hermeneutics: The *Sophist* Lectures", *Journal of the British Society for Phenomenology* **37**(1), 1996, pp. 53–76.

isn't Being itself historical? Does it make any sense to look for a *single* meaning of Being? These are questions that must have given Heidegger pause as he attempted to compose Part One, Division III of *Being and Time*. His later work no longer gives the impression, as *Being and Time* does, that we can find some ahistorical meaning of Being. As we will see in our next chapter, rather than establishing a single concept of Being, he tries to understand how Being "essentially unfolds" in history.

§§78–82: Primordial temporality and the ordinary concept of time

> Of these three divisions of time, then, how can two, the past and the future, *be*, when the past no longer is and the future is not yet? As for the present, if it were always present and never moved on to become the past, it would not be time but eternity. If, therefore, the present is time only by reason of the fact that it moves on to become the past, how can we say that even the present *is*, when the reason why it *is* is that it is *not to be*? In other words, we cannot rightly say that time is, except by reason of its impending state of *not being*. — St. Augustine, *Confessions*, XI, 14[24]

Heidegger has not yet confronted the question of why we ordinarily think of time as something very different from what he has been describing. We can anticipate, however, that he will try to diagnose our usual concept of time as the product of inauthentic falling. This is precisely what he does in the last few sections of *Being and Time*.

Common sense thinks of time by means of pictures, most commonly a clock and a line. Of course a clock is not the *same* as time, but it somehow symbolizes it for us. When we try to think of time *itself*, we usually represent it as a line. The timeline includes an infinite number of points (moments), and extends forever in both directions (past and future). Clocks keep track of our constant progress along the line, in the direction of the future. Everything in the universe is making this march into the future along with us.

This picture is simple enough – but when we consider it more closely, it proves to be full of puzzles. Quite aside from the complexities of the theory of relativity (which Heidegger mentions in note iv, p. 499/417), what are we to make of Augustine's riddle? Time seems to have no objective reality – so is it something subjective, something projected by our mind?

Heidegger claims that puzzles such as these result from focusing on the superficial phenomenon of the timeline instead of on Dasein's temporality. In order to understand why Dasein's temporality is "*primordial time*" (457/405) we have to draw on our ontology of Dasein and examine how our conventional pictures of time *arise* in the first place. As we do so, we have to guard ourselves

24. Augustine, *Confessions*, p. 264.

against crude concepts such as "subjective" and "objective". Heidegger's account here is difficult and complex; what follows may provide a starting-point for exploring it.

When we examine our everyday experience of time (§79) we find that, although it is inauthentic, it is actually much richer than a barren timeline. In everydayness, Dasein is absorbed in its dealings with the ready-to-hand. It *awaits* the results of its dealings, *retains* its equipment and past situations by keeping track of them as necessary, and *makes present* its current situation by paying attention to what it is producing and achieving. Heidegger claims that in this process, "making present has a peculiar importance" (459/407). In everydayness, the past and future matter to us only in relation to the present. (For instance, the auto mechanic keeps track of his tools and uses them to work on the transmission, trying to restore it to its former state of running well. The fact that the transmission once worked well and that it may work well in the future are important to the mechanic only insofar as they affect what he is doing here and now.) Our future and our past, then, are meaningful to us in everyday life because they are relevant to our current practical concerns. This means that time necessarily has a *content* that relates to our practical lives (time is "datable", in Heidegger's terms). I do not keep track of time *primarily* by using numbers: 7 AM, 12 noon, 11 PM. I keep track of time primarily in terms of what it means to my activities: time to get up, time for lunch, bedtime (for Heidegger's own examples, see 461–2/408–9). Time is right or wrong, appropriate or inappropriate. Our ordinary sense of time is part and parcel of our existing in a meaningful, purposive world.

How, then, do we get our picture of time as a sterile line, a "sequence of pure 'nows'" (462/409)? In §80 Heidegger describes how our need to keep track of what we are now doing leads to the use of clocks. Since we *count on* things and on each other to support our activities, we *count* events that help us coordinate and plan our activities – events such as the rising and setting of the sun, which is the most basic clock (465–6/412–13). We use such events to *measure* how late or how early it is – always keeping the present as our main point of reference. For example, I see that the sun is high and my shadow is only one foot long, so I conclude that *now* is the time for me to eat lunch. In our everyday use of clocks, not only are we primarily concerned with the present, but our activity of measuring requires a "specific kind of *making-present*": we apply a present-at-hand standard of measurement to a present-at-hand thing that we are measuring (470/417). (For instance, I treat my shadow as a present-at-hand object that I measure by comparing it to my foot as a present-at-hand object.) Consequently, when we try to conceive of time itself, it is all too easy to focus on the "now" and presence-at-hand, and to focus on the act of measuring instead of on what is being measured (471/418). We can ignore the fact that we were measuring in order to carry out practical projects in the world, and come to think of time as a mere timeline – a sequence of countable "nows" in which objects are present-at-hand. We have then forgotten the richness of our everyday Being-in-the-world. In §§81–82, Heidegger tries to show that this forgetfulness is the origin not only of our common-sense notion of time, but also of all previous philosophical conceptions of time.

To sum up: the notion of time as a timeline is the result of the clock-reading behavior of inauthentic, everyday Dasein. This behavior focuses on counting "nows". But clock-reading behavior is based on the temporality of everydayness, which is much richer than a timeline: it involves purposes and activities, and thus requires the complex structure of the everyday environment that was first described in Division I. In turn, everyday temporality is based on the underlying structure of care. Care is revealed most fully in *authentic* temporality, which involves resolutely facing up to mortality and repeating one's heritage in a moment of vision. When we are authentic, instead of evaluating the past and present in terms of the "now", we recognize that the present gains its significance from the past, and even more so from the future. The authentic temporality of Dasein is far more primordial than any timeline.

Readers are likely to find a paradoxical flavor in Heidegger's claims, to say the least. They will tend to ask the very questions that Heidegger puts in the mouth of the "they": "How is 'time' in its course to be touched even the least bit when a man who has been present-at-hand 'in time' no longer exists? Time goes on, just as indeed it already 'was' when a man 'came into life' " (477/425). In short, isn't human time a tiny and brief phenomenon within the more primordial time in which the entire universe is coming to be?

We may be able to dispel some of the paradox by reviewing what Heidegger means and does not mean when he says that Dasein's temporality is more "primordial" than a timeline. He is not denying that stars and planets were in motion long before we came on the scene. In many contexts, such as paleontology, we can legitimately use linear time: we can correctly place the origin of human beings much later on a timeline than the origin of dinosaurs. Neither does Heidegger deny that we are just a small part of the universe, and that most things are in time in a way that has nothing to do with guilt, mortality, resoluteness and so forth. His point is that "in the order of possible interpretation", Dasein's temporality has to come first (479/426). We cannot truly *understand* what it means for a star to be present-at-hand five million years ago unless we first understand our own relationship to our past and future. Entities show themselves to us as present-at-hand only when we modify our everyday temporality and enter into a theoretical attitude (§69b). Thus, although present-at-hand entities are independent of us, *presence-at-hand* has to be understood in relation to us. (Recall that although entities may be independent of us, Being is not: 255/212.) In other words, our own temporality is what allows other things, which do not have the same sort of temporality, to make a difference to us. We cannot build up an understanding of our own temporality on the basis of the temporality of present-at-hand things.

So is time subjective or objective? Heidegger's answer is: neither (471–2/419). It is not present-at-hand either in subjects or in objects. It is prior to both subject and object, since it makes possible both our own existence as Dasein and the revelation of all other entities to us. What sort of Being does time have, then, or does time have Being at all? Once again, we find ourselves up against the open question: what is the meaning of Being?

Heidegger's account of time is certainly open to dispute and calls for further clarification.[25] But as we wade through its conceptual difficulties, we should not miss the impact that Heidegger wants it to have on our lives. If scientific timekeeping is an alienated, superficial way of relating to time, then we have to get back in touch with our own, living temporality. We should stop pretending to be nothing but "objective" observers, and become individuals once again who care about life and are willing to make choices in the face of death. Behind the sometimes turgid terminology of Heidegger's text, there is a craving for individual authenticity no less vivid than we find in Kierkegaard. The key for both thinkers is that time is not just a medium in which we watch things pass by, and not just an opportunity to get our tasks done; since time is at the heart of human existence, which is a heavy gift that each of us is responsible for carrying, "the time itself is the task".[26]

A glimpse of Division III

The schema of actuality is existence in some determinate time. – Kant[27]

The finished portion of *Being and Time* ends, like many of Heidegger's texts, with a welter of probing questions (§83). These questions lay quite a burden on Part One, Division III – or, since this Division and Part Two were never completed, the burden is laid on those of *us* who wish to think with and beyond Heidegger. Fortunately, we do have some indications not only of the kind of issues Division III was to deal with, but of the general approach it was to take.

Let's begin with the questions that Division III was to resolve. Above all, there is the most fundamental question: what does it mean to *be* in the first place? We have been discussing entities and their particular ways of Being without clarifying what Being itself is. This procedure was necessary, but now we will have to establish a clear idea of Being. Once we have done so, another daunting task faces us: we will have to review our former interpretations of Dasein yet again – just as Heidegger reinterpreted everydayness in terms of temporality in Division II. In addition, we will have to address a series of puzzling problems. For example, Heidegger has distinguished Dasein's existence from readiness-to-hand and presence-at-hand. But we still have to ask what *all* the "variations" of Being are (285/241, 382/333), how these different ways of Being are connected (71/45), and why presence-at-hand keeps "coming back"

25. For some further discussion of the topic, see Dreyfus, *Being-in-the-World*, p. 259.
26. Kierkegaard, *Concluding Unscientific Postscript*, p. 164.
27. I. Kant, *Critique of Pure Reason*, tr. N. K. Smith (New York: St. Martin's Press, 1965), p. 185 (A145/B184).

as the primary meaning of Being (487/437). How are we to understand the Being of negativity (332/286)? What is the relation between truth and Being (272–3/230, 408/357)? What is the difference between a science of Being and a science of entities (272/230)? Does time have some sort of Being (377/328, 458/406, 472/419–20)? If Being is not an entity, and therefore "is" not, how is it given (272/230)?

Heidegger's original plan was to tackle these fundamental questions by treating time as the "horizon" for Being (19/1). In other words, Being is made accessible to us by our own temporality, and must be interpreted in the context of this temporality.

Before we go any farther, it may be worthwhile to warn readers against a basic misunderstanding that is more common than it ought to be. Heidegger never claims that all beings are *temporary*. Maybe there are some entities that last forever, or are eternal (timeless). His claim is that even these would have to be *understood* by us on the basis of time, because *we* are radically temporal beings. (After all, even "timelessness" is a category that refers to time [40/18].) The question "is not whether beings are in time or not. It is rather whether the Being of beings gets understood by reference to time".[28]

Furthermore, one should not make the mistake of picturing Heideggerian time merely as a process of becoming in which things come to be and pass away. Remember that for Heidegger, time is not primarily to be understood in terms of change and motion – or permanence and rest. Time has to be understood in terms of phenomena such as heritage, fate and death. It is time in this richer, historical sense that supposedly undergirds our understanding of Being.

In *Being and Time*, Heidegger occasionally uses the word *Temporalität* ("Temporality") instead of *Zeitlichkeit* ("temporality") to signal that he is considering time not just as the basis of Dasein's Being, but as that which makes possible our understanding of Being in general (40/19). We find the most explicit surviving attempts at an analysis of Temporality in an obscure corner of *Being and Time*, §69c, and at the end of *The Basic Problems of Phenomenology*, a lecture course from 1927.

Recall that there are three aspects of temporality – past, present and future – that come in both authentic and inauthentic varieties. Properly speaking, we should call these aspects of temporality *ecstases*, for Heidegger has claimed that Dasein's temporality is *ecstatical*: because we are temporal, we "stand out". We transcend ourselves and are carried off, as it were, in three directions. In §69c of *Being and Time*, Heidegger briefly introduces the cumbersome expression "horizonal schema" to indicate *that towards which* an ecstasis carries us off. The three ecstases open up three horizonal schemata, which together open up a world and make it possible for us to understand the Being of beings (416–17/365).

This terminology, and the general idea, were apparently suggested to Heidegger by his reading of Kant. In our discussion of §7 we saw that Heidegger

---

28. *The Metaphysical Foundations of Logic*, p. 144.

characterizes his own project as "transcendental" (62/38). For Kant, transcendental knowledge is knowledge of the basic conditions that make experience possible, such as our category of causality. Kant claims that in order to apply to our sensations, the categories have to be "schematized" in terms of time: for instance, the "schema" of causality is succession in time (we expect the cause to precede the effect in time). In very general terms, then, we can describe a schema as a temporal framework that makes it possible for us to understand our experience. This is what the "horizonal schema" does for Heidegger: it is a temporal framework that allows us to understand Being and encounter beings. His account of the horizonal schemata is transcendental, then, in this broadly Kantian sense. But it also involves "transcendence" in the sense that it describes how Dasein *goes beyond* beings to their Being.

Basic Problems attempts to do more to put the concept of the horizonal schema to work. For example, the ecstasis of the present, whether authentic or inauthentic, directs us to a horizonal schema that Heidegger designates with the Latin term *praesens*.[29] It is *praesens* that makes it possible for us to understand the Being of ready-to-hand entities. We understand ready-to-hand entities by projecting them upon *praesens*.[30]

To give a concrete example: I am writing at my computer keyboard. I understand the keyboard – not by staring at it, but by competently using it. In order to do so, I must be able to relate to readiness-to-hand; I have some grasp of the Being of useful things such as the keyboard. In order to have this relationship to Being, I have to engage in the ecstasis of making-present. This ecstasis brings me to *praesens*. *Praesens* is the field in which I can deal with beings such as keyboards and understand their Being.

In 1928 Heidegger has a few more words to say about the horizonal schema of the *future*: this "being-carried-away [provides] futurity as such, i.e., possibility pure and simple. Of itself the ecstasis does not produce a definite possible, but it does produce the horizon of possibility in general, within which a definite possible can be expected".[31]

In general, we understand Being in all its variations in terms of *praesens* and in terms of the other two horizonal schemata to which we are directed by the past and future ecstases of Temporality.[32] (In *Being and Time*, Heidegger calls the past and future schemata *what has been* and the *for-the-sake-of-itself*: 416/365.)

Time thus makes it possible for me to grasp beings in terms of their Being. Time is the origin of the ontological difference between beings and Being – a distinction so crucial to us that, as Heidegger now says, "existence means, as it were, 'to be in the performance of this distinction'".[33]

A nagging question may arise at this point. If we understand beings in terms of their Being, and we understand Being in terms of time, then doesn't time

29. *The Basic Problems of Phenomenology*, p. 305.   30. *Ibid.*, p. 306.
31. *The Metaphysical Foundations of Logic*, p. 208.
32. *The Basic Problems of Phenomenology*, p. 307.   33. *Ibid.*, p. 319.

also need to be understood in terms of some further "horizon"? And if so, aren't we led into an infinite regress?[34] Heidegger says no, but he does not make his reasons very clear. He claims that time does not need any further horizon because primordial time is finite,[35] and because time is "the origin of possibility itself".[36] Readers who want to extrapolate from these remarks should keep in mind that to understand is to project possibilities, and that time is finite because of death – the possibility of having no more possibilities.

Do the few pages at the end of *Basic Problems* complete Heidegger's project of understanding Being in terms of time? Readers must turn to the text and decide for themselves. In my own opinion, not very much is achieved beyond introducing some new terminology. The question of the unity of all the ways of Being is not directly addressed, and many other, equally challenging questions are left hanging. (For instance, there is the question of whether "one might conceive the interpretation of Dasein as temporality in a universal-ontological way". Apparently the problem here is whether Dasein's temporality can illuminate the temporality of other kinds of entities. Heidegger frankly confesses, "This is a question which I myself am not able to decide, one which is still completely unclear to me."[37]) Heidegger himself felt that at this crucial point, his investigation had reached an impasse, a *Holzweg*. He abandoned Division III, and it was not long before he turned in new directions in an attempt to reinvigorate his thought. We are now ready to follow this turn.

34. *Ibid.*, p. 280.   35. *Ibid.*, p. 308.   36. *Ibid.*, p. 325.
37. *The Metaphysical Foundations of Logic*, p. 210.

CHAPTER FIVE

Later Heidegger

With the publication of *Being and Time*, Heidegger's reputation quickly reached international status. But he did not rest on his laurels. If anything, he became increasingly dissatisfied with established philosophical concepts, including his own, and increasingly frustrated with the modern world – its "progress", its popular opinions and its politics.

Heidegger was ready for a revolution not only in thought but in action. When the National Socialists came to power in 1933, Heidegger enthusiastically welcomed the movement. In April 1933, he became the Nazi-approved rector of the University of Freiburg. He officially joined the party on May 1. His rectorate was brief: after conflicts with faculty, students and party officials, he stepped down in April 1934. However, he never gave up his party membership.

For obvious reasons, Heidegger's politics have long been a disturbing and inflammatory topic. From the biographical and psychological viewpoint, his choice is not surprising. He was an intense man who by nature longed for extremes and hated everyday conventionality and comfort; at the same time, he had been raised in a provincial, Catholic environment that turned him against the cosmopolitan liberalism of the Weimar Republic. In a time of crisis, Heidegger was perfectly poised to become one of the many "revolutionary conservative" intellectuals who supported Hitler.

However, for the student of Heidegger's philosophy the main concern should not be his habitual inclinations and temperament, but his thought. To what extent is his *philosophy* embroiled in fascism? Or in more Heideggerian terms, does the error of his existentiell choice taint his reflections on Dasein's existence – reflections which, according to §63 of *Being and Time*, necessarily grow from his existentiell understanding? This question is difficult and highly controversial, and we must postpone discussing it until we have examined some major features of Heidegger's thinking in the 1930s. We will return to the facts about his politics and the various interpretations of his politics later in this chapter. For now, it should simply be noted that he was hardly a typical Nazi.

He viewed the revolution in terms of his idiosyncratic interpretation of Western metaphysics, and he quietly disagreed with several aspects of the official Nazi ideology, including its racism. His political superiors were right to accuse him of a "private National Socialism".[1]

Heidegger returned from administration to teaching. His lecture courses of the thirties and forties relentlessly explore and deconstruct the landmarks of Western thought, while searching for the right way to begin anew. He delivers a series of lecture courses on Nietzsche, in which he concludes that Nietzsche is the last metaphysician, the thinker who exhausts the possibilities of Western metaphysics.[2] He delves into the poetry of Friedrich Hölderlin as a source of an alternative, non-metaphysical vision of human beings' place in the world.[3] He also explores the pre-Socratic thinkers Parmenides and Heraclitus, searching for forgotten possibilities in the beginnings of Western thought.[4]

Meanwhile, Heidegger was writing private, esoteric texts that express his most intense efforts to wrestle with the question of Being. During his lifetime Heidegger shared these texts only with a few friends, and the first was published posthumously in 1989: the dense and enigmatic *Contributions to Philosophy (On Appropriation)*, composed between 1936 and 1938.

The disasters of the Second World War and Germany's defeat were traumatic for Heidegger; in his opinion, a once-promising movement not only had failed to defeat its enemies, but had betrayed itself, becoming just another manifestation of modernity, like liberal democracy and communism. The technological worldview now ruled the planet, treating all beings only as calculable and manipulable objects, while Being itself lay in oblivion.

During the French occupation of Freiburg, a university denazification committee held hearings on Heidegger's political activities, and considered damning testimony from figures such as his former friend Karl Jaspers, who reported that as rector, Heidegger had criticized a colleague in an official letter of evaluation for being "anything but a National Socialist" and associating with a Jewish professor.[5] The committee forbade Heidegger to teach. This was surely the low point in his life, and he experienced a crisis for which he was treated by the psychiatrist Medard Boss. Eventually, however, he regained his equanimity, the guarded respect of the professional philosophical world, and popularity

1. Heidegger, "The Rectorate 1933/34: Facts and Thoughts", in *Martin Heidegger and National Socialism: Questions and Answers*, G. Neske & E. Kettering (eds) (New York: Paragon House, 1990), p. 23.
2. These lectures are available, with some postwar alterations, in *Nietzsche*, D. F. Krell (ed.) (New York: Harper & Row, 1979–87). For a summary of Heidegger's interpretation, see "Nietzsche's Metaphysics", in *Nietzsche*, 3, pp. 187–251.
3. *Hölderlins Hymnen "Germanien" und "Der Rhein"*, GA 39; *Hölderlins Hymne "Andenken"*, GA 52; *Hölderlin's Hymn "The Ister"*, tr. W. McNeill & J. Davis (Bloomington, Indiana: Indiana University Press, 1996).
4. *Heraklit*, GA 55; *Parmenides*, tr. A. Schuwer & R. Rojcewicz (Bloomington, Indiana: Indiana University Press, 1992).
5. K. Jaspers, "Letter to the Freiburg University Denazification Committee (December 22, 1945)", in *The Heidegger Controversy: A Critical Reader*, R. Wolin (ed.) (Cambridge, Massachusetts: MIT Press, 1993), p. 148.

among a new generation of students. Gadamer reports that "after the war Heidegger rode a second wave – much like his global success of the late 1920s and despite official proscription – and elicited an astounding response among academic youth".[6] In 1949, he also regained his right to teach. *What is Called Thinking?*, a lecture course delivered in 1951–52, was Heidegger's first course at the University of Freiburg since 1944. Here he reflects on thought as a calling that responds to the call of Being. The professor emeritus returned to the podium in 1955–56 to present his final lecture series, *The Principle of Reason*, in which he tries to set a limit to our drive to ask *why*, our all-consuming search for explanations. The mysterious revelation of Being is not to be explained rationally, but to be received with gratitude.[7]

Heidegger's thought began to reach new audiences. Medard Boss was influenced by his former patient's philosophy and developed his own brand of Heideggerian psychoanalysis. Boss and Ludwig Binswanger became the leaders of new existential psychology and psychiatry movements, and Heidegger began to give seminars for members of Boss's circle. Meanwhile, the Frenchman Jean Beaufret befriended Heidegger and became his main spokesman in France. In response to some questions Beaufret posed to him about Sartre, Heidegger wrote his influential "Letter on Humanism" (1947), which we will examine below. He made frequent trips to France in his later years, where he met poets, artists and thinkers. Since the immediate postwar period, Heidegger has been an unavoidable point of reference for all French philosophers. In Japan, his writings had been discussed intensively ever since the 1920s, when Japanese philosophers first studied with him; after the war, he paid special attention to Asian thought, even attempting to collaborate with a Chinese scholar on a translation of the *Tao Te Ching*.[8] His thought found an audience even in the United States, although he had always looked upon "Americanism" with nothing but distrust and distaste.

Heidegger's publications and lectures slowed in the 1960s and 1970s, but he continued to teach in forums such as private seminars. Gadamer recalls that while Heidegger's own thinking was as earnest as ever, he had lost the flexibility and capacity for dialogue that he had had in his youth:

> [It] was palpably visible how difficult it was for Heidegger in such discussions to bring himself out of himself, how difficult it was for him to understand others, and how he would open up when one of us came onto the way of thinking he had prepared by means of his answers. This certainly did not always succeed, and then he would become

6. Gadamer, *Philosophical Apprenticeships*, p. 143.
7. *The Principle of Reason*, tr. R. Lilly (Bloomington, Indiana: Indiana University Press, 1991). This volume includes a brief essay that is a concentrated version of the lectures. Heidegger's earlier reflections on this topic (1929) can be found in *The Essence of Reasons*.
8. G. Parkes, "Rising Sun over Black Forest: Heidegger's Japanese Connections", in May, *Heidegger's Hidden Sources*; P. S. Hsiao, "Heidegger and our Translation of the *Tao Te Ching*", in Parkes, *Heidegger and Asian Thought*.

very unhappy and occasionally a bit ungracious. But then Heidegger's simplicity, plainness and warmth won everyone over once we were finished and having an effortless conversation over a glass of wine.[9]

Heidegger's quiet old age was spent largely in his Freiburg home and his beloved mountain cabin – a place for solitude, simplicity and concentration. This private and pensive life was interrupted only by some interviews (with the newsmagazine *Der Spiegel* and with German television)[10] and by Heidegger's own travels (after decades of wrestling with ancient Greek thought, he finally made several visits to Greece). Heidegger died in 1976, at the age of 86, shortly after approving the *Gesamtausgabe*, or collected edition of his writings. His last word was, "Thanks".[11]

A few days before his death, Heidegger penned a motto for his collected edition: "Ways, not works". He explained this motto in some notes for a preface:

> The collected edition should indicate various ways: it is underway in the field of paths of the self-transforming asking of the many-sided question of Being . . . The point is to awaken the confrontation about the question concerning the topic of thinking . . . and not to communicate the opinion of the author, and not to characterize the standpoint of the writer, and not to fit it into the series of other historically determinable philosophical standpoints. Of course, such a thing is always possible, especially in the information age, but for preparing the questioning access to the topic of thinking, it is completely useless.[12]

When we try to sum up the course of Heidegger's thought during the second half of his life, it is all too easy to do nothing but list his opinions, which is exactly what he did not want. This chapter should not be seen as a complete catalogue of Heidegger's later positions. We will focus only on the most important writings from the later period, and we will approach them in a way that is intended to "awaken the confrontation", rather than attempting to summarize these complex texts in detail.

We will begin with the so-called "turn" in Heidegger's thought, the change that follows *Being and Time* and is apparent in certain key texts. These include "What is Metaphysics?", "On the Essence of Truth", *Introduction to Metaphysics*, and "The Origin of the Work of Art". Next, we will turn to some central themes of the *Contributions to Philosophy*. We will then be prepared to return to the troubling question of Heidegger's politics and to understand his views on

9. Gadamer, *Philosophical Apprenticeships*, p. 156.
10. The interviews are well worth reading. The *Spiegel* interview, "Only a God Can Save Us", took place in 1966 and was published at Heidegger's death. It contains some important statements (and misstatements) about Heidegger's politics in the thirties. The *Spiegel* interview is available in Neske & Kettering, *Martin Heidegger and National Socialism*; Sheehan, *Heidegger: The Man and the Thinker*; and Wolin, *The Heidegger Controversy*. The televised interview is available in Neske & Kettering, *Martin Heidegger and National Socialism*.
11. Petzet, *Encounters and Dialogues*, p. 224.   12. GA 1, pp. 437–8.

existentialism and humanism, as explained in the "Letter on Humanism". We will close by considering two topics that are of special interest in Heidegger's postwar thought: technology and language.

Signs of the turn

Some texts of the late twenties essentially continue the project of *Being and Time*. As we have seen, *The Basic Problems of Phenomenology* (1927) makes an attempt to begin Part One, Division III of *Being and Time*. *Kant and the Problem of Metaphysics* (1929) is an unconventional and brilliant confrontation with Kant that fulfills Heidegger's plan for Part Two, Division I.[13] But he was beginning to move in new directions.

It is a rare thinker who can construct an elaborate set of interrelated analyses and a special vocabulary, and then manage to break through this structure in order to think anew. But Heidegger did exactly that. Writing *Being and Time* and the texts mentioned above may have allowed him to set aside an old set of concepts – or perhaps, his love of restless questioning led him to exert himself deliberately to cast off his old concepts. However this may be, in the late twenties we find him working towards fresh formulations and stressing new phenomena. In *The Metaphysical Foundations of Logic* (1928) he emphasizes Dasein's freedom more than he ever did before, waxes enthusiastic about Plato, and tries out new vocabulary: "The freedom towards ground is the outstripping, in the upswing, of that which carries us away and gives us distance. The human being is a creature of distance!"[14] *The Fundamental Concepts of Metaphysics* (1929–30) explores areas that were touched upon only briefly in Heidegger's previous work: the phenomenology of ennui and the ontology of animals.

In texts such as these, Heidegger begins to undergo a transformation that will turn our thinker into the so-called "later Heidegger" or "Heidegger II".[15] This transformation is usually known as the "turn", or *Kehre*. Heidegger uses the word *Kehre* in several senses in various texts, but the best-known such passage is found in the "Letter on Humanism", where he writes:

> The adequate execution and completion of this other thinking that abandons subjectivity is surely made more difficult by the fact that in the publication of *Being and Time* the third division of the first part, "Time and Being", was held back . . . Here everything is reversed. The

---

13. Heidegger's interpretation of Kant was originally developed in a lecture course of 1925–26 (GA 21) and in a course of 1927–28, *Phenomenological Interpretation of Kant's* Critique of Pure Reason, tr. P. Emad & K. Maly (Bloomington, Indiana: Indiana University Press, 1997).
14. *The Metaphysical Foundations of Logic*, p. 221.
15. The expressions "Heidegger I" and "Heidegger II" are used by W. J. Richardson in his *Heidegger: Through Phenomenology to Thought*, 3d edn (The Hague: Martinus Nijhoff, 1974).

division in question was held back because thinking failed in the adequate saying of this turning [Kehre] and did not succeed with the help of the language of metaphysics. The lecture "On the Essence of Truth", thought out and delivered in 1930 but not printed until 1943, provides a certain insight into the thinking of the turning from "Being and Time" to "Time and Being". This turning is not a change of standpoint from *Being and Time*, but in it the thinking that was sought first arrives at the location of that dimension out of which *Being and Time* is experienced, that is to say, experienced from the fundamental experience of the oblivion of Being.[16]

Interpretations of the turn abound. Is it a radical change of opinion on Heidegger's part, or does it fulfill tendencies that were already essential to the project of *Being and Time*? If it is a radical change, was it completed as early as 1930, or only in the forties? Is there a "middle" period between "early" and "late" Heidegger? Although he hardly makes himself crystal clear in the "Letter on Humanism", we can gather from this passage of the "Letter" that according to him, his later writings are not inconsistent with his earlier writings, but instead get at a basic phenomenon that inspired his earlier work and was not fully articulated in this work.[17]

Often the turn is described as a change in focus from Dasein to Being: after all, Heidegger speaks here of abandoning subjectivity, and Division III was supposed to shift from the Being of Dasein to the meaning of Being as such. But this is too simple. We have seen that already in *Being and Time*, Dasein is not a subject in the traditional sense – a self-contained mental thing. Furthermore, Heidegger was clearly never interested in Dasein by itself, to the exclusion of Being; he was interested in Dasein precisely *as* the entity who has an understanding of *Being*. In addition, *Being and Time* holds that neither Dasein nor Being can take place without the other: Dasein has to understand Being in order to be Dasein, and Being is not given except in relation to Dasein (*Being and Time*, 228/183). This is a view that Heidegger maintains throughout his life: in 1969 he says, "the fundamental thought of my thinking is precisely that Being, or the manifestation of Being, *needs* human beings and that, vice versa, human beings are only human beings if they are standing in the manifestation of Being".[18] Both earlier and later, then, he is thinking about *both* Dasein and Being. However, it is true that his later writings rarely return to the texture of human experience with the fine eye for detail shown in *Being and Time*.

16. "Letter on Humanism", in *Basic Writings*, pp. 231–2.
17. In a letter to William J. Richardson, Heidegger puts it this way: "only by way of what Heidegger I has thought does one gain access to what is to-be-thought by Heidegger II. But [the thought of] Heidegger I becomes possible only if it is contained in Heidegger II": "Preface", in Richardson, *Heidegger*, p. xxii. He also claims that the "turn" in the deepest sense is not an event in his own intellectual development, but part of the relationship between time and Being themselves: *ibid.*, p. xviii.
18. "Martin Heidegger in Conversation", in *Martin Heidegger and National Socialism*, Neske & Kettering, p. 82.

When Heidegger says that his earlier "thinking . . . did not succeed with the help of the language of metaphysics", what language does he have in mind? It might seem that in *Being and Time*, Heidegger has invented a vocabulary quite separate from that of the metaphysical tradition. However, he does adopt a few traditional concepts. We have noted that his distinction between *existentialia* and existentiell possibilities looks very similar to the traditional distinction between essential and accidental predicates, and we have found that at certain points, Heidegger's distinction becomes problematic. We have seen, too, that Heidegger speaks in a rather Kantian way of establishing "*transcendental* knowledge" (*Being and Time*, 62/38), and conceives of temporality as the "transcendental horizon for the question of Being" (63/39). In later years, Heidegger takes care to avoid the term "transcendental" (if not the term "transcendence") because the Kantian notion has certain unwelcome connotations.[19] First, it suggests that Dasein has a certain priority over Being, as if Dasein's temporal structure *dictated* what Being could mean. The later Heidegger tends to emphasize that Being holds *us* in its power; we respond to it, we do not create it. Secondly, the Kantian language may make it seem that we can establish a single, fundamental concept of Being, once and for all, and demonstrate its necessity. The later Heidegger understands Being as essentially historical: it is given and withheld unpredictably in history, and takes many forms. But does he object to his earlier language because it could mislead his readers, or because he himself was misled by it? The answer is not altogether clear.

Although the turn is difficult to interpret, it is impossible not to notice the overt signs of a change in Heidegger's thought: the new style and diction that come into his writing around 1930. He was always a powerful writer who exploited the rich resources of the German language. However, his earlier texts tend to have a technical flavor, as if Heidegger, like Husserl, were trying to develop phenomenology as a science with its own specialized terminology. During the 1930s, Heidegger's style becomes distinctly more "poetic". That is, he relies more exclusively on common, basic German words, and by skillfully exploring their sounds and histories, he weaves together texts that flow from question to question without ever crystallizing into a doctrine or a technical vocabulary. The result, although hardly easier to understand than his earlier style, can be more appealing, and even beautiful, as when he writes, "the clearing center itself encircles all that is, as does the nothing, which we scarcely know".[20]

This stylistic change reflects a shift in interest. The nature of poetry and language becomes a major question for Heidegger, as we will see at the end of this chapter. He comes to view philosophy as closer to poetry than to science,

---

19. "The *transcendental* . . . way was only preliminary": *Beiträge zur Philosophie (Vom Ereignis)*, GA 65, p. 305. Heidegger continues to favor the word *transcendence* in some texts written shortly after *Being and Time*, such as "What is Metaphysics?" (1929), *The Essence of Reasons* (1929), and "On the Essence of Truth" (1930).
20. "The Origin of the Work of Art", in *Basic Writings*, 178.

although he never holds that philosophy and poetry are the same.[21] Simply put, both thinkers and poets are sensitive to the richness of meaning in a way that the specialized sciences can never be. Both thinkers and poets are able to draw on the power of language in order to reveal beings or Being anew.

In a related development, Heidegger's claims begin to look less like universal, "scientific" statements about Dasein in general, and more like messages delivered to a particular group of people at a particular juncture in history. Since *Being and Time* already held that Dasein is profoundly historical, it could be argued that Heidegger is not changing his standpoint so much as he is adjusting his language to fit what he was already thinking. We find more talk of "the West" and "the Germans", alongside statements about "Dasein" or "man" in the abstract. The distinction between the "existential" and the "existentiell", which looked much like a distinction between the ahistorical universal and the historical particular, seems to drop out of Heidegger's thought. Heidegger lives up to his claim in *Being and Time* (67/42) that Dasein's characteristics are "possible ways for it to be, and no more than that". Even "care" and "Dasein" are treated as historical *possibilities* rather than universal structures or fixed essences. Dasein is a possible dimension of human beings that we may or may not attain, depending on how we deal with our history.[22] And the meaning of this "we" also becomes problematic: *Who are we?* Heidegger asks with greater and greater intensity.[23]

The language of freedom and decision, which was already important in *Being and Time*, becomes more and more prominent in the 1930s. Heidegger wants "us" to choose. "We" are primarily the Germans, who must decide who they are, what they are to make of themselves, and whether they are willing to shoulder their destiny as "the metaphysical people", the nation called to understand and experience Being.[24] Heidegger has less to say now about everyday practice; he focuses instead on the larger historical developments in which he believes Germany has a crucial role to play. He insists that the Germans have not yet made a genuine decision, because they have not yet undergone the crisis that would lead them to a genuine revolution. He wants them to experience a pressing emergency, a "distress" that will spur them into choice. In the thirties, Heidegger often refers to the current time in terms of "the distress of no distress": no one feels that there is a crisis – and this situation is itself the true crisis![25]

The last major sign of change occurs in the late thirties and early forties. Heidegger gradually tones down this language of decision in order to develop

21. An example of Heidegger's own poetic efforts is "The Thinker as Poet", in *Poetry, Language, Thought.* (The original title of the piece is "From the Experience of Thinking".)
22. Dasein "is something unquestioned and unmastered, which is somehow man and then again is not man": GA 65, p. 313.
23. E.g., GA 65, §19.
24. *An Introduction to Metaphysics*, p. 38 (translation modified). Heidegger's most detailed explorations of freedom are to be found in the lecture courses GA 31, GA 42 and GA 49.
25. See e.g. *Basic Questions of Philosophy*, p. 158.

a language of receptivity. He speaks more and more of listening, waiting and complying. We must learn to stop imposing our will upon beings and instead learn to hear and obey Being. From Meister Eckhart, the medieval German mystic, Heidegger adopts the word *Gelassenheit*, "releasement", to speak of this proper attitude.[26]

This provides another quick and misleading way to characterize the *Kehre*. It looks as if Heidegger switches from activism to quietism – and his late philosophy is sometimes criticized for being *too* passive.

The trouble with this interpretation is that Heidegger himself never accepts the duality that it presupposes. "Releasement lies – if we may use the word lie – beyond the distinction between activity and passivity . . . because releasement does *not* belong to the domain of the will."[27] He points out that already in *Being and Time*, resoluteness (*Entschlossenheit*) was conceived as a kind of disclosedness (*Erschlossenheit*). "Letting be" was already mentioned in *Being and Time*, as well as in "On the Essence of Truth" (1930).[28] Heidegger claims that he never viewed decision as a matter of imposing one's subjective will on the world: true decision involves sensitive clear-sightedness. Of course, Heidegger may not be his own best interpreter, but what he says should give us pause before we claim too readily that in his "turn" Heidegger reversed himself.

The question of the nature of the turn has become a classic topic in the secondary literature. But readers should decide for themselves what the turn means, on the basis of Heidegger's writings rather than from what any commentator says. Furthermore, they must try to interpret the turn not just as an arbitrary change of mind on Heidegger's part, but as a development that makes sense in terms of the questions that are asked in his thinking – although it is probably not the only possible development of these questions. We now turn to some key texts from Heidegger's later period, in search of the questions that drive them.

"What is Metaphysics?": nothingness and the disintegration of logic

In 1929, on the occasion of his inauguration as professor at Freiburg, Heidegger delivered one of his most famous lectures, "What is Metaphysics?" This concentrated, powerful exploration of anxiety and its relation to nothingness owes much to *Being and Time*, but its spirit is one of opening new questions and provoking fresh thought. The lecture was not meant as a clear statement of a doctrine, but as a challenge to philosophize.

In this regard, it had only mixed success. On the one hand, it attracted a great deal of attention and soon became a key text for existentialists. One

26. See "Conversation on a Country Path about Thinking", in *Discourse on Thinking*, pp. 58–90. On the transition from resoluteness to releasement, see Zimmerman, *Eclipse of the Self*. On Heidegger and Eckhart, see J. D. Caputo, *The Mystical Element in Heidegger's Thought* (New York: Fordham University Press, 1990).
27. "Conversation on a Country Path", in *Discourse on Thinking*, p. 61.
28. *Being and Time*, p. 117/84–5; "On the Essence of Truth," in *Basic Writings*, p. 125.

listener reports, "When I left the auditorium, I was speechless. For a brief moment I felt as if I had had a glimpse into the ground and foundation of the world. In my inner being, something was touched that had been asleep for a long time".[29]

On the other hand, "What is Metaphysics?" led indirectly to Heidegger's banishment from the world of Anglo-American philosophy, and for decades this banishment prevented most English-speaking philosophers from using Heidegger as food for thought. For in this lecture, Heidegger makes two statements in particular that are calculated provocations. The first is the pronouncement *das Nichts selbst nichtet*: "Nothingness itself nothings", or "The nothing itself nihilates" (103).[30] The second is the statement, "The idea of 'logic' itself disintegrates in the turbulence of a more original questioning" (105). The first statement sounds like utter gibberish, while the second sounds like reckless irrationalism.

So thought Rudolf Carnap, at least, who denounced Heidegger in his essay "The Elimination of Metaphysics through Logical Analysis of Language" (1932).[31] For Carnap and other logical positivists, philosophy should clarify the rules of coherent, meaningful discourse. Meaningful discourse is scientific; it expresses objective facts in unambiguous propositions. Philosophy, then, is a system of propositions about systems of propositions in general. In other words, philosophy is logic, theory of theory. Now, some sentences seem to be neither science nor logic – for example, "that flower is beautiful" or "justice is good" or metaphysical propositions such as "substantiality implies unity". But these are just pseudo-propositions: they are nonsense, or at best, a symptom of the speaker's emotional state. When we use the tools of logic to clean the Augean stables of philosophy, babble such as *das Nichts selbst nichtet* will be the first to go.

Through Carnap's essay, which was widely read in the Anglophone world, Heidegger's philosophy got the reputation of being the worst sort of verbal trickery, a wooly-headed and dangerously confused concoction that did not deserve the name "philosophy" at all, and certainly was not worth reading. For example, in a popular history of philosophy, Bertrand Russell writes about Heidegger:

> Highly eccentric in its terminology, his philosophy is extremely obscure. One cannot help suspecting that language is here running riot. An interesting point in his speculations is the insistence that nothingness is something positive. As with much else in Existentialism, this is a psychological observation made to pass for logic.[32]

29. Petzet, *Encounters and Dialogues*, pp. 12–13.
30. Within this section of this chapter, parenthesized references will refer to pages of "What is Metaphysics?" in *Basic Writings*.
31. In A. J. Ayer (ed.), *Logical Positivism* (New York: The Free Press, 1959). Also in Murray, *Heidegger and Modern Philosophy*.
32. B. Russell, *Wisdom of the West* (New York: Crescent Books, 1989), p. 303.

That is the entirety of Russell's entry on Heidegger, and it expresses everything that most English-speaking philosophers felt they needed to know about Heidegger until relatively recent times. An analytically trained teacher of mine once quipped, "The argument of *Being and Time* can be summed up in three lines: a ham sandwich is better than nothing; nothing is better than God; therefore, a ham sandwich is better than God". In short, Heidegger is illogical – he says so himself – and thus is not worth taking seriously. This rather smug attitude is often extended to all "continental" philosophy (a misleading term, for the roots of analytic philosophy are at least as German as they are British).

At this point, I recommend that readers turn to Heidegger's brief essay itself, and follow this carefully-constructed piece through its obscurities, its puzzlement, and its final question: "Why are there beings at all, and why not rather nothing?" Carnap's essay is also well worth reading as a statement of an approach to philosophy that is diametrically opposed to Heidegger's. One may then wish to consider the following suggestions for how to interpret "What is Metaphysics?" and how to adjudicate the conflict between Heidegger and Carnap.

Heidegger's lecture begins with an account of "our existence" as researchers (94) and proceeds to the "metaphysical" issue of "the nothing" that he finds in the background of our existence. ("Metaphysics" is an ambiguous term in Heidegger. It refers sometimes to a tradition that needs to be overcome, and sometimes, as here, to genuine thinking about Being.)

Heidegger starts by emphasizing science's "submission to beings themselves" (94–5). Good chemists, economists or historians all have this in common: they want to know what is the case, what is true and only that. They are devoted to beings alone – and *nothing* else.

Heidegger's next move is precisely where Carnap saw the first logical error.[33] Heidegger asks: "what about this nothing?" (95). "What is the nothing?" (96). He immediately anticipates that people will say he is just playing with words (95). In fact, he *is* playing with words: "nothing" does not mean the same in "nothing else" and in "What is the nothing?" In the first phrase, "not anything" can be substituted for "nothing"; in the second phrase, it cannot. But Heidegger is not *just* making a pun: he is claiming that the first meaning of "nothing" ("not anything") is dependent on the second meaning that he is about to explore.

Of course, Carnap would say that there *is* no second meaning: "nothing" makes sense only as a way of expressing a negation, of denying something.[34] We can see this in the ham sandwich joke. The proposition "A ham sandwich is better than nothing" just means that eating a ham sandwich is better than *not* eating anything. The proposition "Nothing is better than God" means that there is *not* anything better than God. "Nothing", it seems, reduces to the "not";

33. Carnap, "The Elimination of Metaphysics", in *Logical Positivism*, Ayer, pp. 69–70.
34. *Ibid.*, p. 71.

it has no independent reality apart from propositions. From the logical point of view, asking what the nothing is makes sense only as a question about how negation works. If we keep insisting, as Russell puts it, "that nothingness is something positive", then by trying to ask about nothing, we will fail to ask about anything. Here Heidegger anticipates Carnap's objection: "the question deprives itself of its own object" (96).[35]

But can "the nothing" have another meaning aside from the "not"? Heidegger now turns to the process of "nihilation", as revealed in the experience of anxiety. As he said in *Being and Time*, anxiety is not about any particular being.[36] It is about beings as a whole. It is impossible to *know* all beings, but it is possible to *feel* the totality of beings in a mood (99). Profound boredom reveals the totality as dull or repellent. The joy of love, when one sees the world in one's lover's eyes, reveals the totality as miraculous and beautiful.

Anxiety, too, reveals beings as a whole in a particular way; as we put it in Chapter 3, in anxiety all entities seem irrelevant, inconsequential, insignificant. This disturbing *meaninglessness* is the "nothing" that Heidegger wants to explore. In a way, Carnap is right: the nothing is nonsense. It is the *non-sense* that constantly threatens the *sense* of the world. If Being is the difference it makes to us that there is something rather than nothing, nihilation is what tends to eliminate this difference. In nihilation, everything threatens to lose its significance: "All things and we ourselves sink into indifference" (101).

This may sound very abstract and nebulous. But to someone actually experiencing anxiety, it is much more concrete and powerful than any logical doctrine. It affects our Being-in-the-world, and not just our propositions. For instance, teenage *Angst*, clichéd though it may be, is a real phenomenon: young adults often experience a crisis of foundations, in which the established interpretation of Being-in-the-world becomes unstable and unsatisfying. According to Heidegger, this experience is always possible for Dasein.

Just as great art often comes from troubled artists, the nothing has the potential to provide fresh illumination. It can help us recognize that, despite the threat of senselessness, there *is* a difference between something and nothing. Beings can now have more meaning than they did in the hackneyed, dull interpretations of everyday life. Being itself is now open to creative transformation.

> Nihilation . . . discloses . . . beings in their full but heretofore concealed strangeness as what is radically other – with respect to the nothing.
>
> In the clear night of the nothing of anxiety the original openness of beings as such arises: that they are beings – and not nothing. [103]

This means that the nothing plays a role in Being. Being can be meaningful only if there are limits to its meaning, a boundary where Being verges on

35. ". . . even if it were admissible to introduce 'nothing' as a name or description of an entity, still the existence of this entity would be denied in its very definition" (*ibid.*).
36. *Being and Time*, p. 230/185–6.

meaninglessness. "Being itself is essentially finite and reveals itself only in the transcendence of Dasein which is held out into the nothing" (108).

We can easily imagine Carnap's response: if by "the nothing" Heidegger means some sort of emotion, such as anxiety, then the expression is a misnomer; it does refer to something. However, it has no relevance to the universe at large, or to the nature of truth or Being itself – it just expresses one possible subjective attitude to life, perhaps an attitude typical of teenagers. Heidegger is trying to put this feeling into ontological language, when it would be expressed better in music.[37] Or as Russell puts it, talk of nothingness is psychology disguised as logic. This is a serious charge (and especially ironic, in view of the fact that the young Heidegger had himself argued against such "psychologism").

What is really at stake in this controversy? One crucial point is that for the logical positivists, there are some propositions that can be stated objectively, independently of the quirks and particularities of mood, language, and culture: "Einstein's theories are expressible (somehow) in the language of the Bantus – but not those of Heidegger, unless linguistic abuses to which the German language lends itself are introduced into Bantu."[38] Philosophy should be logic (not anthropology, linguistics or psychology); it should study the rules of objective, scientific propositions.

Heidegger, in contrast, insists that *all* "unconcealment" is bound up with mood, language and culture. Einstein's theories are meaningful only to someone trained to approach nature in a certain way, the way of Western modernity. Science requires a special mood and a special use of language. Facts are always interpreted in terms of particular, historically grounded ways of thinking: "there are no mere facts, but . . . a fact is only what it is in the light of the fundamental conception, and always depends upon how far that conception reaches".[39]

Two common misinterpretations should be avoided at this point. First, Heidegger does not deny that non-Westerners may participate in modern science. They obviously do, and very successfully. But according to him, this is not because science is independent of culture, but because our planet's cultures are being Westernized. Secondly, Heidegger is not a radical relativist who would say that Einstein's theories are on a par with astrology. Einstein's theories are true: that is, they do unconceal things, and much more so than astrology. However, this unconcealment is made possible for us by a historical context which, like all historical contexts, is limited and is open to innovation. Every theory inherits a past that both submits the theory to certain prejudices and makes possible other approaches that may someday prove to be more illuminating.

37. Music is the "purest" way of expressing an attitude to life "because it is entirely free from any reference to objects": Carnap, "The Elimination of Metaphysics", in Ayer, *Logical Positivism*, p. 80.
38. O. Neurath, "Protocol Sentences", in Ayer, *Logical Positivism*, p. 200.
39. "Modern Science, Metaphysics, and Mathematics" (from *What is a Thing?*), in *Basic Writings*, p. 272.

Heidegger's position, then, is that factors such as culture and mood are always operative in the background of scientific statements. This is so because some particular way of Being-in-the-world is always at work, bringing with it some configuration of sense and non-sense, some relation to Being and to nothingness that precedes and sustains our relationships to particular entities. As Heidegger explains in detail in *Being and Time*, our moods, which are ways of experiencing our thrownness, disclose the world more fundamentally than any propositions, affirmative or negative, that we may express. Our sense of beings as a whole is what allows us to take up particular relationships to entities, including scientific relationships. According to "What is Metaphysics?" we get a sense of beings as a whole, and of Being itself, when we "transcend" the whole of beings in anxiety and experience nihilation. This transcendence makes it possible to relate to particular entities, including *ourselves* – and thus Heidegger writes, "Without the original revelation of the nothing, no selfhood and no freedom" (103).

This is why logic, as a theory of propositional truth, is not of primary importance for philosophy. When Heidegger dramatically declares that logic "disintegrates", he means that logic can deal only with the surface phenomena of meaning – theoretical propositions. These would be meaningless without the more primordial unconcealment that accompanies our existence. As we are about to see, thinking about this *primordial* truth calls for an investigation of the mysteries of human freedom – and here, logic is no help to us.

We may have explained this controversy; we have not resolved it. As late as 1964, Heidegger speculates about "the still hidden center of those endeavors towards which the 'philosophy' of our day, from its most extreme counter-positions (Carnap → Heidegger), tends". He proposes that he and the logical positivists have some common ground. They are concerned with the same questions: what is objectifying, what is thinking, and what is speaking?[40] Today logical positivism has fallen out of fashion, and Heidegger's thought has made inroads into the English-speaking world. This moment should not mark the beginning of a new, Heideggerian dogmatism. It should serve as an opportunity to ask the same questions that were asked by Carnap and Heidegger.

"On the Essence of Truth": unconcealment and freedom

"On the Essence of Truth" (1930) pursues what we can all recognize as characteristic Heideggerian questions: How is it that beings reveal themselves to us

---

40. "The Theological Discussion of 'The Problem of a Non-objectifying Thinking and Speaking in Today's Theology' – Some Pointers to its Major Aspects", in *The Piety of Thinking*, tr. J. G. Hart & J. C. Maraldo (Bloomington, Indiana: Indiana University Press, 1976), p. 24. On the personal and intellectual relationship between Carnap and Heidegger and their common roots in neo-Kantianism, see M. Friedman, "Overcoming Metaphysics: Carnap and Heidegger", in *Origins of Logical Empiricism*, R. N. Giere & A. W. Richardson (eds), Minnesota Studies in the Philosophy of Science, **16** (Minneapolis, Minnesota: University of Minnesota Press, 1996).

as beings? How does truth – that is, unconcealment – come to pass? According to "What is Metaphysics?" beings show themselves to us thanks to "the transcendence of Dasein which is held out into the nothing".[41] In our encounter with the limits of meaning, Being takes on a meaning for us. In "On the Essence of Truth", Heidegger conceives of this transcendence in terms of freedom.

Again, I urge readers to work through Heidegger's dense but brief essay first, and then to consider the following proposals for interpreting it. It should be noted that here, even more than in other texts, Heidegger writes by raising objections to himself. He often shifts into a voice that challenges his own project or the particular steps he is carrying out. Readers will be able to follow these shifts in voice as long as they remember that Heidegger takes issue with the traditional concepts of subject and object and the traditional interpretations of the relationship between the two.

Every word counts in this essay, but we can single out certain statements as particularly important. Here is one possible list of key statements, one each from sections 1–7 of the essay. (I will forego comment on sections 8 and 9, which present a few important afterthoughts on philosophy and Being. The discussion of *Contributions to Philosophy* below may help readers with section 9.)

(1) "The true, whether it be a matter or a proposition, is what accords, the accordant" (117).

(2) "A statement is invested with its correctness by the openness of comportment; for only through the latter can what is opened up really become the standard for the presentative correspondence" (122).

(3) "The openness of comportment as the inner condition of the possibility of correctness is grounded in freedom" (123).

(4) "Freedom, understood as letting beings be, is the fulfillment and consummation of the essence of truth in the sense of the disclosure of beings" (127).

(5) "Precisely because letting be always lets beings be in a particular comportment that relates to them and thus discloses them, it conceals beings as a whole" (129–30).

(6) "*As ek-sistent, Dasein is insistent.* Even in insistent existence the mystery holds sway, but as the forgotten and hence 'unessential' essence of truth" (132).

(7) "Freedom, conceived on the basis of the in-sistent ek-sistence of Dasein, is the essence of truth (in the sense of the correctness of presenting) only because freedom itself originates from the primordial essence of truth, the rule of the mystery in errancy" (134).

Our challenge is not only to understand what Heidegger means by these particular statements, but also to follow the movement that leads him from one

---

41. "What is Metaphysics?", p. 103. Within this section of this chapter, parenthesized references will refer to pages of "On the Essence of Truth" in *Basic Writings*.

to the next – for here he is not presenting a finished system, but is underway. During his train of thought, he considers a number of objections and makes many critical comments about the tradition. We will disregard these objections and comments, valuable though they are, and try to clarify the primary thread of the essay.

Statement (1) is Heidegger's way of expressing the traditional concept of truth as correspondence. He does not reject this concept outright, but he asks (as he did in *Being and Time*, §44) what makes correspondence or "accordance" *possible*. The answer, according to (2), is that correspondence is made possible by "the openness of comportment". In other words, we can formulate correct claims only if we already behave in a way that opens us up to beings and opens up beings for us. I may make the true claim, "On Wednesday we had half an inch of rain". This statement accords with the facts: it harmonizes with the reality of the water that hit the ground a few days ago. My statement is a case of "presentative correspondence": it corresponds to the rain, and presents, or re-presents, the rain to whoever hears my statement. But what allows me to make the statement in the first place? The rain must already be accessible to me, and I must take it as my standard for what I say. So I must pay attention to beings; I must be accessible to them so that they can be accessible to me.

According to statement (3), this openness of comportment is based on freedom. We enter freely into openness, and are free for what we encounter there (123). When he associates truth with freedom, Heidegger does not mean to imply that we can arbitrarily decide what is true and false. Freedom is not just an ability to do whatever we want. More profoundly, freedom is our release into an open area where we can meet with other beings. A rock is not free, not because it is forced to do what it does not want, but because it is totally shut off from everything around it – and consequently cannot want or think anything. Animals are not free either, according to Heidegger, even though they often do what they want, because they are trapped in patterns of responses that do not allow them to encounter other beings, except insofar as these beings stimulate their own instincts. We humans are free, however, because we are able to encounter other beings within a wide-open world. Since my world has been opened up for me by my fundamental freedom, I am now able to like the rain, dislike it, protect myself against it, sing about it, or make a true statement about how much of it fell on Wednesday.

Unlike a rock or a lizard, I am able to *let beings be*. Statement (4) says that letting-be is the essence of freedom, and thus the essence of truth. Of course, rocks and lizards can leave other beings unaffected, "letting them be" in this sense. But Heidegger means that human beings can allow other beings to *show themselves* as they are. I let the rain be: that is, I let it present itself to me in its own raining.

"Letting-be" may sound rather passive, but Heidegger also says, "To let be is to engage oneself with beings" (125). Engagement means being attentively involved with beings in a way that allows them to be exposed. In order to let

128

the rain show itself to me, I cannot just stare at it indifferently; I have to care enough about it, it has to make enough of a difference to me, that I properly notice it. Now we can see how hopelessly crude it is to talk about Heidegger's "turn" in terms of activity and passivity: in this essay from 1930, he is describing human freedom as a sort of active passivity, or better, as an openness that is more basic than either activity or passivity. We stand in this openness because we "ek-sist": we are outside of our own selves, amid other beings, within a region, a "there". In brief, we are Being-there, Da-sein (126).

But according to statement (5), this unconcealment brings concealment with it. Recall that Heidegger claimed in *Being and Time* (§44) that Dasein is essentially both in the truth and in untruth: we are always in a world and encountering beings, but we tend to get absorbed in present beings and forget about our relation to the past and future. We are thrown into the world in some way that is manifested in our attunement, and we project possibilities into the future – but ordinarily we are oblivious to our moods and projects, because we are too concerned with dealing with the things around us. Our own Being is concealed, and this means that the Being of other things is also interpreted in a shallow way.

In "On the Essence of Truth" Heidegger hints at a similar story. He focuses on attunement (128–9). Beings as a whole are disclosed by attunement; they may, for instance, be revealed as oppressive or as uplifting. This revelation of beings as a whole is *mysterious*, because it "cannot be understood on the basis of the beings opened up in any given case" (129). Wednesday's rain will not tell me why the world is oppressive, and neither will anything else I encounter in the world – instead, the oppressiveness is there already, letting me encounter the particular oppressive beings. No particular entity can explain how it makes a difference to me that there are entities rather than nothing. Ironically, the more I gather information about beings (by measuring the rainfall, for instance) the easier it is to forget about the original openness of beings as a whole. We notice "this or that being and its particular openedness" (131) while disregarding the overall meaning of beings. An extreme case would be someone who has collected and memorized vast quantities of correct data, but whose sense of what everything means as a whole is so pallid that it has virtually disappeared. We all know some people like this; they tend to work in educational institutions.

As a result of falling, which Heidegger here rechristens "in-sistence" (132), we approach beings "as if they were open of and in themselves" (132). We forget the original opening of beings as a whole. Since this opening is mysterious to begin with, statement (6) explains that we now have a double concealment: we fail to notice that there is a mystery in the first place.

Statement (7) sums up Heidegger's train of thought and connects it to one last concept: errancy. Much as Heidegger has based the truth of correct propositions on a fundamental unveiling comportment of Dasein, he presents error as much more than the falsehood of propositions; error is part of the human condition, an "errancy" that afflicts us as we wander through existence. He holds out the hope that we can avoid some delusion by recognizing the mystery (134). There is no hope for perfect clarity and certainty, but there is hope that we will remember to notice the enigma of the original opening of the world. If we acknowledge the fact that the revelation of beings as a whole is mysterious, then maybe we will not be seduced into that learned blindness that is burdened with meaningless facts, and we will be open to new ways of experiencing beings as a whole. Once again, Heidegger has led us back to the importance of the simple experience of amazement at the fact that there is something instead of nothing.

Introduction to Metaphysics: the history of the restriction of Being

Introduction to Metaphysics (1935) is one of Heidegger's richest and most artfully constructed lecture courses. When he published it, with some revisions, in 1953, he recommended it in a preface to a new edition of *Being and Time* as an elucidation of the question of Being.[42]

This lecture course can be seen as a continuation of "What is Metaphysics?" It even begins with the question that ended the earlier essay: "Why are there beings at all and not rather nothing?" Heidegger had claimed in "What is Metaphysics?" that Being is essentially finite and is bounded by the nothing. In other words, beings are accessible to us as beings only in certain definite ways, and the sense of beings as a whole is always threatened by nothingness, non-sense. In moments of anxiety, we sense the non-sense: we realize that meaningfulness cannot be taken for granted. After various opening reflections on the question of Being and various deliberately false starts, *Introduction to Metaphysics* explores the determinate way in which Being is opposed to nothingness for us Westerners. Our understanding of Being is restricted to a particular meaning that has been established *historically*. Whether we know it or not, we move within certain tracks that were first laid down in the beginning of Greek philosophy.

Heidegger claims that for us, Being is restricted through the following four oppositions, which he explores in a highly original way.[43] What follows is not a summary of his lectures, but some remarks that can provide an initial orientation to his concerns.

(a) *Being and becoming*. This may be the most hackneyed opposition of all. We associate Being with permanence, and whatever is transitory seems only partially real. For Platonists, the timeless "forms" are what *is* most of all.

42. *Being and Time*, p. 17/vii. The lecture course has been translated as *An Introduction to Metaphysics* by R. Manheim. A new translation, titled *Introduction to Metaphysics*, by G. Fried & R. Polt, is forthcoming.
43. *An Introduction to Metaphysics*, Chapter 4. For a Greek text that briefly illustrates all the oppositions at once, see Plato's *Republic*, 507b–511e.

For modern science, the forms are replaced by invariant, mathematical laws of nature. Anti-Platonist thinkers, such as Nietzsche, assert the priority of change over permanence, becoming over Being. But how did this opposition between Being and becoming arise in the first place? Why do we use time as an ontological criterion, distinguishing between "timeless" Being and "temporal" becoming? Heidegger would insist that we have to ask questions such as these, instead of merely reproducing or inverting the old metaphysical opposition.[44]

(b) *Being and appearance.* We distinguish, naturally enough, between the way things are and the way things seem to be. Certainly this distinction has some use, for appearances can always be misinterpreted. But philosophers have tended to radicalize the distinction: they assume that what appears is *essentially opposed* to what is. The result is a dualistic position that splits apart "the world of appearances" and "the world of things in themselves". We know from the introduction to *Being and Time* (§7) that Heidegger wants to call this dualism into question – while still maintaining room for concealment, illusion and error. In *Introduction to Metaphysics*, he plunges into the origins of the problem.

(c) *Being and thinking.* This is probably the least obvious opposition, but it is the one that Heidegger considers at greatest length. This portion of the lectures develops his announcement of the "disintegration" of logic in "What is Metaphysics?" For the opposition he is challenging sets up thinking, in the sense of making *assertions*, as a court of judgment over Being. Logic, a system of rules about what can be asserted, determines what it means to be.[45] But what gives propositional thinking the right to legislate to Being? In order to reconsider the relationship between thought and Being, Heidegger goes back to Parmenides' enigmatic statement that "Being and thinking are the same" and to the Heraclitean notion of a *logos* that is deeper than logic. He even turns to Sophocles for a poetic expression of the nature of man. In Heidegger's interpretation of antiquity, great human beings, such as philosophers, are not the logical arbiters of Being, but daring adventurers who confront the overwhelming power of Being in an intimate struggle.

(d) *Being and the "ought"*. As Hume said, we cannot derive an "ought" from an "is". For instance, the *fact* that most people are heterosexual does not mean that homosexuality is bad – or that it is good. Judgments about good and bad are *value* judgments, judgments about what we desire as opposed to what there is. At least, this is how we usually think – for this duality certainly pervades much of science and common sense, as well as philosophy. Heidegger's exploration of it is, unfortunately, quite short.

44. Thus, in Heidegger's interpretation, Nietzsche, the anti-Platonist, is still a metaphysician, even if he may be the last metaphysician: "The Word of Nietzsche: 'God Is Dead'", in *The Question Concerning Technology*, p. 53.
45. A twentieth-century example is W. V. Quine's claim that "existence is what existential quantification [in symbolic logic] expresses . . . explication in turn of the existential quantifier itself, 'there is', 'there are', explication of general existence, is a forlorn cause": "Existence and Quantification", in *Ontological Relativity and Other Essays* (New York: Columbia University Press, 1969), p. 97. Quine thus explicitly restricts the question of Being to the logical question of how assertions of existence work within systems of theoretical propositions.

Now, why should we care about these various oppositions? What difference do they make? According to Heidegger, they literally make all the difference in the world. In *Introduction to Metaphysics*, readers will find some of the strongest statements of a conviction that runs throughout Heidegger's later work: human history is guided by the history of Being. A people's relation to Being is the destiny that leads the community through history and lays out its possibilities. According to Heidegger, our current understanding of Being has led us to an empty life of manipulation and calculation – a dead end. We are alienated from ourselves and from the universe, because we thoughtlessly understand beings merely as present-at-hand objects to be described mathematically and controlled technologically. In order to open up new possibilities for Western (and especially German) history, we have to refresh our sense of Being by returning to the source of our old ontological prejudices.

How did Being get restricted in these ways? What was the original experience of Being that led to these distinctions? According to Heidegger, the Greeks originally experienced Being as *physis*. We get our word "physics" from this word, and it is usually translated as "nature". It comes from a verb usually translated "to grow". But Heidegger proposes that *physis* primordially means arising and abiding.[46] A being rises up, appears on the scene, takes its stand for a while, and persists: in other words, it *is*. For instance, an oak has its Being by coming forth from the acorn and unfolding itself: it manifests itself, it actualizes itself, it is present. In this primordial Greek experience, Being is conceived as endurance, and truth is conceived as *aletheia*, unconcealment – truth is a kind of appearing. But in Plato Being becomes mere eternity, and truth becomes mere correctness: our misguided metaphysical tradition has begun. The Romanization, Christianization and modernization of metaphysics succeed only in aggravating the oblivion of Being.

At least, this is one story that Heidegger tells. He will eventually concede that *aletheia* already means correctness as early as Homer.[47] He constantly and almost obsessively revises his "history of Being". He finds both illumination and obscurity in nearly every philosopher, so the details of his history of philosophy are subject to great variation. What remains constant is that the story of Being is a story of decline: it is a fall from a promising Greek beginning that became inflexible and turned into a metaphysics of presence.

Heidegger's exposition of the supposed early meaning of *physis* is so powerful, and is in some respects so consistent with his own claims in other works, that readers often take it to be his own answer to the question of the meaning of Being. But it is safer to say that it is his attempt to recover the original experience of Being as presence that (in his view) founded Western history. Once we have recaptured this experience, we are not done; we have to ask

---

46. *An Introduction to Metaphysics*, p. 14.
47. Heidegger presents Plato as the turning point in "Plato's Doctrine of Truth" (1940), in *Pathmarks*. He retracts this interpretation in "The End of Philosophy and the Task of Thinking" (1964), in *On Time and Being*, p. 70.

about its limits – for Heidegger does believe there are limits to presence. Beings can be present to Dasein only because Dasein itself is more than present – it is temporal. It would seem that a full understanding of Being has to go beyond *physis*, then, and think of Being in relation to time. Heidegger claims at the end of his lecture course that this problem "points in an entirely different direction of inquiry".[48] We must seize the undeveloped Greek possibilities and develop them in a direction that is even more radical than Greek thinking. (Although Heidegger is sometimes classed as a postmodern thinker, he might prefer to be called pre-ancient.) If we succeed, we will be setting Western history on to another path than the one determined by the first beginning, the Greek beginning. We will be initiating "the other beginning", as he likes to say.

Heidegger's reading of the history of philosophy is powerful, but it is also often seen as willful. One has to ask whether he is so attracted to the pre-Socratics partly because they survive only in fragments whose interpretation can easily be skewed in a Heideggerian direction. In the hands of some Heideggerians, as well as of Heidegger himself in his lesser moments, the "history of Being" becomes a formulaic exercise in rehearsing a myth, which is then used to justify a political program.[49]

Heidegger insists on translating phenomenological language into narrative. He is not satisfied, for instance, with examining experience and concluding that unconcealment is more fundamental than correctness; he has to construct a saga in which an original Greek experience of unconcealment degenerated into a focus on correctness, with dire consequences for us all. Granted, it is natural for a philosopher who holds that all truth is historical to develop a history of truth. But it is unlikely that history works as Heidegger portrays it: a mystical beginning followed by a decline, guided not by individual choices, material conditions, or chance, but only by the understanding of Being – which is best expressed, of course, in philosophy. Common sense surely underestimates the importance of philosophy in history – but Heidegger overestimates it.

Introduction to Metaphysics also illustrates another questionable aspect of Heidegger's thought: he relies heavily on his idiosyncratic etymologies of important Greek words. As we saw in Chapter 2, young Heidegger had made a strict distinction between etymology and philosophy. Many wish that he had stuck to this position – for although many of his observations are philologically sound (as when he translates *aletheia* as "unconcealment"), often enough, his etymologies are fanciful, and in the hands of his imitators, this approach often degenerates into a string of bad puns posing as philosophical thought. For the reader who is more concerned with Heidegger than with the Greeks, it is enough to remember that his interpretations are deliberately daring and unconventional. Those readers who want to use Heidegger as a guide to ancient

48. *An Introduction to Metaphysics*, p. 205.
49. For most Heideggerians, the political program is one of postmodernist pluralism. For Heidegger in the thirties, it is fascism. For a postmodern critique of Heidegger's myths (but not of mythmaking in general) see J. D. Caputo, *Demythologizing Heidegger* (Bloomington, Indiana: Indiana University Press, 1993).

philosophy should take his statements with a grain of salt. However, they should also respect his talent for putting the tradition in a fresh light. Translating *logos* as "reason" may not be wrong, but it certainly does less to make us think than does Heidegger's rendition of it as "collecting collectedness".[50]

"The Origin of the Work of Art": the clash of earth and world

Art was hardly mentioned in *Being and Time*, but it may be that artworks are a particularly important kind of entity. If truth cannot be captured in theoretical propositions, then maybe art has a unique role to play in bringing about unconcealment. Art may alert us to the difference between something and nothing, and even open up new ways of relating to Being.

In "The Origin of the Work of Art" (1935) Heidegger carries out his most extended reflection on the nature of art, and develops concepts that are quite important to his late thought. Readers must not expect the essay to set forth a neat doctrine. Instead, as is typical of Heidegger's essays, he follows one of the ramifications of the problem of Being into uncharted territory, blazing a trail by means of questions, pronouncements and sometimes enigmatic plays on words. In his later "Addendum" to the text, he says that art "belongs to the *propriative event* [*Ereignis*] by way of which the 'meaning of Being' (see *Being and Time*) can alone be defined".[51] He thus connects the project of this essay both to his early masterpiece and to the *Contributions to Philosophy (On Appropriation [Ereignis])* – a text that he composed soon after "The Origin of the Work of Art" but which was to appear only posthumously. We will soon consider what Heidegger means by *Ereignis*. For now, we will concentrate on two more obvious features of his essay: he claims, first, that works of art are sites where "the truth of beings has set itself to work" (162) and, secondly, that this truth requires strife between "world" and "earth" (187).

Like all philosophical claims, these statements must be interpreted and tested in the light of our own experience. (When Heidegger warns us against focusing on "lived experience" [204], he means that instead of ruminating on our private feelings, we need to keep focused on the artwork itself. But of course, the artwork cannot have any power unless there is someone who can "preserve" it [192]. We do need to pay attention to our experience, then, but in a way that remains attentive to what is shown to us by the artwork itself.) Although Heidegger says that poetry is the quintessential form of art (198), in this essay his main examples come from architecture (a Greek temple) and painting (a work by Van Gogh). Readers must think of their own examples of powerful artworks, preferably including some types of art that are not analyzed in this essay (such as music), and see how far Heidegger's thoughts can be applied.

50. *An Introduction to Metaphysics*, p. 128.
51. *Basic Writings*, p. 210. Further references to "The Origin of the Work of Art" in this section will take the form of parenthesized page numbers.

Below I will supplement Heidegger's examples with an example of my own: the Vietnam Veterans Memorial in Washington, designed by Maya Lin in 1981 and built in 1984. The fame and impact of this monument, which is often known simply as the Wall, speak to its success as a work of art: it has quickly become a sacred site in the United States, and it has achieved an international reputation. The monument is simple. Sheets of black stone form the wall of a trench. The trench is shaped like a broad V, both horizontally and vertically. On the wall are inscribed the names of all the American soldiers who lost their lives as a result of the war. Heidegger's text and this powerful memorial may be able to shed some light on each other.

True to his phenomenological roots, Heidegger approaches art in terms of what is *manifested* in it. He claims that genuine works of art "make unconcealment as such happen in regard to beings as a whole" (181). Obviously, we are familiar with beings well before we encounter artworks, and even if we never have any contact with art. But this everyday familiarity with beings is superficial and clichéd. What artworks do is "transport us out of the realm of the ordinary" (191). They have the power to make us truly notice the Being of beings, instead of taking it for granted. "The more essentially the work opens itself, the more luminous becomes the uniqueness of the fact that it *is* rather than is not" (190). The fact that the artwork *is*, is inescapable – and through its own Being, it has the power to bring out the Being of all other beings as a whole. It "breaks open an open place, in whose openness everything is other than usual" (197).

This applies very well to the Vietnam Veterans Memorial. Even in photographs, it is an arresting *presence* – something that stands out as striking. Some things, such as new hairstyles, stand out from the ordinary merely because they are clever and innovative, but these are fads that attract our curiosity momentarily and then become passé. The memorial, however, holds one's attention at a level that goes deeper than curiosity; it demands time and reflection. Other things attract our attention because they are complex, bursting with information – for example, music videos. But the memorial is astoundingly simple. Its basic design and conception can be understood at a glance. Nevertheless, it holds the interest of anyone who is willing to pause and to silence the noise of everyday consciousness. The *Being* of this work of art touches us in a way that the shopworn Being of other things does not.

How does the artwork reveal beings other than itself? Heidegger is not claiming that art must be representational, or "realistic". The Wall is certainly not representational. In fact, its lack of images is one reason why it was controversial when it was first proposed, and today a highly realistic statue of three soldiers, by another artist, stands near Maya Lin's black V. But, skillful as it is, the realistic statue draws much less attention than the wall. The representational artwork, in this case, does less to illuminate reality than the non-representational artwork. The names of the soldiers, when they are inscribed in Lin's memorial, bring home the death of these men to us. Each individual death connects to an individual life, each life connects to the lives and deaths of those that surround it, and as the thousands of names gather at the center of the trench, one feels the war in its entirety as an event that is lodged in the American past and present. The monument reveals something about what it is to be American.

But what is the monument saying, specifically? Many veterans initially objected to the design, because they imagined that its message would be one of shame. But now that the artwork is there, almost all visitors recognize that its meaning cannot be summed up in a simple word such as "shame", "pride" or even "mourning". This is not to say that visitors walk away from the monument wrapped up in differing subjective interpretations. Instead, it creates a mysterious solidarity. Any two people who have visited the site share something in common, although they may be hard pressed to put it into words. The artwork speaks on its own terms, and says something that only it could say. It illuminates beings as a whole – for many Americans, at least – by making people pay attention to who they are, who they have been, and who they will be. In Heidegger's words:

> Preserving the work does not reduce people to their private experiences, but brings them into affiliation with the truth happening in the work. Thus it grounds Being for and with one another as the historical standing-out of human existence in relation to unconcealment. [193]

Works of art are capable, somehow, of bringing us home to ourselves; they show us how we dwell together amid things, making us perceive our own existence as something fresh and strange.

Heidegger says that artworks are not the only occasions for the fresh revelation of what is. On pages 186–7 he mentions political revolutions (a remark that gives us a little insight into his own political hopes), divine revelation, "essential sacrifice" (Socrates? Jesus?) and philosophy. In these various fields, truth can come to pass in the strife between *world* and *earth*. These complex concepts are never neatly defined in this essay, but if we apply them to examples and compare Heidegger's concepts to some more familiar conceptual pairs, we may be able to make some progress.

We described "world" in *Being and Time* as a system of purposes and meanings that organizes our identity and our activities. In *Being and Time* Heidegger focused on the everyday world of production, but our world is what gives meaning to *everything* that we can do, all the paths we can follow as we make ourselves who we are. *Being and Time* also focuses on the "individualizing" character of authenticity, but at the same time Heidegger makes it clear that Dasein is Being-with – that I cannot be someone except as a member of a generation in the history of a community. If we keep all these elements in mind, then we can recognize the concept of world in "The Origin of the Work of Art" as a restatement of Heidegger's earlier concept. He now says that in a world, "all things gain their lingering and hastening, their remoteness and nearness, their scope and limits" (170). A world opens up "the broad paths of the simple and essential decisions in the destiny of a historical people" (174).

Let's relate this concept to the Vietnam Veterans Memorial. The monument has the power to open up a world, that is, it shows Americans what is at stake for them as a community. It does not do this by presenting an obvious "message", a particular decision about how to interpret the past. The world is more basic than any particular decisions; it is the context that determines what needs to be decided, which issues are important and which are not. The memorial reminds us of the great issues that structure our existence: life, death, triumph, defeat, shame, glory, justice. Similarly, according to Heidegger, Van Gogh's painting of a pair of shoes exposes the world of a peasant woman, a world oriented by work, need, childbirth and death (159). The Greek temple reveals the Greek world – a world of "birth and death, disaster and blessing, victory and disgrace, endurance and decline" (167). It seems that these various worlds share some common features, some issues that are important to all Dasein at all times. But an artwork reveals these issues in a way that expresses a particular community's way of understanding itself at a particular juncture in history. This gives the artwork its remarkable power to open up a world.

But great art must also involve the *earth*. Heidegger's notion of the earth is new in this essay, and it is elusive. He writes that the earth is the basis on which we dwell, the foundation on which a world is built (168, 174). Earth "shelters" beings that "arise" from it (168). Earth is spontaneous, and also tends to hide itself in concealment (171–2, 174). In short, earth is the mysterious source from which we and other beings spring.

The easiest way to approach the concepts of earth and world may be to see them as an attempt to rethink the trite distinction between nature and culture. A world can be interpreted as a culture: that is, a system of meanings that makes it possible for a group of people to understand themselves and their environment. The earth can be interpreted as nature: that is, the pre-cultural basis for culture, a domain that follows its own laws and resists our attempts to domesticate it. For instance, in Van Gogh's painting, the earth is revealed in its "quiet gift of the ripening grain" in the summer and its "unexplained self-refusal" in winter: the earth is the power of nature, which is not completely under our control, "on which and in which man bases his dwelling" (168).

In *Being and Time*, nature was considered only as something assimilated into culture – something that is available either to be used for practical purposes or to be studied as a present-at-hand object by natural science.[52] "Earth" provides a new, more profound way of relating to nature: we can respect it as something that precedes our manipulations and interpretations, and essentially resists them. (This is the sort of view of nature that has been adopted in today's "deep ecology" movement.)

The vocabulary of nature and culture can also help us understand Heidegger's claims about the *relation* between world and earth. Earth and world are essentially in conflict:

---

52. One passage in *Being and Time* does suggest a deeper understanding of nature: Heidegger speaks of "the Nature . . . which assails us and enthralls us as landscape" (p. 100/70).

The world, in resting upon the earth, strives to surmount it. As self-opening it cannot endure anything closed. The earth, however, as sheltering and concealing, tends always to draw the world into itself and keep it there. [174]

In more familiar terms: culture arises from nature, and tries to understand that from which it arises. Since a culture sheds light on people and their surroundings, it is intrinsically opposed to obscurity and tries to illuminate nature. But (as Heraclitus said) nature loves to hide: there are always limits to what we can understand, and nature tends to reassert itself in its mysterious power.

The limits of understanding are not something so trivial as the fact that our instruments have limited precision, or the fact that there are places where human beings have not yet been. Understanding, according to *Being and Time*, is *intrinsically* finite, because it is a never-perfected process of interpretation. No truth or interpretation is absolute (although some are more revealing than others). The richness of beings will always involve some dimensions that are inaccessible to our current interpretations. Unconcealment thus involves both world and earth – both illumination and its limitations.

A work of art is a point at which the strife between earth and world comes to pass. The artwork opens up a world and at the same time allows the earth to display itself as earth – that is, as something concealed. Art shows us the fact that the earth does *not* show itself. This power to display mystery may distinguish art from science (science can show us only how things show themselves, not how they hide themselves).

But let's return to our example. The Vietnam Veterans Memorial is engaged with the earth in the most obvious sense: it is actually below ground level. It is integrated with its natural surroundings as few monuments are – for this monument is not just a man-made panel, but an opening in the earth itself, almost like an open grave. It is hard to define the limits of the monument; it includes not only the stone blocks, but the whole trench in the ground, and certainly at least some of the surrounding plot. The meaning of this monument tends to extend to the whole field in which it is installed – maybe to the whole territory of the United States, and everything built on it. The monument exposes this land in a special way: it does not reveal any of its secrets, but instead reminds us that it is there, that human beings have built on it, but that they have not wholly understood that upon which they are building. Cultures and political systems are built on mystery, and wars are waged on mysterious grounds – so the Wall seems to say. The artwork succeeds in the difficult task of displaying world and earth in their conflict: it calls on Americans to reflect on their culture and history (their world) while also suggesting the obscure roots of this world. In this way, the memorial provokes people to ask: Who are you? Who are your enemies? What counts as victory and failure for you? What are you willing to risk in your search for victory? How are you going to respond to what you have been and what you might be? Trivial art takes questions such as these for granted, and answers them in some unambiguous way, becoming propaganda or kitsch. Deeper art lets the questions themselves be heard.

The involvement of earth in the monument makes it especially appropriate as a memorial and a site for grieving. If the monument allowed everything to be dissolved into culture, that is, into a range of clear, neat interpretations of war and death, it would not allow room for the sense of an inexplicable burden that is crucial to mourning.

The danger of equating world and earth with culture and nature is that we will believe that this equation spares us the work of thinking. "Nature" and "culture" are two of those all-too-familiar words that seem obvious until we actually try to define them. We then find that we hardly understand what we mean by them. This is doubtlessly why Heidegger avoids them. Still, if they are taken as beginnings of thought rather than as endings, they can be useful tools for interpreting the essay on the artwork.

A few other familiar concepts can also be useful. Although Heidegger makes it very clear that he does not want to think of art in terms of form and matter, these concepts are not completely foreign to what he is saying. A form is, roughly, a scheme that stems from our culture or world, by means of which we understand or manipulate nature or the earth. We may, for instance, shape clay as matter into the form of a jug. Although an artwork is qualitatively different from a jug, both involve the interaction between world and earth. The difference is that in an everyday thing of use, earth is normally *absorbed* into cultural utility and does not stand out as such.[53]

Earth and world also have affinities to some concepts from *Being and Time*. Thrownness, like earth, is not of our own making, and we can never get it into our grip; it is a basis that we must take over and can never produce (*Being and Time*, 329–30/284). Projection, like world, involves understanding ourselves and other beings by laying out possibilities. One could also argue that anxiety reveals the earth by calling into question the web of meanings that constitutes the world.

One more approach to earth and world may be useful to those who have read Nietzsche's first book, *The Birth of Tragedy*. This book is clearly an inspiration for Heidegger's essay, even down to the titles of the two texts. Nietzsche is no easier to understand than Heidegger, but the parallels between the two philosophers are thought-provoking. According to Nietzsche, tragedy reflects its own origin in the conflict between two fundamental forces, "the Apollinian" and "the Dionysian". Nietzsche associates the Apollinian with the realm of dreams, and claims that in "our dreams we delight in the immediate

---

53. In his essay "The Thing", in *Poetry, Language, Thought*, Heidegger evokes an extraordinary experience of a jug as pointing to "the fourfold", including the earth. See pp. 151–2 of this book.

understanding of figures; all forms speak to us; there is nothing unimportant or superfluous".[54] In other words, the Apollinian – like Heidegger's "world" – is an all-embracing order within which everything makes sense and has a place. In the Dionysian, however, this intelligibility collapses. But at the same time, a "mysterious primordial unity" is achieved: "nature which has become alienated, hostile, or subjugated, celebrates once more her reconciliation with her lost son, man".[55] The affinities to Heidegger's "earth" are clear.

None of these parallels are meant as attacks on Heidegger's originality. He was not concerned with originality in the sense of being different from everything past; what he wanted was originality as contact with the origin, "that from which and by which something is what it is and as it is" (143). "The Origin of the Work of Art" remains profoundly original, precisely because Heidegger draws on deep currents within our philosophical tradition in order to reveal what is at work in works of art.

Contributions to Philosophy: fragments of another beginning

In the essays we have been considering so far, Heidegger gestures rather indirectly at what would be involved in experiencing Being in an original way. It is in the challenging Contributions to Philosophy (On Appropriation) that his struggle to bring about such an experience plays itself out most directly and intensely. The Contributions are an esoteric text in many ways. Heidegger composed this long manuscript in private between 1936 and 1938, and during his lifetime showed it only to a few confidants. He specified that it should appear in print only after the publication of all his lecture courses – thus implying that dozens of volumes of introduction are the prerequisite to understanding this book. The editors of the collected edition bent Heidegger's rule a little, and published the Contributions once editors had been assigned to all the available manuscripts of his lecture courses. The book appeared in 1989, the centenary year of Heidegger's birth.

The Contributions attracted instant attention, but also created bewilderment, for the most important sections of the text seem to be written in pure Heideggerese. Even more than in his other, already difficult writings, Heidegger exploits the sounds and senses of German in order to create an idiosyncratic symphony of meanings. The translators of this text have faced an immense challenge.[56]

In addition, the organization of the text is loose. It consists of 281 sections; some are polished short essays, but others are not even written in complete

54. *The Birth of Tragedy*, tr. W. Kaufmann (New York: Vintage, 1967), p. 34.
55. *Ibid.*, p. 37.
56. A translation by P. Emad & K. Maly is forthcoming from Indiana University Press. I will refer to the text by parenthesized section number in order to facilitate reference to the translation. I will also add a page reference to the German edition (GA 65) when sections are long. The translations here are my own.

sentences. The sections are grouped thematically, but the book does not follow a systematic plan, as did *Being and Time*. The style is deliberately fragmentary: this text "is no edifice of thoughts anymore, but blocks apparently fallen at random in a quarry where bedrock is broken and the rock-breaking tools remain invisible" (§259, p. 436). This is not to say that Heidegger's statements here are really chaotic and groundless, but he expects readers to work hard to discover unspoken connections.

Heidegger is not just being secretive. He is trying as hard as he can to respond to Being with appropriate language, but he holds that it is simply impossible to say "the truth of Being" directly: nothing we can say will make Being unconceal itself with perfect clarity. Being is *intrinsically* mysterious. We have to learn to give up our ambition to represent things perfectly and directly when we are trying to deal with Being, for "every saying already speaks *from* the truth of Being, and cannot leap over itself immediately to reach Being itself" (§38). We cannot turn Being into an object and describe it with scientific precision, because we do not control it; we are already plunged into a way of experiencing the difference between something and nothing. So instead of trying to dominate Being conceptually, we should respond to it with cautious and tentative respect. Heidegger believes that only "the few and the rare" are capable of thinking this way (§5).

Given the esoteric nature of the *Contributions*, Heidegger would certainly object to any attempt to sum them up in an introductory book, and especially to any suggestion that his thoughts here can be made easy. He even warns us theatrically that "when philosophy makes itself intelligible, it commits suicide" (§259, p. 435). Readers should keep in mind, then, that the comments that follow are not meant as a summary of the entire *Contributions to Philosophy*. They are simply explorations of a few key words and concepts from the text, explorations that may serve as the beginnings of paths for those who want to wander farther into the thickets of the *Contributions*.

Machination and lived experience

At this day, when the Psycho-Erg, a combination of the Psych, the unit of esthetic satisfaction, and the Erg, the unit of mechanical energy, is recognized as the true unit of value, it seems difficult to believe that in the twentieth century and for more than ten centuries thereafter, the dollar, a metallic circular disk, was being passed from hand to hand in exchange for the essentials of life. — Harry Stephen Keeler[57]

Before we examine Heidegger's way of addressing Being in the *Contributions*, we should consider the features of modern life to which he objects so strongly that he searches for an alternative to the entire Western tradition.

---

57. H. S. Keeler, "John Jones's Dollar", in *Fantasia Mathematica*, C. Fadiman (ed.) (New York: Copernicus, 1997), p. 250.

In Chapter 3 we saw that the division between subject and object, which finds its classic expression in Cartesianism, is linked to a technological understanding of our existence. From this point of view, non-human beings are objects that can be represented accurately and effectively by the mathematical means of modern natural science. Human beings, in contrast, are conscious, willing subjects. Through science, we can become the masters of nature; we can harness natural forces and use beings as resources in the service of our will. Things have value, then, only insofar as they supply energy for our technological projects or satisfy our subjective desires. We may continue to use dollars for some time, but one could argue that the Psycho-Erg has been our true unit of value ever since Descartes.

For Heidegger, this modern condition is a disaster, and the *Contributions* express his horror at it. We can say that this horror even determines the structure of the whole book. After a general overview (Part I), Heidegger describes the degenerate condition of the modern world (II). This leads him to a confrontation with the philosophical tradition of the West (III). Fresh from this confrontation, he ventures a "leap" which will establish new conceptions of Being, Dasein, and truth (IV–VII). Another overview (VIII) concludes the *Contributions*.

In Part II, titled "The Echo", Heidegger listens to the distant sound of a departed Being echoing in the hollowness of modern existence. He diagnoses this hollowness as a combination of the Erg and the Psych, objectivism and subjectivism – or in his terms, "machination" and "lived experience".

The word "machination" (*Machenschaft*) is Heidegger's expression in the *Contributions* for what he will later call *Technik* (technology) or *Ge-stell* (enframing). Machination is not just a human behavior, the act of manipulation; it is a *revelation of beings as a whole* as exploitable and manipulable objects (§61). The world seems to be a collection of present-at-hand things with no intrinsic meaning or purpose, a cold place where we cannot put down any roots. All we can do is calculate and control. We observe and measure everything, we make things go faster and faster, our power and efficiency are ever increasing – but questioning and reflection are withering away (§57). Quality is reduced to quantity (§70). This mathematization of the world does away with all sacredness: Heidegger speaks of "the flight of the gods" and "the death of the moral, Christian God" (§56).

In the world of machination, beings become "unbeings" (§§2, 58). This expression does not mean that everything has been destroyed, but that the *importance* of everything is being destroyed. Heidegger complains that "beings *are* [but] Being has abandoned all 'beings'" (§5, p. 15). In other words, the difference it makes to us that there is something rather than nothing has dwindled away to mere presence-at-hand. The wealth of meaning has faded away, leaving only a bleak, gray wasteland.

In order to compensate for the impoverishment of our objective world, we pile up "lived experience" (*Erlebnis*) that will enrich our subjectivity. Here we should make it clear that Heidegger is not against experience in general. There are two German words for "experience" that have very different connotations for him. An *Erfahrung* (related to *fahren*, to travel) is a journey that transforms the journeyer; this can be very desirable, and Heidegger likes to think of his own philosophy as a "path" along which he travels. But an *Erlebnis* (related to *leben*, to live) is merely a superficial stimulus that leaves the one undergoing the experience fundamentally untouched.[58] This is the target of Heidegger's attack (§§62–68). In our search for lived experience, we consume neverending quantities of entertainment and information. We represent beings and play with our representations of beings. But we never open ourselves up to Being itself. Instead, we make our own means of representation the standard for "what can count as a 'being'" (§63). Today, when we are so capable of creating "virtual realities", Heidegger's diagnosis seems truer than ever; the distinction between beings and our own representations is becoming harder and harder to maintain.

Heidegger's more thorough reflections on these themes can be found in the postwar essay "The Question Concerning Technology", which we will consider later. But we have seen enough to understand that he wants an alternative to the modern worldview. From *Being and Time* one might get the impression that we can find such an alternative simply by taking a fresh look at our own, everyday existence. But Heidegger now seems to believe that in the modern age, everyday existence is so impoverished and corrupted that what we need is a radical revolution in our relationship to Being itself. In order to understand this revolution, we can begin with the title of his book.

Being as appropriation

Contributions to Philosophy is a deliberately bland, empty and conventional title (see Heidegger's note before §1). But the "proper heading" – (*On Appropriation*), in parentheses – uses a mysterious word, *Ereignis*, that has never been an important philosophical term before. It points to the central message of this text. To put it in a sentence, *das Seyn west als das Ereignis* (§10). This sentence can be translated, "Being essentially unfolds as appropriation". But what does this mean? We will have to take the words one by one, and look closely at some German vocabulary.

In the *Contributions*, Heidegger often spells the word for "Being" as *Seyn* instead of *Sein*. *Seyn* is an old-fashioned, nineteenth-century spelling that gives the word a faint flavor of something archaic and forgotten. He wants to recall a mysterious sense of Being that lies hidden behind the conventional way of conceiving of Being.

Heidegger claims that traditional metaphysics has focused on *beings*, and the question of the Being of *beings* has been the "guiding question" of Western philosophy (§34). Here "Being" just means whatever can be said *in general* about all beings – horses, planets, houses, redness, running and whatever *is*

---

58. See R. Bernasconi, *The Question of Language in Heidegger's History of Being* (Atlantic Highlands, New Jersey: Humanities Press, 1985), pp. 81–2.

in any way. All of these entities, as entities, are presumed to have certain characteristics in common, or at least to be classifiable according to one general scheme. (For example, Aristotle holds that although not all beings are substances, they can all be understood with reference to substances. Modern physics tries to understand all beings as mathematically describable patterns of mass-energy in space-time. Nietzsche, according to Heidegger, interprets all beings as manifestations of the will to power. In philosophy departments, many metaphysicians are still busy counting up the types of beings and trying to determine their essences according to some scheme.) Traditional metaphysics also tends to look for a particular entity that most fully exemplifies what it means to be. This entity is the perfect being, or God. Metaphysics thus becomes what Heidegger likes to call "onto-theology": the discipline that classifies and explains beings in general and subordinates them to a supreme being.

Heidegger wants to ask a new question now, a "grounding question" that can found "the other beginning" of Western thought and Western history. In this context he uses the spelling *Seyn* (§34):

> If in contrast [to the question about the Being of beings] we now ask about *Seyn*, we are not starting from beings, that is, from this and that particular being, nor are we starting from what is, as such and as a whole; instead, what is accomplished is a leap into the *truth* (clearing and concealing) of *Seyn* itself. Here, at the same time, we are experiencing and interrogating . . . the *openness for essential unfolding* as such, that is, *truth*.

In other words, Heidegger wants to think about Being without basing his thought on beings at all, and he wants the question of truth to form part of this project.

If we look back at the goal of *Being and Time* and at essays such as "On the Essence of Truth", we can see what he means. He is asking how it is that beings are unconcealed to us in the first place. He wants to pay attention to the difference it makes to us that there are beings, rather than nothing. We can never approach this question by looking at beings themselves, because *before* we start to investigate the characteristics of houses, horses, or even the entire universe, it must *already* make a difference to us that there is something rather than nothing. *Being* must already be at work.

We are still trying to understand the claim, "Being essentially unfolds as appropriation". We can now turn to the expression "essentially unfolds" (*west*, infinitive form *wesen*). In the *Contributions*, Heidegger does not ask, "What is Being?" or "What is the meaning of Being?" but "How does Being *wesen*?" *Das Wesen*, a noun, is the standard German counterpart to our word "essence". But *wesen*, a verb, is an archaic word that today is used only by poets – and Heideggerians. It originally means to live, exist or work. Like "be", it is a fundamental word for what things *do* at a primordial level. No English expression is really a satisfactory equivalent to *wesen* (to transpire? to "escence"?), but the word has often been rendered as "essentially unfold".

The verb *wesen* is useful to Heidegger in two ways. First, it gives him a fresh way of talking about the search for what is most important about something. The noun "essence" carries a lot of undesirable metaphysical baggage; it suggests that we are looking for some timeless abstraction, or some everlasting core of things. But the verb *wesen* suggests that we simply have to pay attention to how things actually happen. For instance, if we ask how poetry *west*, we do not have to look for some universal essence of poetry that applies to all poets at all times. Instead, we listen to a poem and focus all our attention on what is really going on in this poem. This shift in emphasis helps to free philosophers from what Nietzsche called their "Egyptianism". ("They think they're *honoring* a thing if they de-historicize it . . . if they make a mummy out of it. Everything that philosophers have handled, for thousands of years now, has been conceptual mummies; nothing real escaped their hands alive.")[59]

The second way in which Heidegger takes advantage of the verb *wesen* is by reserving it for Being, and thus using it to help us avoid thinking of Being as a being. To put it succinctly: *Das Seiende ist. Das Seyn west.* "Beings are. Being essentially unfolds" (§10). If we said that Being *is*, we would be treating it as an entity, when instead, it is the difference it makes to us that there are entities in the first place. According to Heidegger, it would be hopelessly naïve to try to understand Being as if it were a being. For example, we might try to understand how entities make a difference to us by means of some science that studies some particular realm of entities: psychology, biology or anthropology. But then we would be *taking it for granted* that there are entities, including human beings, whereas Heidegger's question necessarily involves a sense of wonder at the fact that beings in general are *granted* at all. He wants us to notice the *granting* of beings as such. Otherwise, we will be far too likely to treat all beings merely as present-at-hand entities. We can then discover all the facts we want about beings, both human and non-human, but fail utterly to reflect on the meaning of Being itself.

When we ask how Being essentially unfolds, then, we are trying to pay attention to what is going on when the unconcealment of beings is granted to us. We are trying to notice the happening of the disclosure of what is.

The next word we have to consider in Heidegger's sentence, "Being essentially unfolds as appropriation", is the treacherous little word "as". Is Heidegger saying that (a) Being is the *same* as appropriation, (b) Being is a *kind* of appropriation, or (c) appropriation is a kind of Being? Heidegger discusses this issue most explicitly in the late essay "Time and Being" (1962). He clearly rejects (b) and (c).[60] But his position on (a) is harder to discern. In "Time and Being", Heidegger exploits the German expression *es gibt*, which is used like our expression "there is", but literally means "it gives". Time and Being *are* not

59. F. Nietzsche, *Twilight of the Idols: Or, How to Philosophize with the Hammer*, tr. R. Polt (Indianapolis: Hackett, 1997), p. 18.
60. "Time and Being", pp. 21–2. This lecture and the summary of a seminar on the lecture, both available in *On Time and Being*, are important but difficult texts that are of limited use to beginners.

(they are not entities), but instead, it is better to say that "it gives" time and Being. What is the "it" that gives them? – Appropriation.[61] (Or, to play with our favorite phrase: if Being is the difference it makes that there is something rather than nothing, then appropriation is the "it" that makes this difference.)

Appropriation, then, is the source of Being and time, as well as of their interconnection. But appropriation is not a source in any normal sense: it is not a cause or an entity. It is not a thing that gives us another thing, namely Being, but is more like the very event of giving. Is it separable, then, from Being itself? Maybe not. Heidegger claims it is also acceptable to say, as he does in his "Letter on Humanism", that the "it" that gives Being is Being itself.[62] "*Essential unfolding* is not supposed to name something that lies still *beyond* Being, but it expresses what is innermost in Being, *ap-propriation*" (§164).

It is easy to get lost in these vague musings, and more than one reader has concluded that Heidegger is just playing pseudo-mystical word games. But it seems fairly safe to say, at least provisionally, that Being is the same as appropriation – with the caution that, in this realm, our most basic commonsense concepts, such as "same", may fail us. It may be more precise to put it this way: whatever the content of Being may be (whether Being means presence for us, or has some other meaning), appropriation is Being's own way of *happening*, of *giving* itself to us. (Although this may sound like some divine act, we have to keep in mind that Being is not an entity, not even a god, but an illumination or meaningfulness.)

So: what *does* Heidegger mean by "appropriation", *Ereignis*? The word is so crucial that, in a sense, the only way to answer this question is to study all of the *Contributions*, and other later writings of Heidegger as well. There is also the short and sweet answer: "Appropriation appropriates".[63] But maybe we can find an explanation between these extremes.

Ordinarily *Ereignis* is used just as we use the word "event", but Heidegger wants us to hear an echo of the adjective *eigen*, "own", which is the root of words such as *Eigenschaft* (property), *geeignet* (appropriate), and even *eigentlich* (authentic). (*Eigen* is not actually the root of *Ereignis*, which in fact is related to *Augen*, "eyes". In this case Heidegger does not claim anything about etymology; he is just relying on a similarity in sound to suggest a connection in meaning.) Hence the usual translations: "appropriation", "event of appropriation" or "propriative event".

Heidegger had exploited the word *Ereignis* as early as 1919, when he used two German words for "occurrence" to distinguish between, on the one hand, occurrences as they are described by theory, and on the other hand, occurrences that are genuinely part of someone's experience.[64] A *Vorgang* (etymologically, a process or procession – that which goes by before me) is an occurrence

---

61. "Time and Being", p. 19.
62. "Summary of a Seminar on the Lecture 'Time and Being'", in *On Time and Being*, p. 43. Cf. "Letter on Humanism", in *Basic Writings*, p. 238.
63. "Time and Being", p. 24.   64. GA 56/57, pp. 74–5.

from which I am detached, and which I merely watch as it passes by. But an *Ereignis* is an event that is my *own*. In an *Ereignis*, beings find a significant place within my own life and world. "The *Ereignis* happens to *me*, I make it my own, it relates to me."[65] One might think of the difference between watching a sport on television and playing the sport oneself: it may be the same game, but it shows itself much more intensely and meaningfully to the participants.

The expression *Ereignis*, both in this early text and in the *Contributions*, points to the fact that meaning and truth require involvement. Like "care", the word *Ereignis* suggests that we can never truly be detached from the world and become timeless, placeless observers. The world opens up for us only because we are engaged participants in it.

If *Ereignis* is not a further thing above and beyond Being, but is Being's own way of occurring, then to say that Being *west* as *Ereignis* is to say both (a) that Being is an event, a happening, and (b) that Being involves owning, or appropriation. Let us consider both these claims in turn.

(a) With the claim that Being is an event, Heidegger may have succeeded in leaving behind philosophical "Egyptianism" once and for all. Being is not some eternal object (this would only be a special kind of *entity*). Being is essentially timebound; this most fundamental of all phenomena, the condition that allows us to encounter beings at all, is *historical*. There is a "history of Being" that, according to Heidegger, provides the key to *all* history. This history of Being involves a series of transformations of the way in which it makes a difference to Dasein that beings are, rather than are not. Much of the *Contributions* – and of Heidegger's other later writings – is devoted to telling the story of these transformations.

But when we say that Being is temporal or historical, we should not make the mistake of supposing that this means only that Being is always changing. Being does in fact change over the course of history, but that is not Heidegger's main point. History is not just a series of changes; when we consider it this way, we are looking at history just as a *Vorgang*, a present-at-hand process that "goes by" in front of us.

In order to develop a vocabulary that can talk about history in an adequate way, Heidegger's later writings exploit a series of plays on words: history (*Geschichte*) is a happening (*Geschehnis*) in which our fate and destiny (*Schicksal* and *Geschick*) are wrapped up in how Being is sent (*geschickt*) to us.[66] History is a drama into which we are thrown, and in which Being is thrown to us, so that we may catch it and in turn cast it forwards into the future. We cannot avoid inheriting a meaning of Being, and it is our responsibility to appreciate it, question it and keep it alive by keeping it open to further unfolding. We cannot detach ourselves from the event of Being, because

---

65. G. Walther's notes to Heidegger's lecture course *Die Idee der Philosophie und das Weltanschauungsproblem*, quoted in Kisiel, *The Genesis of Heidegger's* Being and Time, p. 65.
66. E.g. "Time and Being", pp. 8–9.

our participation in it is what makes us human – or rather, makes us Dasein, "the thrown thrower" (§182).

(b) Precisely because Being is an event, not as a present-at-hand process but as a sending which is thrown to us, Being involves *owning*. Being is not universal and eternal, but instead *belongs* to us, as the destiny of our particular community – and just as Being belongs to us, we belong to Being. We are appropriated by Being: it seizes us and turns us into Dasein, instead of a closed-off animal or thing. And in turn, we can appropriate Being: we can stop taking it for granted and allow it to come alive for us as a question. When we do so, history happens. At such truly historical moments, an entire culture and era can be founded. When human beings appropriate Being, through poetic, philosophical and political creativity, they lay a new basis for a community.

This means that Being not only is timebound, but also is bound to a site. Being literally *takes place*. Here we have to understand "place" not just as a point on a map, but as a home in which people dwell. The great revolutionary acts, the acts that can institute a new way of dwelling and set up a new place, are acts through which Being itself shows itself with fresh intensity. At such moments, the "there" is founded, and we leap into the fullness of Being-there, Dasein. Our task as Dasein is to be "steadfast" (*inständig*), to stand courageously and clearly within the site that we have opened up (§174). This means keeping aware of the limits of this site, and staying open to new paths, instead of getting so comfortable in our routes that they become ruts.

For example, Egypt was founded (from a Heideggerian point of view) when an Egyptian meaning of Being was established – an Egyptian sense of what was at stake for the community and what was important about beings. This foundation may have occurred through great religious, poetic, philosophical or political achievements. The spark of the culture was sustained in times of innovation and reinterpretation, when the Egyptian destiny underwent a renaissance. But the long periods of stability and the fixed patterns for which ancient Egyptian culture is known lay it open to the charge of so-called "Egyptianism". Heidegger would view this stability as stagnation: at these times, the meaning of Being has come to seem so obvious that its historicity can no longer be recognized. Then, patterns of meaning appear to be eternal, and we can be consumed by the illusory ambition to be absorbed in eternity. This "Egyptianism" is hardly limited to ancient Egypt, but is a permanent danger for Dasein. Heidegger claims to see it happening all around him.

The founding of a site is always crucial to how Being takes place: "Being essentially unfolds as the *propriative event of the grounding of the there*, or in short: as *appropriation*" (§130).

How should we understand the phrase *das Seyn west als das Ereignis*? Maybe as follows: beings make a difference to us thanks to an historical happening that lays claim to us, and which we, in turn, can make our own at certain rare, foundational moments. Great moments in history happen when we wrestle with pre-existing patterns of illumination, and encounter things in their splendor and mystery.

Truth as sheltering

Heidegger has said that he wants to think about Being without starting with entities. His "Being" is not a supreme being, and it is not a generalization of the characteristics of beings. It is an event in which the "there" opens up, so that beings can first become accessible to Dasein.

But this does not mean that he wants to ignore beings altogether. Being does, of course, necessarily relate to entities. Being – in the formulation that we have been using in this book – is the difference it makes to us that there are *beings* rather than nothing. All beings have the capacity to indicate Being itself if we approach them in the right way. Certain beings, such as artworks, have this capacity to a remarkable degree. (We can now see why art "belongs to *Ereignis*".[67])

In this connection, the *Contributions* speak of "sheltering" (*Bergung*). In order to embrace history and found a site, we have to *shelter* the truth of Being in beings (§243):

> Sheltering belongs to the essential unfolding of truth . . . The clearing must ground itself in what is open within it. It requires that which it contains in openness, and that is a being, different in each case (thing – equipment – work). But this sheltering of what is open must also and in advance be such that openness comes into beings in such a way that self-concealment, and thereby Being, essentially unfolds in it.

Let us try to rephrase this. The "clearing", the open region of unconcealment, has to be "grounded" in particular beings. These particular beings "shelter" truth when they hint at the whole realm of unconcealment – when they suggest the depths of the meaning of Being. This suggestion is never a complete revelation, because Being, as Heidegger repeats throughout the *Contributions*, is intrinsically mysterious.

Recall our description of the Vietnam Veterans Memorial. The monument is not just another everyday, relatively insignificant thing, like a billboard or parking lot. It is a powerful, unique being that opens up the whole world of American history – while also making room for the earth, the unmastered and uninterpreted depths that lie beneath the world. By embodying the strife between world and earth, the monument *shelters* the truth of Being.

In "The Origin of the Work of Art", Heidegger discussed the conflict between world and earth only in relation to artworks, but in the *Contributions* it is clear that it can apply to any entity, as long as that entity shelters Being (§269). To use an example other than art: ordinarily we may glance at a mountain and naïvely assume that it is just "there", an object that is given to us. Being and truth are then dimmed down. But if we allow the mountain to shelter the truth of Being, we can experience its "thereness" more fully. We will acknowledge all the ways in which the mountain makes a difference in our world: for example,

---

67. Addendum to "The Origin of the Work of Art", in *Basic Writings*, p. 210.

as a ski resort, a source of copper, and the traditional home of a god. Now the mountain will reveal itself as much more than a meaningless object; it is a point at which various dimensions of significance itself are gathered and displayed. Furthermore – and this is crucial – we will allow the mountain to exceed and challenge our interpretations. By recognizing and respecting its mystery, we will experience the way it sets forth the "earth" as well as the "world".

Heidegger's talk of sheltering is a good example of the intricate wordplay that runs throughout the *Contributions* and that makes this text so hard to translate. Consider these interrelated words:

bergen: to shelter
verbergen: to conceal
Unverborgenheit: unconcealment
Wahrheit: truth
wahren, bewahren, verwahren: to safeguard and preserve

When Heidegger lets these words resonate with each other in his sentences, the German language helps him make his point: when truth is sheltered in beings, it is preserved and safeguarded in a way that involves both concealment and unconcealment. No wonder Heidegger believed that German was matched only by Greek as a language for philosophy!

Sheltering happens only at times of greatness. In Heidegger's bleak vision, we are currently suffering from "the oblivion of Being" (e.g. §50), and consequently beings are not sheltering Being – they have been reduced to "unbeings". We are becoming indifferent to the difference between beings and nothing (§47). For us, the universe is turning into a wasteland.

In response to this crisis, Heidegger intends nothing less than "to give historical humanity a goal once again: *to become the grounder and preserver of the truth of Being*, to *be* the there as the ground that is required by the essence of Being itself: *care* [for] the Being of beings as a whole" (§5, p. 16). Note that Dasein ("to *be* the there") and care are now historical possibilities, rather than invariant features of human beings. Heidegger challenges us to leap into another beginning, in which humanity will have a double role (§266, p. 467):

> The relation to Being, as a grounded relation, is steadfastness in *Being*-there, standing within the truth of Being (as appropriation).

> The relation to beings is the creative safeguarding of the preservation of Being in that which, in accord with such preservation, sets itself as beings into the clearing of the there.

The way from beings to Being

To review:

If we think of Being on its own terms, without basing it on beings, then it reveals itself as the event of appropriation.

But although Being cannot be *reduced* to beings, it does need beings in order to occur: the truth of Being needs to be sheltered in beings.

This opens up the possibility of a different, and perhaps more accessible, route to understanding Being. "It must be possible . . . to find the way from 'beings' to the essential unfolding of truth, and on this way to reveal *sheltering* as belonging to truth" (§243). We can *start with particular beings* and train ourselves to see them as sheltering the truth of Being. This is not to be confused with the traditional procedure of metaphysics, which constructs a concept of Being by finding *general* features of beings. Traditional metaphysics might begin with the mountain and the Vietnam Veterans Memorial, and ask what is common to them both as beings. They are both present substances that have various qualities – so Being, according to this way of thinking, involves presence, substance, quality, and so on. But Heidegger would approach the mountain or the memorial by looking for the unique way in which it embodies the conflict between world and earth, and thus points to the essential unfolding of Being.

A helpful passage in the *Contributions* sketches just such an approach:

> The opposite way can be taken most securely if an interpretation reveals the spatiality and temporality of the thing, equipment, the work, machination, and all beings as the sheltering of truth . . . The interpretation must awaken new experiences, beginning with the thing . . . The way starting from here [Being] and the way starting from beings must meet each other.[68]

This programmatic statement gives us the key to unifying many of Heidegger's late essays. His plan is to focus on various realms of beings in a way that will point to Being as appropriation – a theme that is discussed most directly, of course, in the *Contributions* themselves. Let us see how this plan was realized:

(a) *The work.* Heidegger means the artwork. This part of "the way starting from beings" was fulfilled in "The Origin of the Work of Art".

(b) *Machination.* As we have seen, this is not just the realm of machines, but beings as they are revealed in the modern, technological worldview – beings as calculable, manipulable resources. This theme is explored further in postwar essays such as "The Question Concerning Technology", which we will discuss below.

(c) *Equipment.* This word (*Zeug*) points back to the analysis of "ready-to-hand entities" in *Being and Time*. In his later essays, Heidegger drops this terminology in favor of an even more ordinary word that has a broader meaning:

(d) *The thing.* Some of Heidegger's best-known postwar essays are devoted to exploring "things", such as a jug or a bridge.[69] Heidegger attempts to use

68. GA 65, §242. The context of this passage is a discussion of "time-space", a concept that I cannot discuss here but that is essentially connected to the *Contributions*' concepts of Being and truth as I have explained them.
69. See "Building Dwelling Thinking" and "The Thing", both in *Poetry, Language, Thought.* "Building Dwelling Thinking" is also available in *Basic Writings.*

these things to reveal what he calls "the fourfold": earth, sky, gods and mortals. For example, he describes a jug as follows:

> In the gift of the outpouring that is drink, mortals stay in their own way. In the gift of the outpouring that is a libation, the divinities stay in their own way, they who receive back the gift of giving as the gift of the donation. In the gift of the outpouring, mortals and divinities each dwell in their different ways. Earth and sky dwell in the gift of the outpouring. In the gift of the outpouring earth and sky, divinities and mortals dwell *together all at once.*[70]

The fourfold is a strange creation. It is likely to provoke responses such as Gadamer's first reaction to "The Origin of the Work of Art": "Metaphors? Concepts? Were these expressions of thought or announcements of a neoheathen mythology?"[71] Is Heidegger trying to describe our actual experience of a jug? Is he trying to recapture some lost, primal experience? Is he trying to create a new one?

In any case, it is clear that he wants us to perceive things as more than just dull, meaningless, present-at-hand objects. He wants us to perceive them as sheltering the truth of Being – a truth that involves, or at least could involve, the four dimensions of the fourfold.

Readers who want to investigate the origins of the fourfold should begin with Heidegger's readings of Hölderlin. Those who are intrigued by the mention of "divinities" will want to examine the many references to gods in the *Contributions*, particularly §§253–6 on "the final god". We cannot treat this important topic here, except to give a few hints. In his later thought, Heidegger is neither a theist nor an atheist. He wants to point to the lack of the divine in contemporary existence, and point the way to the dimension of the sacred as a realm where divinity might someday reappear. His enemy is not atheism, but *indifference* to the question of the holy. True godlessness is not the absence of gods, but a state in which their presence or absence makes no difference to us. Heidegger wants us to recognize that a people's relation to the divine plays a crucial role in its relation to Being (§251).

We have, then, a program for Heidegger's late essays: they will explore various fields of beings in a way that is meant to point us toward Being as appropriation. In addition, of course, he will continue to write about the history of Western philosophy, about the relation of Being and Dasein in general, and increasingly, as we will see, about language as a mode of appropriation.

Heidegger's politics: facts and thoughts

We turn now from the hermetic depths of the *Contributions to Philosophy* to Heidegger's failed attempt at a contribution to politics. Following a formula

70. "The Thing", p. 173.   71. Gadamer, *Philosophical Apprenticeships*, p. 51.

used by Heidegger himself in a postwar apologia, we can roughly divide the issues into "facts" and "thoughts".[72] In other words, (a) what are the facts about what Heidegger did and said in the political realm during the Nazi period? Here we will concentrate on his words. (b) How should these facts be interpreted in relation to his philosophy in general? The "thoughts" can in turn be divided into Heidegger's own postwar self-interpretation and the interpretations of others.

The facts are complex, and we cannot review them in detail here.[73] While he was rector of the University of Freiburg in 1933–34, Heidegger certainly supported Hitler, opposed academic freedom, and attempted some steps towards reorganizing the university along "revolutionary" lines by evaluating faculty in terms of their commitment to the party. The well-known Heidegger's public speeches played a not insignificant role in giving the Nazis cultural prestige.

What were Heidegger's opinions during this time? The most notorious and most interesting of Heidegger's speeches as rector is his first, the so-called "Rectoral Address" he gave upon assuming the office. It is titled "The Self-Assertion [Selbstbehauptung] of the German University". But the grim joke at the time was that it should have been called "The Self-Beheading [Selbstenthauptung] of the German University" – for here Heidegger makes it very clear that he wants the university to participate in the new National Socialist order, and he condemns academic freedom as "arbitrariness" and "lack of restraint".[74] However, he is very vague about specific policies, and concentrates on the deeper significance of the revolution rather than on its concrete effects. He describes this significance not in the favored Nazi terms of race and domination, but in terms of his own history of Being. For Heidegger, what is essential is that the university's quest for knowledge be grounded in and unified by the confrontation with Being that is part of the German destiny – "the historical spiritual mission of the German Volk as a Volk that knows itself in its state".[75] In order to fulfill their mission, students will now be bound to "labor service", "military service" and "knowledge service".[76] And if Germany fails to fulfill its destiny? Heidegger paints a grim scenario in which "the spiritual strength of the West fails and the West starts to come apart at the seams . . . this moribund

72. See "The Rectorate 1933/34: Facts and Thoughts" (1945), in *Martin Heidegger and National Socialism*, G. Neske & E. Kettering (eds).
73. The best-known account is V. Farías, *Heidegger and Nazism*, J. Margolis & T. Rockmore (eds) (Philadelphia, Pennsylvania: Temple University Press, 1989). A less polemical and better-documented study is Ott, *Heidegger: A Political Life*, 1993. Some crucial documents, including selected political speeches by Heidegger, can be found in G. Neske & E. Kettering, *Martin Heidegger and National Socialism*, 1990, and Wolin, *The Heidegger Controversy*, 1993. The most complete collection of such documents in German is G. Schneeberger (ed.), *Nachlese zu Heidegger: Dokumente zu seinem Leben und Denken* (Bern, 1962). H. Sluga, *Heidegger's Crisis: Philosophy and Politics in Nazi Germany* (Cambridge, Massachusetts: Harvard University Press, 1993) provides some helpful context and compares Heidegger's actions to those of other academic philosophers in Germany at the time.
74. "The Self-Assertion of the German University", in Wolin, *The Heidegger Controversy*, p. 34.
75. *Ibid.*, p. 30.   76. *Ibid.*, p. 35.

pseudocivilization collapses into itself, pulling all forces into confusion and allowing them to suffocate in madness".[77]

Among other documents of the time, several are notable for supporting Hitler's proposal to withdraw from the League of Nations. Heidegger presents this not as an act of aggression, but as a step towards "a true community of nations" that will "stand by one another in an open and manly fashion".[78] If he believed this, his statement shows a good amount of naïveté – but it also provides an intriguing glimpse of a Heideggerian ideal of international relations.

Shortly after resigning as rector, in the summer of 1934, Heidegger delivered a lecture course titled *Logic*. The text has not been published in the *Gesamtausgabe*, but a series of notes marked as a partial transcript of the lecture course were discovered among the effects of one of Heidegger's best students, Helene Weiss.[79] If these notes can be trusted – and they are completely compatible with Heidegger's other lecture courses in both style and content – they show that Heidegger is committed to thinking philosophically about the issues raised by National Socialism, primarily the issue of what it means to be a people (*Volk*).

The text moves quickly from logic to language to people. "The questioning [of logic] happens as care for knowledge about the Being of beings, and this Being comes to power insofar as the might of the world happens in language."[80] But language is always the language of a people: "Language is the might of the world-building and preserving center of the historical Dasein of the people."[81] Amid many passionate questions and exhortations, the lectures assert that true Being-a-people requires decisiveness and requires a strong state. This authoritarian order leaves little or no room for individual liberty:

> Freedom is not doing things and leaving them undone without restraint. Freedom is the imposition of the ineluctability of Being, it is the incorporation of historical Being into will that knows, it is the recasting of the ineluctability of Being into the mastery of a structured order of a people. Care for the freedom of historical Being is in itself the empowerment of the power of the state as the essential structure of an historical mission. Because the Being of the historical Dasein of man is grounded in temporality, that is, care, therefore the state is essentially necessary. "The state" not as an abstraction, and not as derived from an imagined right linked to a timeless human nature in itself, but the state as the essential law of historical Being, owing to whose arrangement the people can first secure for itself historical endurance, and this means the preservation of its mission and the struggle for its task. The state is the historical Being of the people.[82]

77. *Ibid.*, p. 38.
78. "German Men and Women!" in Wolin, *The Heidegger Controversy*, p. 48.
79. The text has been published only in a bilingual German–Spanish edition: *Lógica: lecciones de M. Heidegger (semestre verano 1934) en el legado de Helene Weiss*, intro. & tr. V. Farías (Barcelona: Anthropos, 1991).
80. *Lógica*, p. 128.　　81. *Ibid.*, p. 126.　　82. *Ibid.*, p. 118.

It is disturbing to watch Heidegger use concepts from *Being and Time* to justify an authoritarian and nationalistic vision – vague though this vision is. He obviously had high hopes for Nazism, of a peculiarly metaphysical kind. His version of "the movement" interprets it in relation to Being itself: "Socialism . . . means care for the standards and the essential structure of our historical Being, and this is why it wills ranking according to profession and work, it wills the untouchable honor of all labor, it wills the unconditionality of service as the fundamental relationship to the ineluctability of Being."[83]

The National Socialists' talk of nation, labor, rank and service appealed to Heidegger. But he did not adopt their rhetoric of race. Race is a non-historical, biological factor, and Heidegger insists throughout his life on separating human beings from lower animals. Thus the *Logic* lectures try to find some way to accommodate Nazi ideas without accepting Nazi biological racism: "Blood, bloodline [*Geblüt*], can be a fundamental determination of human beings only if it is determined by temperament [*Gemüt*]. The voice of blood comes from the fundamental mood of a human being."[84] On one occasion, the lectures verge on what we might call a non-racial racism – that is, they suggest the inferiority of a racial group using "history" rather than blood as a criterion. This chilling passage suggests that while Hitler's airplane is historic, the historicity of Africans is questionable:

> One will object that our assertion that history is what is distinctive about human beings is arbitrary. Blacks are human beings too, after all, but they have no history. There is also a history of animals, plants, which is thousands of years old and much older than all human history . . . Even nature has its history. But then blacks also have history. Or does nature have no history, after all? It can, to be sure, pass away into the past, but not everything that passes away passes into history. If the propeller of an airplane turns, then nothing is really "happening". However, when this airplane brings the Führer to Mussolini, then history is happening.[85]

The best that can be said about this passage is that Heidegger is speaking in the form of a dialogue; he does not commit himself outright to any statements about black people, either negative or positive.

In 1936, Heidegger still praises Hitler and Mussolini from the podium as "the two men who have introduced countermovements [to nihilism] on the basis of the political formation of the nation or the people".[86] But the *Contributions to Philosophy* show Heidegger's growing uneasiness with certain aspects of fascism. He insistently objects to the biologism of Nazi ideology and its crude concept of the *Volk* (§§56, 117, 268, 273). He also objects to its self-centered nationalism: rather than merely trying to ensure its own survival and expand its power, a nation should open itself up to the meaning of Being that

83. *Ibid.*, p. 120.   84. *Ibid.*, p. 100.   85. *Ibid.*, pp. 38, 40.   86. GA 42, p. 40.

is destined for it (§§196, 251). He compares "total political faith" to "total Christian faith" and writes that "their struggle is not a creative struggle, but 'propaganda' and 'apologetics'" (§14, p. 41). Another private text, written in 1939, begins by quoting a speech by Hitler: "the ultimate justification for every attitude" is to be found in its "usefulness for the [social] totality". Heidegger then lets loose a storm of questions: "Who is the totality?" "How is it determined? What is its goal?" "Why is *usefulness* the standard for the legitimacy of a human attitude? What is the basis for this claim? Who determines the essence of humanity?"[87] Heidegger's frustration is obvious. A revolution that had appeared to promise a rebirth of the German spirit has turned out to be dogmatic and totalitarian. He had hoped to become the public intellectual leader of the movement, but has been reduced to asking himself his philosophical questions about Nazism in private notes.

This is not to suggest that Heidegger wants to return to the liberal democracy of the Weimar Republic, or that he has any sympathy for the Allies when war finally breaks out. His references to liberalism in the *Contributions* (e.g. §§14, 196) make it clear that he sees it as a dead end. When America declares war against Germany, he reacts with fury: "America's entry into this planetary war is not its entry into history; rather, it is already the ultimate American act of American ahistoricality and self-devastation".[88]

It has often been asked whether Heidegger was an anti-Semite. Since the Nazi platform included much more than anti-Semitism, hatred of Jews was not necessarily the main reason for joining the party. However, since Hitler's anti-Semitic views were obvious enough, clearly anyone who supported the Nazis was at best indifferent to the welfare of the Jews. There are some signs of Heidegger's prejudice: notably, in 1929 he wrote a letter of recommendation in which he praised a candidate as providing an alternative to the growing "Jewification" (*Verjudung*) of German culture.[89] And yet, he had close relationships with many people of Jewish descent, such as his teacher Husserl, his student and sometime lover Hannah Arendt, his protégés Karl Löwith and Helene Weiss, and his lifelong friend and correspondent Elisabeth Blochmann.[90] But anyone who is familiar with prejudice knows that no number of particular cases is enough to defeat someone's bigotry – these cases can always be seen as "exceptions".

Does a prejudice against Jews infect Heidegger's philosophical thought? There seem to be no anti-Semitic statements in his books or lecture courses,

---

87. GA 66, pp. 122–3.   88. *Hölderlin's Hymn "The Ister"*, pp. 54–5.
89. U. Sieg, "Die Verjudung des deutschen Geistes: Ein unbekannter Brief Heideggers", *Die Zeit* **54** (22 Dec 1989). For a cautious assessment of the evidence regarding the question of Heidegger's anti-Semitism, see J. Young, *Heidegger, Philosophy, Nazism* (Cambridge: Cambridge University Press, 1997), pp. 38–43.
90. The Heidegger–Blochmann letters are printed in *Martin Heidegger, Elisabeth Blochmann: Briefwechsel, 1918–1969,* J. W. Storck (ed.) (Marbach am Neckar: Deutsche Schillergesellschaft, 1989). The Heideggers and the Husserls were on poor terms during the 1930s, although it is unclear whether Heidegger betrayed his teacher in the particular ways of which he has been accused, such as by barring Husserl from the university library.

and it is very clear that he did not share the official Nazi doctrine of racial superiority. However, not all anti-Semitism is racist; it can also be cultural. It can be argued that Heidegger's view of the inauthentic modern individual is disturbingly similar to the anti-Semitic cultural caricature of "the Jew": a calculating, rootless cosmopolitan. It can also be argued that Heidegger's focus on "the" people and "our" history implicitly condones violence against marginalized outsiders. For reasons such as these, some critics find a symbolic or implicit anti-Semitism in Heidegger's philosophical writings. However, national identity is not a given for him; it is a problem, an open question, as when he reacts to Hitler by asking, "Who is the totality?" Heidegger recognizes that the boundaries of a community are debatable – so he cannot correctly be called an uncritical nationalist.

This brings us to some thoughts about the facts. We begin with Heidegger's own postwar reflections on the Nazi period. It was believed for some time that he had said nothing after the war about his own behavior, the Nazis, or the Holocaust. "Heidegger's silence" became notorious – and it was especially striking, given his claim in *Being and Time* that silence can be more telling than loquacity.[91] What was his silence trying to tell us? The most charitable interpretation was that he recognized that the horror of the Holocaust was literally unspeakable.

However, Heidegger did *not* actually keep silent. A number of postwar documents, some published only recently, make his opinions clear. He does admit that he supported the Nazis and that he was wrong. He made mistakes, and did not foresee "what was to come".[92] But he is quick to add excuses, and tries to minimize the extent of his involvement. He interprets himself as offering subtle resistance to Nazi ideas. For instance, he says that in his 1934 *Logic* lectures, he "sought to show that language was not the biological-racial essence of man, but conversely, that the essence of man was based in language as a basic reality of *spirit*".[93]

Heidegger typically leaps from the question of personal responsibility to an analysis of the technological understanding of Being that is supposedly taking over the planet. Nazism proved to be just another product of modern metaphysics, along with all other current forms of political organization. Fascist nationalism is just another kind of "anthropologism", along with liberal individualism and communist internationalism.[94]

Heidegger's few references to the Holocaust tend to downplay its uniqueness. In a letter to Herbert Marcuse, he defensively insists that the East Germans are

91. *Being and Time*, p. 208/164–5. For recent treatments of the theme, see R. J. Bernstein, "Heidegger's Silence? *Êthos* and Technology", in R. J. Bernstein, *The New Constellation: The Ethical-Political Horizons of Modernity/Postmodernity* (Cambridge, Massachusetts: MIT Press, 1992), and B. Lang, *Heidegger's Silence* (Ithaca, New York: Cornell University Press, 1996).
92. "The Rectorate 1933–34: Facts and Thoughts", in *Martin Heidegger and National Socialism*, G. Neske & E. Kettering (eds), p. 19.
93. "Letter to the Rector of Freiburg University, November 4, 1945", in *The Heidegger Controversy*, R. Wolin (ed.), p. 64.
94. "Letter on Humanism", in *Basic Writings*, p. 244.

157

victims no less than the Jews.[95] An essay that we will discuss later compares genocide to mechanized agriculture: both are "essentially the same" in the sense that they are symptoms of modern, technological nihilism.

One recently published text is especially valuable as a statement of Heidegger's thinking at the very moment of Germany's collapse: "Evening Dialogue in a Prisoner-of-War Camp in Russia between a Younger and an Older Man", dated 8 May 1945, one day after Germany's surrender.[96] (Heidegger's own two sons were prisoners in such a camp at this time.) The dialogue develops the idea that the attitude of "pure waiting" is the key to genuine freedom, genuine thinking, genuine poetry and genuine Germanness. Heidegger's spokesmen leave us with no doubt that he views the Nazi regime as a calamity – for the Germans themselves (the non-German victims are not mentioned). The Germans have been led astray, and their youth has been stolen from them.[97] Germany is prone to "tyrannizing itself with its own ignorant impatience" and mistakenly believing that it must "fight to win recognition from other peoples".[98]

However, Heidegger emphatically rejects the moral judgments that are being passed on Germany. Evil must be understood not in moral terms, but as a manifestation of a fundamental "malignancy" and global "devastation".[99] The essence of this devastation is not the destruction of beings, but "the abandonment of Being".[100]

The defeat of Germany is just a triumph of the same metaphysical force that was responsible for the aberrations of Nazism itself. "Nothing is decided by the war."[101] Heidegger bitterly dates his dialogue "on the day when the world celebrated its victory, and did not yet recognize that for centuries already, it has been defeated by its own rebellion".[102]

Heidegger's postwar view of Nazism may have some value as a serious analysis of the phenomenon. But we should not overlook the *psychological* value it also had for Heidegger himself and for his audiences. He is faced with the unbearable charge that he and his country are implicated in unparalleled murder and destruction. He tries to elude the guilt through a typical series of moves that can be found in text after text. First, he shifts the focus from the crude realm of beings, such as corpses and gas chambers, to the "essential" realm of Being, which can be tamed with his conceptual resources. Next, the responsibility is transferred from human beings to Being itself, which "destines" history. Then the disaster becomes global, or at least pan-Western, and envelops not just Nazi Germany, but thousands of years of European history. Finally, the Germans themselves are presented as victims of this sweeping destiny. By the end of this interpretive process, the guilt has been diluted

95. Letter to Herbert Marcuse, January 20, 1948, in *The Heidegger Controversy*, R. Wolin (ed.), p. 163.
96. "Abendgespräch in einem Kriegsgefangenenlager in Rußland zwischen einem Jüngeren und einem Älteren", in *Feldweg-Gespräche (1944/45)*, GA 77.
97. "Abendgespräch", in GA 77, pp. 206, 219–20.
98. *Ibid.*, p. 233.   99. *Ibid.*, pp. 207–8.   100. *Ibid.*, p. 213.
101. *Ibid.*, p. 244.   102. *Ibid.*, p. 240.

and depersonalized enough that it can be repressed and ignored. Was Heidegger indulging in wishful thinking when he said, "The greater the master, the more completely his person vanishes behind his work"?[103]

It is hard to avoid the conclusion that Heidegger's postwar self-interpretation is cowardly and self-deceptive. To speak the language of *Being and Time*: it is glaringly *inauthentic*.

Thus, it is essential to consider others' interpretations as we ask: what is the relation between Heidegger's philosophical thought and his involvement with Nazism? Heidegger's politics have been the occasion for countless articles and books, which range from sensationalist demonizations to worshipful apologetics, with some very thoughtful analyses scattered here and there. I will make no attempt to survey all this secondary literature.[104] However, readers will soon find that interpretations of Heidegger's politics tend to fall into the following seven types. I offer a quick summary of each type of interpretation – which is necessarily somewhat of a straw man – followed by my own criticism of each. This is not meant as a comprehensive account of this controversy; it is only a set of suggestions for further reading and reflection.

1. "Heidegger? Bad man; must be a bad philosopher" – as Gilbert Ryle is reputed to have said. Heidegger's Nazism proves that his philosophy is false.

This position assumes that what philosophers think is in complete harmony with what they do. Is it really necessary to point out that this assumption is wrong?

This position also betrays a very simplistic notion of truth in philosophy: a philosophy is either correct or incorrect, and if it is correct on any point, then it is correct on all points, including ethics. Heidegger's own understanding of philosophy seems much more reasonable: a philosophy is a tentative path that necessarily has limitations, but which may provide some illumination if one is willing to follow it.

The advocates of position #1 are generally not willing to follow the path: they use Heidegger's politics as an *a priori* excuse not to read his books. But if we timidly restrict ourselves to reading books with which we agree, which were written by people with impeccable moral judgment, we will read very few philosophers, if any, and we will never learn anything from our reading.

Of course, Heidegger's politics may be cause for *suspicion*, and may encourage us to read him carefully and critically. This is the intelligent way to read *any* philosopher.

2. "Being an original philosopher . . . is the result of some neural kink that occurs independently of other kinks . . . Philosophical talent and moral character

---

swing free of each other."[105] There is no relationship between how people think and how they act, so we can ignore Heidegger's politics.

This position is the mirror image of #1, and it is just as dogmatic. Like #1, it is an *a priori* assumption that exempts one from wrestling with the real problems at stake. Furthermore, although this position may pose as an attempt to judge Heidegger's philosophy on its own merits, in fact it peremptorily rejects some of his own most basic philosophical convictions. For Heidegger, thoughts and ideas grow out of one's own Being-in-the-world. Philosophical propositions get their meaning from their roots in concrete experience, so in order to do philosophy well, one must exist authentically (*Being and Time*, §63).

It is foolish to insist that someone who is good at philosophizing has to be good at making moral choices – but it is also foolish to insist that there can never be any relation between thought and action.

3. Heidegger was naïve: he was an impractical dreamer who thought he could become a philosopher-king, and he simply did not understand the brutal realities of Nazism.

Heidegger himself sometimes suggests this interpretation, and there is some truth to it. There is something ridiculous and hopelessly unrealistic about a philosophy professor who imagines that brownshirts will pore over the pre-Socratics.

However, this does not get us out of the problem. For the sake of argument, let us accept the claim that Heidegger's fantasies about Nazism bore little relation to reality. Even if this is so, Heideggerian fantasy fascism is disturbing enough; it is obviously nationalistic, authoritarian and anti-democratic. We are still faced with the difficult question: does Heidegger's thought encourage tyranny, or at least, does it not do enough to discourage tyranny?

4. Heidegger's actions are understandable when we put them in context. He was not the only one who viewed Nazism as the best solution under the circumstances.

This position is correct, but it is incomplete. We do need to know a lot about history in order to make good judgments about Heidegger's choices. Certainly, Heidegger was not unique – Hitler had his supporters and collaborators everywhere, including the academy.[106] However, the basic question still remains: was Heidegger's *bad decision* linked to his philosophical thought? For Heidegger did make a decision, and it is hard to deny that it was a bad one.

Those who take position #4 as the *last word* on the problem of Heidegger's politics imply that Heidegger's reasons for supporting the Nazis were completely situational – that is, they were never meant to apply beyond the confines of Germany in the thirties. But this is not so. Although he does not claim to have universally applicable answers, he does link his political stance to a wide-ranging vision of history, Dasein, and Being, a vision that is certainly meant to have some broad significance.

105. R. Rorty, "Taking Philosophy Seriously", *The New Republic* **88**, April 11, 1988, pp. 32–3.
106. On the behavior of other German philosophers during the Nazi regime, see Sluga, *Heidegger's Crisis*.

An interpretation that focuses exclusively on position #4 can also imply that our knowledge of *circumstances* should somehow exempt us from discussing *choices*. But this is an illusion – not to mention that it seems to fly in the face of the insistence on "decision" that permeates Heidegger's texts, at least through the mid-thirties. The most complete historical account does not eliminate the element of human choice. After all, many people in the same circumstances made different choices. Futhermore, even if everyone else had been doing the same as Heidegger, this would not eliminate Heidegger's responsibility. The appeal to what "everyone" is doing is a classic manifestation of the "they", and it does not make responsibility disappear, but only masks it.

5. This brings us to an interpretation that, unlike 1–4, actually depends on Heidegger's philosophical texts: if he had stuck to his concept of authenticity in *Being and Time*, he could never have become a Nazi.

The best evidence for this position is the discussion of authentic and inauthentic Being-with in *Being and Time*, §26. In particular, Heidegger distinguishes between leaping ahead, which opens up possibilities for others, and leaping in, which does things for others, relieving them of responsibility. Defenders of position #5 may hold that Hitler's leadership was a form of leaping in, and that when Heidegger succumbed to the charms of Nazism, he behaved as a they-self.

Unfortunately, as we saw in Chapter 3, the ethical or pseudo-ethical remarks in *Being and Time* are sketchy, and their grounds are unclear. Furthermore, many people were inspired by Hitler to see new possibilities for themselves and Germany. It is hard to deny that *der Führer* (the Leader) was an "authentic" leader in Heidegger's sense. Certainly, the possibilities revealed by Hitler were evil – but *Being and Time* does not seem to give us a clear philosophical basis for this judgment. The concept of authenticity is so formal that it looks as if almost any possibility could be chosen authentically.

Defenders of position #5 may also argue that Heidegger behaved as a they-self because he went along with the masses at a time when he should have stood up for the individual conscience. This is unconvincing. According to *Being and Time*, what distinguishes behavior as authentic is neither its similarity nor its dissimilarity to what everyone else is doing, but the fact that it is chosen resolutely. There is no reason to believe that Heidegger's choice was not resolute. Granted, it was a choice that was based on the options that were currently available in his community – but according to *Being and Time*, there *are* no other options. An authentic deed is not the private invention of an individual, but is the individual's appropriation of a publicly accessible opportunity.

One may argue that *Being and Time* implies that it would be an ontological error to treat any Dasein as a mere thing. Is this not what the Nazi regime did? This may be a more promising line of argument, but it does require us to take several steps beyond what *Being and Time* actually says.[107]

107. For one of the most persuasive examples of this line of argumentation, see Young, *Heidegger, Philosophy, Nazism*, pp. 102–8.

Those who hold position #5 ultimately have to argue that Heidegger misunderstood his own book. The argument can be made, but it takes ingenuity.

6. If we reject position #5, we may be tempted to adopt the opposite position: *Being and Time* is a crypto-fascist book. Its ontology of Dasein is really a "political ontology" that prepares the way for Nazism.[108]

This interpretation has the advantage that it seems to have been endorsed by Heidegger himself during the years of his greatest enthusiasm for "the movement". We saw that the 1934 *Logic* course claims that because "the Being of the historical Dasein of man is grounded in temporality, that is, care, therefore the state is essentially necessary" – namely, a nationalist and authoritarian state.[109] When he met Karl Löwith in Rome in 1936, Heidegger, who was wearing a Nazi pin, told Löwith that his political commitment grew from his concept of historicity.[110]

There are indeed elements of *Being and Time* that not only allow for a pro-Nazi decision, but appear to point in that direction. No one can avoid a shudder upon encountering the words *Volk* and *Kampf* (people and struggle) in Heidegger's discussion of authentic historicity.[111] Here he makes it clear that authentic choices involve breaking with everyday complacency, appropriating a communal heritage and resolutely choosing a "hero". It is not surprising, then, that the author of *Being and Time* would be attracted to a revolutionary movement headed by a charismatic leader who promised to reawaken the German spirit, and who used the rhetoric of will and decision. Presumably factors such as these lie behind Heidegger's statement to Löwith.

One can argue that other elements in *Being and Time* would tend to discourage Heidegger from subscribing to the other main political alternatives of the age: liberal democracy and communism. His aversion to materialistic explanations of Dasein seems incompatible with traditional Marxist theory.[112] His opposition to conceptions of Dasein as a completely autonomous individual subject seems incompatible with liberal theory in its more individualistic forms. His contempt for the idle talk of the "they" would tend to undermine the principle of majority rule: if most people, most of the time, are "in untruth", then why should their opinions deserve respect?

---

108. I adopt the phrase from Pierre Bourdieu, *The Political Ontology of Martin Heidegger*, tr. P. Collier (Palo Alto, California: Stanford University Press, 1991). Bourdieu's short book, which ranges throughout Heidegger's writings, is one of the most sophisticated examples of this approach.

109. *Lógica*, p. 118.

110. Löwith, *My Life in Germany Before and After 1933*, p. 60.

111. *Being and Time*, p. 436/384. In German, Heidegger even emphasizes the word *Volk* by referring to *das Volk* – "the people", not "a people", as the translations have it.

112. Until 1933, however, Herbert Marcuse believed that Heidegger's thought complemented and completed Marxism: see Marcuse, "Contribution to a Phenomenology of Historical Materialism", *Telos* 4 (Fall), 1969, pp. 3–34 (written 1928). In a postwar remark, Heidegger himself gives Marx credit for viewing history in terms of alienation: "Letter on Humanism", *Basic Writings*, p. 243.

Having said this, I must reassert that on the whole, I agree with Heidegger's claim in *Being and Time* that the text does not "discuss what Dasein *factically* resolves in any particular case".[113] In my view, authentic choices can include communism or liberal democracy – at least if these political programs can be purged of their traditional theoretical underpinnings (and probably even if they cannot, for authenticity involves existentiell understanding and not necessarily existential, ontological understanding). Nearly all the ontological claims in *Being and Time* are simply too general to be branded fascist, and defenders of position #6 have to rely on a heavy dose of suspicion and innuendo in order to find Nazism between the lines of what Heidegger actually wrote.

There is a further problem with position #6. Even if we granted that fascism is the logical outcome of Heidegger's views, this would not count as a *refutation*. If one wants to reject *Being and Time*, one is still under the obligation of coming up with a better description of the human way of Being. There is no political shortcut around ontology.

7. Heidegger succumbed to Nazism because he was still under the sway of the metaphysics of presence. With the completion of the "turn", Heidegger realized that fascism was just another symptom of metaphysics, instead of the cure.

This interpretation is also often put in terms of "humanism", in a sense that we will explain below. The idea is that just as liberalism involves imposing the individual human will upon beings, fascism involves imposing a national or racial human will upon beings. With the overcoming of metaphysics, we can enter a new era that involves responding to Being rather than dominating beings.

The essence of this position is in complete agreement with Heidegger's own postwar self-interpretation. But it deserves to be listed alongside positions 1–6 because it is espoused not only by orthodox Heideggerians, but also, surprisingly enough, by many left-leaning postmodernists. These interpreters stress that capitalist liberal democracy is akin to fascism (both are "metaphysical"), and they hold out hope for a postmodern, radically pluralistic politics. According to this position, Heideggerian ideas are not necessarily chauvinistic. By deconstructing the metaphysics of presence, we supposedly undermine authoritarian and repressive regimes. Authoritarian politics (according to this interpretation) spring from the metaphysical project of representing and dominating all beings according to some ultimate principle. But the later Heidegger has supposedly shown us that this project must fail, and that we should be open to a plurality of meanings of Being. This will translate – somehow – into a politics of tolerance and diversity.

This position obscures far more than it reveals when it equates liberal democracy with fascism. The "metaphysical" concept of individual rights makes life in a liberal democracy dramatically different from life under fascism. A constitution based on individual rights still seems to be the best way to provide the pluralism and tolerance that postmodernists themselves want.

113. *Being and Time*, p. 434/383.

Furthermore, it is not clear that the "turn" occurred after Heidegger's engagement with National Socialism; Heidegger's ideal Nazism may already be post-metaphysical. However this may be, it is certain that his vision of authentic communal existence never resembles the multicultural paradise of the post-modernists. It is an elitist vision, in which only those of higher existential rank are privileged to encounter Being. It is a pluralist vision – but for Heidegger, plurality involves struggle and confrontation, rather than tolerance and play.[114] Heidegger never showed sympathy for democracy in any form. As late as 1974, he complained to a friend, "Our Europe is disintegrating under the influence of a democracy that comes from below against the many above".[115] These are reasons enough for us to be suspicious of the standard postmodern reading of Heidegger.

If all these positions have problems, this is a sign that thinking about Heidegger's politics is not a way around his philosophy, but leads us straight into the heart of it. One must reflect deeply on our Being in order to decide how human thought relates to human life, whether there are absolute moral or political guidelines, and to what degree we are responsible for our choices. Heidegger's writings are still invaluable stimulants to such reflection.

In a sense, it is a blessing that Heidegger's life makes it impossible for us to be completely comfortable with his writings. For Heidegger never respected Heideggerians. He never wanted his thought to be a comfortable party line; he wanted it to be thought-*provoking* and highly questionable. Finally, regardless of what he himself wanted, the most fruitful way to read any philosopher is to wrestle with and against what the philosopher says.

"Letter on Humanism": existentialism, humanism and ethics

The "Letter on Humanism" (published 1947) is an open letter addressed to Jean Beaufret, who had asked Heidegger certain questions in regards to Jean-Paul Sartre's "L'existentialisme est un humanisme" (1946). Students of Heidegger are well-advised to read Sartre's short and clear essay, which catapulted him to fame. Here, Sartre defines existentialism as the view that, for human beings, "existence precedes essence". In other words, there is no fixed human nature – only human freedom. It is up to us to create our own values and make ourselves into whoever we choose to be. Sartre defends himself against charges of nihilism and pessimism by claiming that his position constitutes the only true humanism, and that it is the basis for an ethics of freedom and responsibility.

---

114. See G. Fried, "Heidegger's *Polemos*", *Journal for Philosophical Research* **16**, 1991, pp. 159–95.
115. Letter to Heinrich Wiegand Petzet, March 12, 1974, quoted in Petzet, *Encounters and Dialogues with Martin Heidegger*, p. 222. For other postwar anti-democratic remarks, see *What is Called Thinking?* p. 67; "Only a God Can Save Us", in *The Heidegger Controversy*, R. Wolin (ed.), pp. 104–5.

In the course of his essay, Sartre invokes Heidegger as an ally, claiming that both Heidegger and he are "atheistic existentialists".[116]

Is this claim correct? The question turns out to be more complex than it seems – and more complex than Heidegger himself makes it seem in the "Letter".

First, the problem of atheism. We know that Heidegger began as a Catholic and even had plans to become a Jesuit. During the First World War, however, he became dissatisfied with Catholic theology and sought more authentic sources of religious experience. In the early twenties, he seems to take an anti-religious turn. He declares that philosophy is fundamentally "atheistic". But this does not seem to mean that philosophers have to deny the existence of God. Instead, it means that philosophy does not *rely* on God or faith, and is not in the service of religion. "I do not behave religiously in philosophizing, even if as a philosopher I can be a religious person."[117] In *Being and Time*, religious questions are systematically treated as "ontical" issues that lie outside the scope of Heidegger's project. However, in the *Contributions to Philosophy*, he speculates incessantly about "the god" or "the gods". He can no longer accept the Christian God, but he wants to leave room for the possibility of a new revelation of the divine. In 1966, in his interview with *Der Spiegel*, he makes the striking statement, "only a god can save us".[118] For Sartre, atheism fundamentally means that "even if God did exist, that would change nothing": we would still be completely responsible for our own actions.[119] But for Heidegger, at least in his later period, the presence of the divine can transform our lives.

The problem of existentialism is even more difficult. What is an existentialist, after all? Sartre has a tidy definition, and Heidegger will reject it just as neatly. But the word "existentialism" is used in many ways, and often refers to a wide variety of thinkers. The term seems to have been invented only in the 1940s, when Gabriel Marcel used it to describe Sartre. Marcel meant it in a pejorative sense, but Sartre decided to adopt it, and Marcel ended up being classified as a religious existentialist himself. The label was then applied retroactively to many philosophers.

Kierkegaard is usually counted as the first existentialist – and understandably so, because he stressed the "existing individual". According to Kierkegaard, I am faced with fundamental choices that will define how I am to exist and who I am to be (for example, will I exist religiously or aesthetically?). These personal decisions cannot be made on the basis of rational rules that apply to everyone (that would already presuppose a personal decision to exist in accordance with rational rules!). Life-determining decisions require a "leap"

---

116. J-P. Sartre, "The Humanism of Existentialism", in *Essays in Existentialism*, W. Baskin (ed.) (New York: Citadel Press, 1990), p. 34.
117. *Phänomenologische Interpretationen zu Aristoteles: Einführung in die phänomenologische Forschung*, GA 61, p. 197. For statements from both Heidegger's earlier period and his later period on the relation of philosophy to theology, see *The Piety of Thinking*. In both periods, he tends to insist that faith and philosophy are distinct and should be kept distinct.
118. "Only a God Can Save Us", in *The Heidegger Controversy*, R. Wolin (ed.), p. 107.
119. Sartre, "The Humanism of Existentialism", p. 62.

and "passion". Since Kierkegaard held that existence could never be captured by a system, he would have a good laugh at the term "existentialism". However, views such as Sartre's are clearly indebted to Kierkegaard's thought.

Nietzsche is also often called an existentialist, although his thought is too individual to fit neatly into the category. Nietzsche tries to cast off the shackles of metaphysics and theology in order to embrace life as a creative, dynamic process.

In Germany in the 1920s, "philosophy of existence" was associated with figures such as Karl Jaspers. Heidegger respected Jaspers' *Psychology of World-views* (1919), where Jaspers describes existence as a confrontation with "limit situations", such as death and guilt.

It is clear that Jaspers' approach helped to stimulate some analyses in *Being and Time*, as did Kierkegaard's writings on anxiety, guilt, the moment of decision, and individualization.[120] Heidegger is thus clearly linked to thinkers considered existentialists – even though the "existential" terminology was added to *Being and Time* only in its final draft. Like Kierkegaard, Nietzsche, Jaspers and Sartre, Heidegger wants to think about concrete human existence and life-determining choices. Like all "existentialists", he rejects the traditional ontological concepts that treat human beings as substances, or present-at-hand things with predetermined essences. Instead, he conceives of Dasein as an entity whose own Being is an issue for it.

In the "Letter on Humanism", Heidegger will refuse to acknowledge these connections. It cannot be said that he does justice to intellectual history. However, there is much more to the "Letter". It is not primarily meant as an essay on intellectual history, but instead is meant to provoke us to reflect on a series of basic questions: what is it to exist, what is it to be human and what is it to act?

The "Letter" is indeed a letter, and not a traditional academic essay; it is written in a meandering style that follows several trails of thought without being reducible to a single thesis. In fact, Heidegger stresses the "multidimensionality" of genuine thinking.[121] However, for introductory purposes we can focus our analysis on a single three-part question: *why does Heidegger refuse to associate himself with existentialism, humanism and ethics, as these have formerly been defined?* Our focus on this question will leave out many details of the letter. The letter's remarks on language will be discussed in a separate section on language below.

We must first point out that in rejecting the established understanding of existentialism, humanism and ethics, Heidegger is not endorsing essentialism, inhumanity or unethical behavior. He is trying to practice a new way of thinking that will not fall into stereotyped oppositions such as these (249–50).

---

120. Kierkegaard and Jaspers each receive only three mentions in footnotes in *Being and Time*, but all are interesting and rather laudatory footnotes. On Kierkegaard, see *Being and Time*, pp. 492/190, 494/235, and 497/338; on Jaspers, see pp. 495/249, 496/301, and 497/338.
121. "Letter on Humanism", in *Basic Writings*, p. 219. Further references to this essay in this section will take the form of parenthesized page numbers.

It should also be noted that if we are willing to redefine the terms "existentialism", "humanism" and "ethics", they *can* be applied to Heidegger. He does hold that the human essence is "ek-sistence" (229); he does admit that his thought can be called " 'humanism' in an extreme sense" (245); and he also says that his thought can be called "the original ethics" (258). But instead of giving these old terms new meanings, he would prefer to do without "isms" and labels altogether.

Why does Heidegger refuse to associate himself with existentialism, as it has formerly been defined? To put it briefly, he accuses Sartre of using the terms "essence" and "existence" in their traditional senses, without rethinking the meaning of Being (232).

Heidegger's accusation is not altogether fair. Sartre's essay is a popularization, and for his better statements of his position we have to turn to *Being and Nothingness*. Heidegger is said to have read only the first few pages of his own copy of *Being and Nothingness*. If Heidegger had not given up on this treatise, he might have admitted that the "existence" of human consciousness, for Sartre, is a rather untraditional sort of Being. Sartrean "existence" is certainly not presence-at-hand, as Heidegger seems to imply. Instead, Sartre holds that consciousness ("the for-itself") is only pure freedom and pure awareness of the non-conscious ("the in-itself"). Consciousness is not a thing, but a no-thing – a free opening *on to* things. And didn't Heidegger himself distinguish Dasein from present-at-hand entities, interpret Dasein as a kind of opening, and claim that the essence of unconcealment is freedom?

Still, the Sartrean distinction between the for-itself and the in-itself is heavily indebted to the opposition of subject and object that runs throughout modern philosophy, culminating in Hegel (who is the source of Sartre's terminology). Sartre does little to investigate the historical roots of this opposition. Neither does he ask about Being, in Heidegger's sense. "Ontology" for Sartre means describing the basic features of the two kinds of *beings*; he does not ask, with Heidegger, how it is that we understand the "to be".

Heidegger also rejects Sartre's *voluntarism*. As we saw in "On the Essence of Truth", Heidegger thinks of freedom primarily in terms of unconcealment, rather than in terms of self-determination, as does Sartre. Meaning, for Heidegger, is not purely the product of human will, but is projected by Dasein on the basis of *thrownness*. Thus, we do not have complete control over how to interpret ourselves and our world. In other words, we respond to Being, we do not make it.

When Heidegger says that our essence is ek-sistence, then, what does he mean? He means that "man occurs essentially [*west*] in such a way that he is the 'there', that is, the clearing of Being" (229). Ek-sistence means "standing out into the truth of Being" (230). "Ek-sistence", then, for Heidegger, is another way of referring to our most fundamental trait: we are the beings who are connected to Being, the beings to whom it makes a difference that there is something rather than nothing.

Now, according to *Being and Time*, we are connected to Being and stand in unconcealment thanks to our *temporality*. This temporality involves thrownness, fate, death, guilt and anxiety – precisely the themes that are near and dear to the hearts of philosophers labeled "existentialist". So it is disingenuous of Heidegger to disassociate himself completely from existentialism. However, he would stress that if we analyze phenomena such as death and guilt without keeping in mind the overarching question of Being, we will be limited to studying facts about a particular entity (ourselves) without ever reflecting on the unconcealment of entities as such. This is what Heidegger misses in Sartre – a close examination of truth and Being.

Why does Heidegger refuse to associate himself with humanism, as it has formerly been defined? In short, humanism represents humans as centrally important beings within a *metaphysical* interpretation of beings as a whole.

Since Heidegger uses the term "metaphysical" in various ways, and not always pejoratively, we have to pay close attention to his definition of metaphysics in this text. "Every determination of the essence of man that already presupposes an interpretation of beings without asking about the truth of Being, whether knowingly or not, is metaphysical" (225–6).

> Metaphysics does indeed represent beings in their Being, and so it thinks the Being of beings. But it does not think the difference of both. Metaphysics does not ask about the truth of Being itself. Nor does it therefore ask in what way the essence of man belongs to the truth of Being. [226]

Metaphysics, then, is a kind of thinking that considers beings as a whole and tries to discover their basic principles, but fails to ask how it comes to pass that we have an understanding of what it means to be at all. We know from the *Contributions to Philosophy* that Heidegger wants to think about Being itself, not just "the Being of beings" (a generalization on the basis of beings). He wants to ask how it is that Being opens up for us in the first place. He also wants to stress that our belonging to the truth of Being, our sensitivity to the difference between something and nothing, is what is most crucial about us. Metaphysics fails to ask about Being itself, and consequently fails to see how Dasein is necessarily linked to Being. Humanism considers human beings valuable, but it does not understand what it is to be human.

For instance, a Christian humanism may view human beings as precious creatures because they are created in God's image. This humanism presupposes an interpretation of beings as a whole in terms of creation: all beings are either creatures or their Creator. Man is the creature who somehow resembles the Creator. But this interpretation misses what is really most distinctive about us, according to Heidegger – the fact that we have an understanding of what it means to be. Heidegger wants us to recognize this understanding of Being, explore it, and ask about its history. Similar criticisms could presumably be made of atheistic, agnostic and other religious versions of humanism.

But if Heidegger claims that human beings are given the unique destiny of standing in the truth of Being, isn't this just another form of humanism, since it gives us center stage in the universe? In response, he would first stress that his position, unlike all humanisms, is not "metaphysical": he thinks about our relation to Being, and not merely our relation to other beings. Secondly, he puts Being at the center, and not ourselves (248). Humanity is not "the lord of beings", but "the shepherd of Being" (234, 245). Heidegger is thinking of a shepherd not as one who exploits the sheep, but as one who cares for his flock in obedience to some authority. In this case, Being is both the flock and the authority: we are "called by Being itself into the preservation of Being's truth" (245). Being appropriates us, giving us the opportunity to be Dasein – and we are to appropriate Being, protecting its unconcealment by sheltering it in beings (as the *Contributions* say). In more ordinary language, human beings need to take responsibility for cultivating the meaningfulness that they have inherited.

Why does Heidegger refuse to associate himself with ethics, as it has formerly been defined? For Heidegger, action cannot be understood adequately in terms of *rules* or *values*.

We have already noticed his refusal to provide rules for action (*Being and Time*, 340/294). According to *Being and Time*, decisions must be made in the light of a particular situation, and no rule can make it any easier to decide. In the "Letter", he implies that the demand for rules is a symptom of the technological approach to the world, an approach that tries to manage and control the behavior of all entities, including human beings. Such management may in fact be necessary sometimes, but it is not the thinker's job to provide it (255).

The alternative to a rule-based ethics (such as Kant's) may be a value-based ethics (such as that of Max Scheler, the phenomenologist who criticized Kantian ethics in his *Formalism in Ethics and Non-Formal Ethics of Value* [1913–16]). Talk of "values" is certainly popular in our own times, when every politician harps on their importance. But the opposition to "values" is a constant in Heidegger's mature thought. For example, *Introduction to Metaphysics* accuses official Nazi philosophy of "fishing in the troubled waters" of value theory.[122]

What could be wrong with values? In his youth, Heidegger associated with philosophers such as Rickert, for whom even truth was a "value". But he soon recognized that the ontological status of values is very unclear. No politician will be able to define what a "value" is, and a philosopher will resort either to Platonism (values exist in some eternal realm) or to subjectivism (values are created by human concepts, desires or will). The Platonic answer is embroiled in the traditional oppositions between Being and becoming, and Being and the "ought", that Heidegger challenged in *Introduction to Metaphysics*. The subjectivist answer elevates us to the rank of lords of beings, but like all metaphysics, it fails to recognize our openness to Being. Valuing imposes our standards on

122. *An Introduction to Metaphysics*, p. 199.

beings instead of acknowledging how they are (251). As Heidegger insisted in *Being and Time*, beings already reveal themselves to us as meaningful *before* we make any value judgments about them.[123]

What is his alternative to rules and values, then? "More essential than instituting rules is that man find the way to his abode in the truth of Being" (262). Once again, the key is to recognize our relation to Being, and as he often does, Heidegger appeals to etymology to bolster his position. The fundamental meaning of *ēthos* is "abode" (256–8): we inhabit an open area, the truth of Being, within which we can encounter beings. Since to think is essentially to recognize Being, thinking turns out to be the highest form of action (217), for it is the deepest way to find our *ēthos*.

Heidegger proposes that good and evil are to be understood as healing and raging (260–61), and that these have their origin in the interplay of Being and nihilation, which he first discussed in "What is Metaphysics?" One can find similar suggestions in several other texts from this period, such as the dialogue between prisoners of war that we discussed above (p. 158). However, Heidegger never develops this thought at length, and it has usually been neglected by his interpreters. Maybe we can begin to explain it as follows. When we appreciate Being and shelter it in beings, we respect and care for what is. An experience of the limits of meaning – nihilation – can help us appreciate the meaningfulness of the world. However, this experience can also be perverted into nihilism, which manifests itself as destructiveness and reckless malice. Possibly suggestions such as these can take us farther in understanding evil than any analysis in terms of rules and values.

Many critics find the "Letter's" position on ethics intolerably vague. As in *Being and Time*, Heidegger leaves us with no concrete directions. *Being and Time* told us: be resolute! But it did not explain upon what we were to resolve. Now Heidegger says: listen to Being! But he does not tell us what Being is saying, at least not in enough detail to affect how we treat each other. Readers must decide for themselves – is Heidegger's vagueness a flaw, or is it the honest acknowledgment that truth and freedom cannot be captured in any system of morality?

One point to consider is that ethics need not be based primarily either on rules or on values; it can also be based on the concept of virtue, which in fact has experienced a philosophical revival since Heidegger wrote the "Letter on Humanism".[124] In some ways, one can even argue that Heidegger himself is close to Aristotle, the great philosopher of virtue. For both, our highest purpose is to become what we essentially are by practicing our highest activity: the activity of openness to what is, and to Being itself.[125]

---

123. *Being and Time*, p. 132/99.
124. See e.g. A. Macintyre, *After Virtue*, 2d edn (Notre Dame, Indiana: University of Notre Dame Press, 1984).
125. See Aristotle's discussion of the "theoretical life" in *Nicomachean Ethics*, Book X. Of course, Heidegger's understanding of our relation to Being differs from Aristotle's.

Yet another way of approaching ethics is in terms of our responsibility to "the other". Emmanuel Levinas, perhaps the most influential contemporary thinker on this topic, develops it in a way that involves a sustained and rather persuasive critique of Heidegger. "To affirm the priority of *Being* over *beings*," writes Levinas, "is to subordinate the relation with *someone*, who is a being (the ethical relation), to a relation with the *Being of beings*, which is impersonal."[126]

"The Question Concerning Technology": beings as manipulable resources

As we saw, the *Contributions to Philosophy* already reflect at length on the technological approach to the world, which in that text is called "machination". The technological attitude involves much more than simply constructing and using complex machines; it is *a way of understanding beings as a whole*. Heidegger believes that he can diagnose this understanding of beings as a symptom of modern metaphysics. Ultimately, according to him, machination reflects the limitations not just of modernity, but of the "first beginning" of Western thought.

The technological approach to beings (which from now on we will call "technology" for short) implies an understanding of Being itself. For technological Dasein, to *be* means to be either a present-at-hand object that is available for exploitation and manipulation, or a subject that is the manipulator and exploiter of the object. "Technology is a way of revealing."[127] Technology reveals beings as resources available for our use: they present themselves as "standing-reserve" (322), or to put it more graphically, as one big gas station.

When we look at today's language, we can see that there is something to what Heidegger is saying. Natural things are routinely called "natural resources" – a far cry from the mysterious, self-concealing "earth" that Heidegger described in "The Origin of the Work of Art". Human beings are "human resources". Books and artworks become "information resources", and writing becomes "word processing", as if language, too, were just a resource to be manipulated. Time itself has become standing-reserve: witness software tycoon Bill Gates' pronouncement, "Just in terms of allocation of time resources, religion is not very efficient".[128]

It seems that the universe has been dissolved into a supply of raw material that can be processed and reprocessed. By digitizing all our representations of objects, computer technology is greatly increasing the accessibility and manipulability of data. But what is the purpose of all this manipulation? Heidegger proposes that it is simply "the will to will": there *is* no purpose aside

126. *Totality and Infinity*, tr. A. Lingis (Pittsburgh, Pennsylvania: Duquesne University Press, 1969), p. 45 (translation modified).
127. "The Question Concerning Technology", in *Basic Writings*, p. 318. Further references to this essay in this section will take the form of parenthesized page numbers.
128. Quoted in W. Isaacson, "In Search of the Real Bill Gates", *Time*, January 13, 1997, p. 51.

from sheer self-assertion, sheer power. We are in the grip of the compulsion to grip things.

What exactly is wrong with this? Some negative consequences of technology are easy to see: we are destroying much of our planet, and have the potential to destroy our entire species with our machines. Furthermore, the cult of power and control can lead to political nightmares. O'Brien, George Orwell's totalitarian ideologist, explains: "Power is not a means; it is an end . . . Power is in inflicting pain and humiliation . . . If you want a picture of the future, imagine a boot stamping on a human face – forever."[129] Can't the totalitarian horrors of the twentieth century be seen as consequences of the technological worldview?

In one of his rare references to the Holocaust, Heidegger proposes that this is, in fact, the case. But he says so in a way that is most disturbing: "Agriculture is now a motorized food industry, essentially the same as the manufacture of corpses in gas chambers and extermination camps, the same as the blockade and starvation of countries, the same as the manufacture of hydrogen bombs."[130] Most interpreters find this passage shocking, and understandably so. For although Heidegger does not condone mass murder, the implication of his claim seems to be that modern farming is just as bad. In addition, the references to blockades and hydrogen bombs allude to the Soviet Union and the United States, and imply that there is no significant difference between these countries and Nazi Germany. Do all these phenomena really spring from the same root, and does that mean they are all "essentially the same"?

This brings us to the more controversial aspects of Heidegger's view of technology. Everyone will agree that nuclear war, global warming and the Holocaust are bad. But for Heidegger, even if we achieve world peace, guarantee human rights, and save the planet, technology may be a disaster. As the German prisoners of war say in his dialogue:

> *Younger man:* . . . devastation also rules precisely where land and people are untouched by war's destruction.
> *Older man:* Where the world shines in the radiance of advances, advantages and material goods, where human rights are respected, where civil order is maintained, and where, above all, there is a guaranteed supply that constantly satisfies an undisturbed comfort, so that everything can be overseen and everything remains calculable and manageable in terms of utility.[131]

Heidegger's fears for the future are less Orwellian than Huxleyan. In Aldous Huxley's *Brave New World*, the planet has been transformed into a place where everyone is satisfied and pleased, amply supplied with sex, drugs and rock and roll (or its equivalent in the 1930s imagination). Nature has been tamed and turned into a well-managed golf course. There is no dissent. But what has

129. G. Orwell, *1984* (New York: New American Library, 1961), pp. 217–20.
130. "Das Ge-Stell", in *Bremer und Freiburger Vorträge*, GA 79, p. 27.
131. GA 77, p. 216.

been lost is depth, awareness and freedom. In Huxley's vision, traditional ways and feelings survive only on Indian reservations. Similarly, Heidegger once wrote, "Today the authentic thinking which explores the primordial lore of Being still lives only on 'reservations' (perhaps because it, in accordance with its origin, is as ancient as the Indians are in their fashion)."[132] Heidegger's fear is that once we have gained complete control over ourselves and our natural environment, we will have lost our openness to Being. We will no longer be Dasein, because we will be so entrapped in technology that we will have no suspicion that there are other, richer ways in which beings can show themselves. We will be completely insensitive to mystery, to the possibility of historical transformation, and to Being as something that is worth asking about (332–3).

How should we respond to this bleak possibility? Most ways of reacting to technology do not address the fundamental problem. For example, we may notice that we are killing off other species and destroying the wilderness, and we may call for laws that will preserve the rain forests; we may point out that the rain forests contain thousands of useful natural products, even possible cures for cancer, which will be lost if we continue to ruin this environment. This is all well and good, but notice that this approach continues to view nature as a collection of natural resources that it is up to us to control and manage. We are still on the way to reducing all other living things to food, drugs, pets and zoo specimens. A menagerie is not a wilderness.

What should we do about the basic problem, then? Maybe this very question perpetuates technology: when we approach things as problems to be fixed, we are already thinking technologically. But then, are we just supposed to lie back and do nothing at all?

Heidegger would respond that, as he writes in the opening of "Letter on Humanism" (217), "We are still far from pondering the essence of action decisively enough." The simple opposition between activity and passivity is too crude. There is a kind of letting-be that is not just inert suffering. This letting-be involves waiting, listening, responding – attentively receiving what is given to us.

But what is given to us above all is Being. We have to learn to stop taking Being for granted, and instead notice it precisely *as* something that is granted – as a gift. Even the technological meaning of Being is a gift that springs from mysterious historical sources, and that may be followed by other gifts, new revelations of Being (337). Being is neither a resource, nor something we can make and manipulate; it is an event that must be gratefully appreciated. Thinking – as Heidegger says – is thanking.[133] The proper response to technology, then, is not to abandon technological devices, but to recognize that a historically developed understanding of Being is at work in our lives, and that this is an occasion for thoughtful gratitude.

132. Heidegger, *Aufzeichnungen aus der Werkstatt*, quoted in O. Pöggeler, *Martin Heidegger's Path of Thinking*, tr. D. Magurshak & S. Barber (Atlantic Highlands, New Jersey: Humanities Press International, 1987), p. 191.
133. *What is Called Thinking?* pp. 139ff.

Heidegger does not want to smash all machines. He just hopes that we can achieve a balanced life that keeps technology in its place. When he expresses this view in a popular lecture, he says quite simply, "We can use technical devices as they ought to be used, and also let them alone as something which does not affect our inner and real core."[134] (Heidegger never owned a television set, but enjoyed watching sports on others' sets. He hated the idea of composing on a typewriter, and wrote all his texts by hand – but then had his brother type them.)[135] He suggests that we can learn to use our machines in the way the windmill was once used – as a device that works with nature, instead of assaulting it (320). "Little things", quiet changes in the way we dwell in the world, may help keep alive the possibility of a post-technological era (338).

Two objections have often been made to Heidegger's position on technology. The first is that, despite his attempt to rethink the nature of action, and although he claims that "destining is never a fate that compels" (330), Heidegger still ends up being too passive, too quietist and even fatalistic. Is there really nothing we can do other than to let Being play with us? This late-Heideggerian attitude seems to lead to an overly pessimistic assessment of what we can achieve – as when, in the *Spiegel* interview, Heidegger says that "only a god can save us".

The second objection is that Heidegger views life in a monochromatic way that blurs fundamental distinctions. The Holocaust is essentially *not* the same as mechanized agriculture, totalitarianism is essentially *not* the same as democracy, and there are important differences in the purposes to which we put technological devices. They can be used for good or evil, and to ignore these differences is to view human beings as robots.

At their worst, Heidegger's analyses of technology are themselves "technological": he writes as if he has a technique for unlocking the mechanism of history. But at their best, essays such as "The Question Concerning Technology" are effective ways of initiating reflection on the deeper trends that lie behind the terrifying events of our age.

Poetry and language

> Now I am tempted to say that the right expression in language for the miracle of the existence of the world, though it is not any proposition *in* language, is the existence of language itself. — Wittgenstein[136]

> What abides is established by the poets. — Hölderlin, "Remembrance"

---

134. "Memorial Address", in *Discourse on Thinking*, p. 54.
135. On Heidegger and television, see Petzet, *Encounters and Dialogues*, pp. 209–10. Heidegger's tirade against the typewriter is in *Parmenides*, p. 85.
136. Wittgenstein, "A Lecture on Ethics", in *Philosophical Occasions*, pp. 43–4.

We have not yet discussed one of Heidegger's best-known lines from the "Letter on Humanism": "Language is the house of Being."[137] It is a memorable but enigmatic dictum. Obviously Heidegger wants to link language and Being closely together. But what does he mean by "house"? Why – we automatically ask – does he resort to speaking so poetically, so metaphorically?

Our question betrays certain assumptions about language itself that are ingrained in common sense.

(a) We assume that *language is essentially a tool used by human beings to communicate information.* Heidegger must have in mind some fact he wants to point out, and he is using words in order to do so. In a more ordinary example, if my head aches and I want to tell the doctor about it, I say, "I have a headache". If I were in a Spanish-speaking country I'd say, "Me duele la cabeza". The same fact can be expressed in many different languages. A competent speaker is in *control* of the language, and can use it to convey data efficiently to his or her audience. In their quest for greater efficiency in communication, people have devised artificial languages that give them more control, such as Esperanto, symbolic logic, computer programming languages, and the technical languages of the sciences. The goal is to set up a system in which each sign can be interpreted only one way – each sign points so unambiguously at what it represents that the sign itself becomes completely unobtrusive. The perfect language is a technique for perfect representation.

(b) We also assume that *everyday, prosaic language is the norm, and poetic language is derivative.* "My house is on Vine Street" is a normal, everyday statement; it efficiently communicates a fact. "Language is the house of Being" is a metaphorical statement, since of course, language is not *literally* a house built with bricks and timber. Heidegger could have made his point more prosaically, but for some reason he wants to speak poetically. Poetry – we assume – takes everyday language and applies certain techniques to it (rhyme, meter, alliteration, metaphor, and so on) in order to create an artwork. The resulting poem makes us notice the words themselves, the means of communication, in addition to the information that is being communicated. The result can be a pleasant aesthetic experience.

Heidegger's concern with language is especially obvious in his later essays, but it was always a part of his thought.[138] Let's return for a moment to a lecture course of 1925 in order to challenge the two common-sense assumptions we listed.

(a) Using the example of Latin in Catholicism, Heidegger discusses the phenomenon of "dead languages":

> . . . as "dead" this language is no longer subject to changes in meaning
> . . . whereas in any "living" language contexts of meaning change with

137. "Letter on Humanism", in *Basic Writings*, p. 217.
138. For Heidegger's own reflections on the developing role of language in his thought, see "A Dialogue on Language between a Japanese and an Inquirer", in *On the Way to Language*.

175

changes in the interpretation of historical Dasein at the time . . . A language has its genuine Being only as long as new correlations of meaning and so – although not necessarily – new words and phrases accrue to it from understanding . . .[139]

This passage suggests that it is misguided to try to fixate language and turn it into an unambiguous tool for communicating information and representing beings. Representation – or in more Heideggerian terms, the unconcealment of beings – always occurs historically, in the context of some communal understanding that is in a process of development. Even an ordinary headache presents itself to me thanks to my historical Being-in-the-world: because I am modern and not medieval, I experience the headache as something that interferes with my work and should be fixed, rather than as a sign of the fallen condition of the flesh, which should be endured piously and patiently. This is not to suggest that there is no truth, but that truth is always linked to historically evolving interpretations. These "correlations of meaning", as Heidegger calls them, tend to become language.

If Heidegger is right, the same fact *cannot* be expressed in many different languages, because beings and "information" present themselves differently according to different cultural contexts. The quest for a universal, unambiguous language can only succeed in creating stillborn languages – languages that are locked into a particular interpretation and are incapable of responding creatively to new experience. Artificial languages are not more objective than natural ones – they are just narrower and more rigid.

Language can never be just a tool that we control, because in a sense, we owe our own Being to language. Language plays a part in the fundamental revelation of the world; it is part of what enables us to be someone and notice things in the first place. Even before I choose the right words in which to express the fact that I have a headache, the headache has been revealed to me within a context that is partly linguistic.

When Bertrand Russell complains of Heidegger, "language is here running riot",[140] Russell's own language may be revealing more than he knows about how he *thinks* of language. Do we speak well by policing our words, which are always on the verge of breaking into mob violence? Or do we learn to speak well by learning to *respect* the mysterious powers of language?

(b) On everyday language and poetic language, Heidegger remarks:

. . . even relatively original and creative meanings and the words coined from them are, when articulated, relegated to idle talk. Once articulated, the word belongs to everyone, without a guarantee that its repetition will include original understanding. This possibility of genuinely entering into the discourse nevertheless exists . . . discourse, especially

---

139. *History of the Concept of Time*, p. 271.
140. Russell, *Wisdom of the West*, p. 303.

poetry, can even bring about the release of new possibilities of the Being of Dasein.[141]

Here, Heidegger thinks of poetry not as a source of some special aesthetic pleasure, but as a force that can reveal our world and transform our existence. Poetry is certainly much less *common* than ordinary prose, but that does not mean that it is less *fundamental*. Poetic language is fundamental because it is "the elementary emergence into words, the becoming-uncovered, of existence as Being-in-the-world".[142] Everyday "idle talk" is a pale, dull reflection of "creative meanings" such as those achieved in poetry.

This view of poetry fits perfectly with Heidegger's understanding of authenticity and history. Both in an individual life and in the history of a people, the lucid and creative moments are few; the rest is inauthentic and derivative.

This approach tends to undermine our usual distinction between literal and metaphorical uses of language. Consider the possibility that everyday statements such as "my house is on Vine Street" are idle talk derived from poetry. The word "house" in this sentence, then, does not really have a perfectly clear, unambiguous, "literal" meaning – its meaning is just well-worn, familiar, and *seemingly* obvious. What is a house, after all? It is a place to live in, a dwelling. But what is it to dwell? This is already getting puzzling. Maybe dwelling is something like abiding in an abode and resting in it. But what is abiding? – We find ourselves forced into more and more "poetic" language, not because we are abandoning reality but because we are looking at it more deeply (*dwelling* on it, we might say).[143] Perhaps when Heidegger says that language is the house of Being, he means it "literally": Being abides in language as its abode. There may be no prosaic way of saying this well, because ordinary prose is just poetry that has lost its disclosive force. What makes poetry poetry is not that it uses special poetic techniques, but that it recaptures the illuminating power that secretly resides in our ordinary words, letting us see the world as if for the first time. We cannot write poetry in symbolic logic, because artificial languages have been constructed precisely by restricting the revealing power of language. I quote the complaint of a scientifically minded student upon reading Keats in a class taught by my wife: "Poetry *means* too much!"

If Heidegger is right, then our most authentic relation to language is poetic. Instead of using language as a tool for representation, we should respect it as a rich source of poetic revelation. Heidegger's own writings after *Being and Time* reflect this insight. Not only does his style become less technical and more poetic, but he writes about poets – Georg Trakl, Rainer Maria Rilke, Stefan George, and above all, Friedrich Hölderlin. In the thirties and forties, Heidegger delivered three lecture courses on Hölderlin's concentrated, challenging

---

141. *History of the Concept of Time*, p. 272.
142. *The Basic Problems of Phenomenology*, pp. 171–2.
143. For Heidegger's exploration of dwelling, see "Building Dwelling Thinking", in *Basic Writings*.

poetry.[144] He also wrote a series of shorter essays on Hölderlin between 1936 and 1968.[145] For Heidegger, his early discovery of Hölderlin was an "earthquake".[146] He comes to see Hölderlin as the poet who opens up new paths for Germany and the West. Through Hölderlin, Heidegger explores issues such as the mission of the West, the German encounter with other cultures, and the nature of poetry itself, in its intimate connection with the Being of Dasein – for it was Hölderlin who wrote, "Poetically man dwells upon the earth".

In the 1950s, Heidegger composed a series of essays that take poetry as the clue to the essential unfolding of language.[147] These are subtle, tentative pieces that are often focused on poems, and even sound like poems. They are difficult essays, but readers will have a good foothold on them if they are willing to question the two common-sense assumptions about language we discussed above. We thus find Heidegger claiming that "language speaks" (*die Sprache spricht*):[148] we human beings are not the primary speakers, but are participants in an event of meaningfulness. We do not fully control this process, and language is not a mere tool at our disposal. Heidegger thus thinks we can learn nothing about the essence of language by constructing formal languages and "metalanguages".[149] Language is not just a human construct or a human act, but a deeper "Saying" that should be understood as showing – an event of unconcealment.[150] Heidegger always insists on the primacy of poetry: "Everyday language is a forgotten and therefore used-up poem, from which there hardly resounds a call any longer."[151]

Alert readers will also notice that Heidegger connects his explorations of language to his thoughts on *Ereignis*. Language is a medium in which Being takes hold of us, appropriates us, and allows us and all beings to come into our own. "Language is the house of Being because language, as Saying, is the mode of Appropriation."[152]

The final analysis?

Heidegger's influence is as powerful today as it ever was. His ideas work in surprising and indirect ways in fields as diverse as architecture, literary theory,

---

144. GA 39, GA 52 and *Hölderlin's Hymn "The Ister"*.
145. *Erläuterungen zu Hölderlins Dichtung*, GA 4. The essays "Remembrance of the Poet" and "Hölderlin and the Essence of Poetry" are translated in Heidegger, *Existence and Being*, W. Brock (ed.) (Chicago, Illinois: Henry Regnery Company, 1949).
146. "The Nature of Language", in *On the Way to Language*, p. 78.
147. Heidegger's most important essays on language are available in *On the Way to Language* and *Poetry, Language, Thought*. The essay "The Way to Language" is also contained in *Basic Writings*.
148. "Language", in *Poetry, Language, Thought*, p. 190.
149. "The Nature of Language", p. 58; "The Way to Language", in *On the Way to Language*, p. 132.
150. "The Way to Language", in *On the Way to Language*, pp. 122–3.
151. "Language", in *Poetry, Language, Thought*, p. 208.
152. "The Way to Language", in *On the Way to Language*, p. 135.

and even the study of nursing. As his writings continue to be published and interpreted, his thought is poised to indicate unexpected directions.

Existentialism may be out of fashion, and Heidegger never accepted the label – but for those who want to do justice to the experience of being an existing individual, *Being and Time* is still a rich resource. It is at least a courageous attempt to conceptualize our existence without forcing it into concepts that are suited only to mere objects.

For those who want to explore the situatedness of knowledge, its character as an ongoing interpretive process, Heidegger is a major figure in hermeneutics, the theory of interpretation. His reflections do much to help us understand understanding.

For postmodernists, Heidegger's deconstruction of the metaphysics of presence points to an era in which there are no absolute beginnings or boundaries. Heidegger was a centripetal thinker: he always sought the center, the gathering power of Being. But postmodern thinkers are centrifugal, exploring the margins of meaning, hoping to practice an ethics and politics that are not about an "ownmost" possibility, but about "the other". Despite this difference in direction, it was Heidegger who first made many of the moves that are now part of the postmodern dance.

For many English-speaking philosophers, Division I of *Being and Time* releases us from our obsession with propositions and mental contents. It shows us that our everyday practices and skills are more fundamental than our theoretical assertions. Heidegger becomes a route back to pragmatism, and gives us hope for escaping from the conundrums of analytic epistemology and metaphysics, as well as from the computational model of human consciousness.

The future impact of Heidegger's thought is so unpredictable partly because the thought itself is so mixed, even paradoxical. At his best, Heidegger masterfully combines phenomenological insight with sensitivity to history. At his worst, he replaces insight with harangue and history with melodrama. When it comes to the problem of Being, his creativity and resourcefulness are unmatched – but his insistence on viewing everything in terms of this problem betrays a certain lack of imagination. The more he tries to efface his own personality in the vast scope of the history of Being, the more unmistakably his idiosyncrasies show through.

Heidegger often insisted that philosophy is not a worldview.[153] Philosophy is the activity of questioning Being; a worldview is a rigid representation of beings. But Heidegger himself fell prey to a worldview, a vision that for a time led him into politics that were deluded at best. His later thought returns obsessively to this worldview, now de-politicized but still impossibly simplistic; it is a view of human beings as dominated by the technological understanding of Being,

153. E.g. *The Basic Problems of Phenomenology*, p. 10; GA 65, §14. Heidegger's most thorough exploration of this issue is in *Einleitung in die Philosophie*, GA 27. Here Heidegger concludes that philosophy *can* be understood as a kind of worldview – but it is a worldview as an attitude (*Haltung*) rather than as a foundation or foothold (*Halt*). See especially pp. 376–90.

demoted to servants of the metaphysics of presence. This picture is inadequate, even on purely Heideggerian grounds. Although it is suggestive and sometimes illuminating, it conceals more than it unconceals. It hides the richness and diverse texture of life that Heidegger himself once wanted to discover. This worldview is rationalistic: it proposes a single, unifying explanation of all cultural phenomena – even though Heidegger himself had tried to curb our thirst for explanations and point us back to the phenomena themselves. Finally, this worldview in effect treats life as determined by theory, whereas Heidegger had originally tried to view theory as an outgrowth of life. For the early Heidegger, human existence is permeated with a rich significance that is artificially restricted in theory, reduced *in theory* to a meaning of Being as presence-at-hand. For late Heidegger, at his most apocalyptic, the weight of presence first overwhelms the philosophers and then crushes the Dasein out of all humans, reducing us *in fact* to mere functionaries of metaphysics.

Is Heidegger's philosophy, in the final analysis, a success or a failure? – one wants to ask. But maybe the categories of this "final analysis" are always inadequate for understanding a philosopher. When it comes to philosophy, no analysis is final: every analysis of a philosophy is the continuation of that philosophy, an exploration of its ongoing possibilities. And if success means establishing an unassailable and total truth, then no philosopher has succeeded. Heidegger writes, "every philosophy, as a human thing, intrinsically fails; and God needs no philosophy".[154] But despite the failure of philosophy, despite its finitude, we human beings do need what it offers.

> The finitude of philosophy consists not in the fact that it comes up against limits and cannot proceed further. It rather consists in this: in the singleness and simplicity of its central problematic, philosophy conceals a richness that again and again demands a renewed awakening.[155]

154. *The Metaphysical Foundations of Logic*, p. 76.   155. *Ibid.*, p. 156.

Selected Bibliography

This bibliography includes (I) German editions of Heidegger's works to which I refer in this book; (II) important English translations of works by Heidegger; (III) recommended secondary works in English; and (IV) other works cited in this book.

In I and II, I have indicated the date of the composition of the text when this date is significantly earlier than the publication date. I have briefly noted the contents of some works that are not discussed in this book or whose contents are not apparent from their titles.

In III, I concentrate on the best older studies, commentaries on *Being and Time*, recent monographs likely to be helpful to beginners and important anthologies. I have supplied a brief comment on each text.

The inclusion of a work about Heidegger in IV rather than III does not necessarily mean that this source is *not* recommended, but simply that it is less useful to the beginner than sources cited in III.

For a very complete older bibliography, see H-M. Sass, *Martin Heidegger: Bibliography and Glossary* (Bowling Green, Ohio: Philosophy Documentation Center, 1982). Two more recent bibliographies of writings by and about Heidegger in English are J. Nordquist, *Martin Heidegger: A Bibliography* (Social Theory: A Bibliographic Series, 17) (Santa Cruz, California: Reference and Research Services, 1990) and *Martin Heidegger (II): A Bibliography* (Social Theory: A Bibliographic Series, 42) (Santa Cruz, California: Reference and Research Services, 1996).

I. Heidegger in German

A. Volumes of Heidegger's *Gesamtausgabe*, or collected edition (Frankfurt am Main: Vittorio Klostermann, 1976–). These are designated throughout this book by "GA" and the volume number. Readers interested in textual history should be aware that the *Gesamtausgabe* is an "edition of the last hand" rather than a critical edition: that is, it includes changes that Heidegger made to his manuscripts after their original composition, without indicating these changes as such.

GA 1, *Frühe Schriften* (1978). (Written 1910–16.)

GA 4, *Erläuterungen zu Hölderlins Dichtung* (1981). (Written 1936–68.)

GA 13, *Aus der Erfahrung des Denkens (1910–1976)* (1983). A collection of short pieces.

GA 21, *Logik: Die Frage nach der Wahrheit* (1976). (Written 1925–26.) An important exploration of unconcealment.

GA 27, *Einleitung in die Philosophie* (1996). (Written 1928–29.) Investigates the relationships among science, philosophy, and worldviews.

GA 31, *Vom Wesen der menschlichen Freiheit. Einleitung in die Philosophie* (1982). (Written 1930.)

GA 39, *Hölderlins Hymnen "Germanien" und "Der Rhein"* (1989). (Written 1934–35.)

GA 42, *Schelling: "Vom Wesen der menschlichen Freiheit" (1809)* (1988). (Written 1936.)

GA 49, *Die Metaphysik des deutschen Idealismus. Zur erneuten Auslegung von Schelling: "Philosophische Untersuchungen über das Wesen der menschlichen Freiheit und die damit zusammenhängenden Gegenstände" (1809)* (1991). (Written 1941.)

GA 52, *Hölderlins Hymne "Andenken"* (1982). (Written 1941–42.)

GA 55, *Heraklit* (1979). (Written 1943–44.)

GA 56/57, *Zur Bestimmung der Philosophie* (1987). (Written 1919.) Important early reflections on theory and life.

GA 61, *Phänomenologische Interpretationen zu Aristoteles: Einführung in die phänomenologische Forschung* (1985). (Written 1921–22.)

GA 63, *Ontologie (Hermeneutik der Faktizität)* (1988). (Written 1923.)

GA 65, *Beiträge zur Philosophie (Vom Ereignis)* (1989). (Written 1936–38.)

GA 66, *Besinnung* (1997). (Written 1937–39.) Like GA 65, to which it forms a kind of sequel, this is a long and wide-ranging series of private reflections.

GA 77, *Feldweg-Gespräche (1944/45)* (1995).

GA 79, *Bremer und Freiburger Vorträge* (1994). (Written 1949 and 1957.)

B. Other works in German cited in this book.

Lógica: Lecciones de M. Heidegger (semestre verano 1934) en el legado de Helene Weiss, bilingual German–Spanish edn, intro. and tr. V. Farías (Barcelona: Anthropos, 1991).

Martin Heidegger, Elisabeth Blochmann: Briefwechsel, 1918–1969, J. W. Storck (ed.) (Marbach-am-Neckar: Deutsche Schillergesellschaft, 1989).

Martin Heidegger–Karl Jaspers Briefwechsel, 1920–1963, W. Biemel & H. Saner (eds) (Frankfurt-am-Main: Klostermann/Piper, 1990).

Sein und Zeit, 14th edn (Tübingen: Max Niemeyer Verlag, 1977). First edition in *Jahrbuch für Philosophie und Phänomenologische Forschung*, E. Husserl (ed.) **8** (Halle: Max Niemeyer, 1927) and as *Sein und Zeit: Erste Hälfte* (Halle: Max Niemeyer, 1927).

II. Heidegger in English

Aristotle's Metaphysics *Θ 1–3: On the Essence and Actuality of Force*, tr. W. Brogan & P. Warnek (Bloomington, Indiana: Indiana University Press, 1995). (GA 33, written 1931.) An original exploration of potentiality and actuality in Aristotle.

"Art and Space", tr. C. H. Seibert. *Man and World* **6** (1), 1973, pp. 3–5. (Written 1969.)

Basic Concepts, tr. G. Aylesworth (Bloomington, Indiana: Indiana University Press, 1993). (GA 51, written 1941.) A short, powerful presentation of some theses on Being.

The Basic Problems of Phenomenology, tr. A. Hofstadter (Bloomington, Indiana: Indiana University Press, 1982). (GA 24, written 1927.)

Basic Questions of Philosophy: Selected "Problems" of "Logic", tr. R. Rojcewicz & A. Schuwer (Bloomington, Indiana: Indiana University Press, 1994). (GA 45, written 1937–38.) An exploration of truth as unconcealment.

Basic Writings, 2nd edn, D. F. Krell (ed.) (San Francisco, California: HarperSanFrancisco, 1993). An excellent starting point for reading Heidegger, this anthology contains various pieces first published in German between 1927 and 1964, including "What is Metaphysics?", "On the Essence of Truth", "The Origin of the Work of Art", "The Question Concerning Technology" and "Letter on Humanism".

Being and Time, tr. J. Macquarrie & E. Robinson (New York: Harper & Row, 1962). (First published 1927.)

Being and Time, tr. J. Stambaugh (Albany, New York: State University of New York Press, 1996). (First published 1927.)

The Concept of Time, tr. W. McNeill, bilingual edn (Oxford: Basil Blackwell, 1992). (Written 1924.) An important early lecture on Dasein's temporality.

Contributions to Philosophy (On Appropriation), tr. P. Emad & K. Maly (Bloomington, Indiana: Indiana University Press, forthcoming). (GA 65, written 1936–38.)

Discourse on Thinking, tr. J. M. Anderson & E. H. Freund (New York: Harper & Row, 1966). Contains part of a dialogue written 1944–5 and a public lecture written 1955, both about releasement.

Early Greek Thinking, tr. D. F. Krell & F. A. Capuzzi (New York: Harper & Row, 1975). (Written 1943–54.) Four essays on pre-Socratic thought.

The End of Philosophy, tr. J. Stambaugh (New York: Harper and Row, 1973). (Written 1941–54.) Difficult essays on the history of Being.

The Essence of Reasons, tr. T. Malick, bilingual edn (Evanston, Illinois: Northwestern University Press, 1969). (Written 1929.)

The Essence of Truth, tr. T. Sadler (London: Athlone, 1998). (GA 34, written 1931–32). Interesting lectures on Plato's allegory of the cave and *Theaetetus.*

Existence and Being, W. Brock (ed.) (Chicago, Illinois: Henry Regnery Company, 1949). (Written 1929–43.) A selection that today is useful primarily for its translations of two essays on Hölderlin.

The Fundamental Concepts of Metaphysics: World, Finitude, Solitude, tr. W. McNeill & N. Walker (Bloomington, Indiana: Indiana University Press, 1995). (GA 29/30, written 1929–30.)

Hegel's Concept of Experience, tr. J. G. Gray & F. D. Wieck (New York: Harper & Row, 1970). (Written 1942–43.)

Hegel's Phenomenology of Spirit, tr. P. Emad & K. Maly (Bloomington, Indiana: Indiana University Press, 1988). (GA 32, written 1930–31.)

Heraclitus Seminar 1966/67, with E. Fink, tr. C. Seibert (Evanston, Illinois: Northwestern University Press, 1993).

History of the Concept of Time: Prolegomena, tr. T. Kisiel (Bloomington, Indiana: Indiana University Press, 1985). (GA 20, written 1925.) A valuable discussion of phenomenology, and a draft of part of *Being and Time.* The title is misleading.

Hölderlin's Hymn "The Ister", tr. W. McNeill & J. Davis (Bloomington, Indiana: Indiana University Press, 1996). (GA 53, written 1942.) Includes an interpretation of an ode from Sophocles' *Antigone* as well as readings of Hölderlin.

Identity and Difference, tr. J. Stambaugh, bilingual edn (New York: Harper & Row, 1969). (Written 1957.) Short but challenging reflections on the relation between Dasein and Being.

An Introduction to Metaphysics, tr. R. Manheim (New Haven, Connecticut: Yale University Press, 1959). (Written 1935, revised 1953.)

Introduction to Metaphysics, tr. G. Fried & R. Polt (New Haven, Connecticut: Yale University Press, forthcoming). (Written 1935, revised 1953.) This version will be closer to the original than the Manheim translation.

Kant and the Problem of Metaphysics, tr. R. Taft, 4th edn (Bloomington, Indiana: Indiana University Press, 1996). (Written 1929.) Includes an account of Heidegger's disputation regarding Kant with Ernst Cassirer in 1929.

"Kant's Thesis about Being", in *Thinking about Being: Aspects of Heidegger's Thought*, R. W. Shahan & J. N. Mohanty (eds) (Norman, Oklahoma: University of Oklahoma Press, 1984). (Written 1962.)

Logic: The Question of Truth, tr. T. Sheehan & R. Lilly (Bloomington, Indiana: Indiana University Press, forthcoming). (GA 21, written 1925–26.)

The Metaphysical Foundations of Logic, tr. M. Heim (Bloomington, Indiana: Indiana University Press, 1984). (GA 26, written 1929.) An interpretation of Leibniz and an exploration of the ontological preconditions of logical necessity.

Nietzsche, D. F. Krell (ed.) [4 vols] (New York: Harper & Row, 1979–87), [2 vols] (New York: Harper & Row, 1991). (Written 1936–46.)

On the Way to Language, tr. P. D. Hertz & J. Stambaugh (New York: Harper & Row, 1971). (Written 1953–59.)

On Time and Being, tr. J. Stambaugh (New York: Harper & Row, 1972). (Written 1962–64.)

"Only a God Can Save Us", *Der Spiegel's* 1966 interview with Heidegger, is translated in the anthologies edited by Sheehan, Wolin, and Neske & Kettering listed in III below. The version in Neske & Kettering includes some phrases that were deleted by *Der Spiegel* when the interview was first published in 1976.

Ontology (Hermeneutics of Facticity), tr. J. van Buren (Bloomington, Indiana: Indiana University Press, forthcoming). (GA 63, written 1923.)

Parmenides, tr. A. Schuwer & R. Rojcewicz (Bloomington, Indiana: Indiana University Press, 1992). (GA 54, written 1942–43.)

Pathmarks, W. McNeill (ed.) (Cambridge: Cambridge University Press, 1998). An important collection of essays. (GA 9, written 1919–1958.)

Phenomenological Interpretation of Kant's Critique of Pure Reason, tr. P. Emad & K. Maly (Bloomington, Indiana: Indiana University Press, 1997). (GA 25, written 1927–28.)

"Phenomenological Interpretations with Respect to Aristotle: Indication of the Hermeneutical Situation", tr. M. Baur, *Man and World* **25**, 1992, pp. 355–93. (Written 1922.) An early effort to express Heidegger's approach to interpreting concrete human life.

The Piety of Thinking, tr. J. G. Hart & J. C. Maraldo (Bloomington, Indiana: Indiana University Press, 1976). A selection of essays from the 1920s to the 1960s relevant to theology.

Plato's Sophist, tr. R. Rojcewicz & A. Schuwer (Bloomington, Indiana: Indiana University Press, 1997). (GA 19, written 1924–25.) Heidegger's most detailed reading of Plato and of Book VI of Aristotle's *Nicomachean Ethics.* Knowledge of Greek is almost indispensable.

Poetry, Language, Thought, tr. A. Hofstadter (New York: Harper & Row, 1971). (Written 1950–59.)

The Principle of Reason, tr. R. Lilly (Bloomington, Indiana: Indiana University Press, 1991). (Written 1955–56.)

The Question Concerning Technology and other Essays, tr. W. Lovitt (New York: Harper & Row, 1977). (Written 1938–1955.) Reflections on science, nihilism, and technology.

Schelling's Treatise on the Essence of Human Freedom, tr. J. Stambaugh (Athens, Ohio: Ohio University Press, 1985). (Written 1936–1943.)

Towards the Definition of Philosophy, tr. T. Sadler (London: Athlone, 1998). (GA 56/57, written 1919.) Important lecture courses that document Heidegger's early critique of the theoretical attitude.

What is a Thing? tr. W. B. Barton & V. Deutsch (Chicago, Illinois: Henry Regnery Company, 1967). (Written 1935–36.) A study of Descartes, Kant and the nature of modern philosophy and science.

What is Called Thinking? tr. F. D. Wieck & J. G. Gray (New York: Harper & Row, 1968). (Written 1954.)

What is Philosophy? tr. W. Kluback & J. T. Wilde (New Haven, Connecticut: College & University Press, 1958). (Written 1955.)

"Why Do I Stay in the Provinces?" in *Heidegger: The Man and the Thinker*, T. Sheehan (ed.) (Chicago, Illinois: Precedent, 1981). (Written 1934.)

III. Recommended secondary works

Biemel, W. *Martin Heidegger: An Illustrated Study*, tr. J. L. Mehta (New York: Harcourt Brace Jovanovich, 1976). This introductory work by a student of Heidegger successfully combines photographs, personal observations and analyses of some important texts.

Blitz, M. *Heidegger's* Being and Time *and the Possibility of Political Philosophy* (Ithaca, New York: Cornell University Press, 1981). One of the more careful approaches to the political dimension in Heidegger. Also serves as a clear review of the major ideas of *Being and Time*.

Caputo, J. D. *Demythologizing Heidegger* (Bloomington, Indiana: Indiana University Press, 1993). A postmodern critique by a formerly faithful Heideggerian.

Cooper, D. E. *Heidegger* (London: Claridge Press, 1996). A very good although compressed survey. Sensible remarks on many important topics.

Dreyfus, H. L. *Being-in-the-World: A Commentary on Heidegger's* Being and Time, *Division I* (Cambridge, Massachusetts: MIT Press, 1991). A detailed work, influential in the English-speaking world. Stresses practical "coping" as the basis of intelligibility; presents Division II as an "existentialist" side of Heidegger that is separable from Division I.

Dreyfus, H. L. & H. Hall (eds). *Heidegger: A Critical Reader* (Oxford: Basil Blackwell, 1992). A collection of careful, closely argued essays. Most interpret Heidegger in terms of "everyday practices".

Gadamer, H-G. *Heidegger's Ways*, tr. J. W. Stanley (Albany, New York: State University of New York Press, 1994). Essays by one of Heidegger's most important students.

Gelven, M. *A Commentary on Heidegger's* Being and Time, 2nd edn (DeKalb, Illinois: Northern Illinois University Press, 1989). A helpful, plain-spoken analysis. Holds that Heidegger is not urging his readers to exist authentically.

Guignon, C. B. *Heidegger and the Problem of Knowledge* (Indianapolis, Indiana: Hackett, 1983). An unusually clear exposition of Heidegger in general, with special attention to the problems of Cartesianism and epistemology.

Guignon, C. B. (ed.). *The Cambridge Companion to Heidegger* (Cambridge: Cambridge University Press, 1993). An excellent collection of essays by leading scholars on a wide variety of topics. Most are helpful for beginners. Guignon's introduction provides an overview of Heidegger's work.

Inwood, Michael. *Heidegger* (Oxford: Oxford University Press, 1997). A short but generally helpful survey of some central ideas, written in a lively style. The focus is *Being and Time* and "The Origin of the Work of Art".

Kaelin, E. *Heidegger's* Being and Time: *A Reading for Readers* (Tallahassee, Florida: Florida State University Press, 1988). An interesting if sometimes obscure analysis. Stresses the structure of Heidegger's text and its relevance for literary criticism.

Kisiel, T. *The Genesis of Heidegger's* Being and Time (Berkeley, California: University of California Press, 1993). The most detailed account available of Heidegger's development through the writing of *Being and Time*. Difficult but very valuable.

Kisiel, T. & J. Van Buren (eds). *Reading Heidegger from the Start: Essays on his Earliest Thought* (Albany, New York: State University of New York Press, 1994). A good resource for students exploring this topic.

Kockelmans, J. J. (ed.). *A Companion to Heidegger's* Being and Time (Washington, DC: University Press of America, 1986). A collection of excellent essays on topics relevant to *Being and Time*. Not all are directly about *Being and Time*.

Kockelmans, J. J. *Heidegger's "Being and Time": The Analytic of Dasein as Fundamental Ontology* (Washington, DC: Center for Advanced Research in Phenomenology and University Press of America, 1989). This careful, reliable commentary stays quite close to Heidegger's own language.

Marx, W. *Heidegger and the Tradition*, tr. T. Kisiel & M. Greene (Evanston, Illinois: Northwestern University Press, 1971). Compares Heidegger to Aristotle and Hegel. Challenging but enlightening.

Mehta, J. L. *Martin Heidegger: The Way and the Vision* (Honolulu, Hawaii: University Press of Hawaii, 1976). An extensive, faithful survey of Heidegger's work; emphasis on *Being and Time*.

Mulhall, S. *The Routledge Philosophy Guidebook to Heidegger and* Being and Time (London: Routledge, 1996). A compact commentary on *Being and Time*. Does not cover other texts. Tends to misinterpret Being-in-the-world in terms of having concepts.

Murray, M. (ed.). *Heidegger and Modern Philosophy* (New Haven, Connecticut: Yale University Press, 1978). Interesting and diverse essays.

Neske, G. & E. Kettering (eds). *Martin Heidegger and National Socialism: Questions and Answers*, tr. L. Harries (New York: Paragon House, 1990). Contains important original documents by Heidegger (including his 1933 rectoral address, his 1966 interview with *Der Spiegel*, and his 1969 television interview with Richard Wisser) as well as a range of interesting essays, many of which defend Heidegger.

Ott, H. *Heidegger: A Political Life*, tr. A. Blunden (New York: BasicBooks, 1993). The most complete historical study of Heidegger's political involvement; paints an unattractive picture of his personality and behavior.

Pöggeler, O. *Martin Heidegger's Path of Thinking*, tr. D. Magurshak & S. Barber (Atlantic Highlands, New Jersey: Humanities Press International, 1987). A classic German study of Heidegger's development, rich in references to intellectual history.

Richardson, W. J. *Heidegger: Through Phenomenology to Thought*, 3d edn (The Hague: Martinus Nijhoff, 1974). This monumental work discusses Heidegger's entire career, but the emphasis is on texts published during the second half of his life. Includes a letter from Heidegger to Richardson on the development of his thought.

Rockmore, T. & J. Margolis (eds). *The Heidegger Case: On Philosophy and Politics* (Philadelphia, Pennsylvania: Temple University Press, 1992). A sampling of approaches to the question of Heidegger's politics.

Safranski, R. *Martin Heidegger: Between Good and Evil*, tr. E. Osers (Cambridge, Massachusetts: Harvard University Press, 1998). The most thorough biographical study; includes thoughtful observations about Heidegger's philosophy as well as about his personality and actions.

Sallis, J. *Echoes: After Heidegger* (Bloomington, Indiana: Indiana University Press, 1990). Challenging essays by one of the more influential American readers of Heidegger.

Sallis, J. (ed.). *Reading Heidegger: Commemorations* (Bloomington, Indiana: Indiana University Press, 1993). Wide variety of essays, most quite good, from a conference on the occasion of the hundredth anniversary of Heidegger's birth.

Schmitt, R. *Martin Heidegger on Being Human: An Introduction to* Sein und Zeit (New York: Random House, 1969). Carefully discusses critical objections to key claims in *Being and Time* about ready-to-hand entities, language, phenomenology and understanding. Also discusses Heidegger's relation to Husserl. Best for readers who have already studied *Being and Time* and who have some background in analytic philosophy.

Shahan, R. W. & J. N. Mohanty (eds). *Thinking about Being: Aspects of Heidegger's Thought*. (Norman, Oklahoma: University of Oklahoma Press, 1984). An interesting collection, including Heidegger's 1962 essay "Kant's Thesis about Being".

Sheehan, T. (ed.). *Heidegger: the Man and the Thinker* (Chicago, Illinois: Precedent, 1981). This fine anthology includes Heidegger's 1934 essay "Why Do I Stay in the Provinces?" and his 1966 interview with *Der Spiegel*.

Steiner, G. *Heidegger*, 2d edn (London: Fontana, 1992). An interesting short study, good on stylistic analysis and Heidegger's relationship to his culture at large, but sometimes unreliable.

Waterhouse, R. *A Heidegger Critique: A Critical Examination of the Existential Phenomenology of Martin Heidegger* (Atlantic Highlands, New Jersey: Humanities Press, 1981). Includes a good summary of *Being and Time* with special attention to Husserl and the hermeneutic tradition, as well as criticisms of Heidegger that are worth considering.

Wolin, R. (ed.). *The Heidegger Controversy: A Critical Reader* (Cambridge, Massachusetts: MIT Press, 1993). Contains important original documents by Heidegger as well as interesting essays by others relevant to the question of Heidegger's politics.

Young, J. *Heidegger, Philosophy, Nazism* (Cambridge: Cambridge University Press, 1997). A well-argued and vigorous defense of Heidegger's thought.

Zimmerman, M. E. *Eclipse of the Self: The Development of Heidegger's Concept of Authenticity*, 2nd edn (Athens, Ohio: Ohio University Press, 1986). A very clear discussion of Heidegger's views on resoluteness and releasement. Holds that understanding Heidegger requires a personal transformation and authentic existence.

IV. Other works cited

Aristotle. *Nicomachean Ethics*, tr. T. Irwin (Indianapolis, Indiana: Hackett, 1985).

St. Augustine. *Confessions*, tr. R. S. Pine-Coffin (Harmondsworth: Penguin, 1961).

Ayer, A. J. (ed.) *Logical Positivism* (New York: The Free Press, 1959).

Bambach, C. *Heidegger, Dilthey and the Crisis of Historicism* (Ithaca, New York: Cornell University Press, 1995).

Barash, J. A. *Martin Heidegger and the Problem of Historical Meaning* (Dordrecht: Martinus Nijhoff, 1985).

Bernasconi, R. *The Question of Language in Heidegger's History of Being* (Atlantic Highlands, New Jersey: Humanities Press, 1985).

Bernstein, R. J. *The New Constellation: The Ethical-Political Horizons of Modernity/Postmodernity* (Cambridge, Massachusetts: MIT Press, 1992).

Bourdieu, P. *The Political Ontology of Martin Heidegger*, tr. P. Collier (Palo Alto, California: Stanford University Press, 1991).

Braig, C. *Vom Sein: Abriß der Ontologie* (Freiburg im Breisgau: Herder, 1896).

Brentano, F. *On the Several Senses of Being in Aristotle*, tr. & ed. R. George (Berkeley, California: University of California Press, 1975).

Caputo, J. D. *The Mystical Element in Heidegger's Thought* (New York: Fordham University Press, 1990).

Descartes, R. *Selected Philosophical Writings*, tr. J. Cottingham, R. Stoothoff & D. Murdoch (Cambridge: Cambridge University Press, 1988).

Descartes, R. *Discourse on Method and Meditations on First Philosophy*, tr. D. A. Cress, 3d edn (Indianapolis: Hackett, 1993).

Dewey, J. *Experience and Nature*, 2nd edn (La Salle, Illinois: Open Court, 1929).

Edwards, P. *Heidegger on Death: A Critical Evaluation* (La Salle, Illinois: Hegeler Institute, 1979).

Ettinger, E. *Hannah Arendt/Martin Heidegger* (New Haven, Connecticut: Yale University Press, 1995).

Farías, V. *Heidegger and Nazism*, J. Margolis & T. Rockmore (eds) (Philadelphia, Pennsylvania: Temple University Press, 1989).

Fried, G. Heidegger's *Polemos*, *Journal for Philosophical Research* **16**, 1991, pp. 159–95.

Friedman, M. Overcoming Metaphysics: Carnap and Heidegger. In *Origins of Logical Empiricism*, R. N. Giere & A. W. Richardson (eds) Minnesota

Studies in the Philosophy of Science, **16** (Minneapolis, Minnesota: University of Minnesota Press, 1996).

Gadamer, H-G. *Philosophical Apprenticeships*, tr. R. R. Sullivan (Cambridge, Massachusetts: MIT Press, 1985).

Gadamer, H-G. *Truth and Method*, 2nd edn, tr. J. Weinsheimer & D. G. Marshall (New York: Continuum, 1997).

Hawking, S. *A Brief History of Time: From the Big Bang to Black Holes* (New York: Bantam Books, 1988).

Husserl, E. *Logical Investigations*, tr. A. J. Findlay (London: Routledge & Kegan Paul, 1970).

Huxley, A. *Brave New World* (New York: Harper & Row, 1969).

Isaacson, W. In Search of the Real Bill Gates, *Time*, January 13, 1997.

Jaspers, K. *Psychologie der Weltanschauungen*, 6th edn (Berlin: Springer-Verlag, 1971).

Kant, I. *Critique of Pure Reason*, tr. N. K. Smith (New York: St. Martin's Press, 1965).

Keeler, H. S. John Jones's Dollar. In *Fantasia Mathematica*, C. Fadiman (ed.) (New York: Copernicus, 1997).

Kierkegaard, S. *The Concept of Anxiety: A Simple Psychologically Orienting Deliberation on the Dogmatic Issue of Hereditary Sin*, tr. & ed. R. Thomte & A. B. Anderson (Princeton, New Jersey: Princeton University Press, 1980).

Kierkegaard, S. *Concluding Unscientific Postscript to* Philosophical Fragments, tr. H. V. Hong & E. H. Hong (Princeton, New Jersey: Princeton University Press, 1992).

Kockelmans, J. J. *Edmund Husserl's Phenomenology* (West Lafayette, Indiana: Purdue University Press, 1994).

Kuhn, T. *The Structure of Scientific Revolutions* (Chicago, Illinois: University of Chicago Press, 1962).

Lang, B. *Heidegger's Silence* (Ithaca, New York: Cornell University Press, 1996).

Levinas, E. *Totality and Infinity*, tr. A. Lingis (Pittsburgh, Pennsylvania: Duquesne University Press, 1969).

Löwith, K. *My Life in Germany Before and After 1933: A Report*, tr. E. King (Urbana, Illinois: University of Illinois Press, 1994).

Macintyre, A. *After Virtue*, 2d edn (Notre Dame, Indiana: University of Notre Dame Press, 1984).

Makkreel, R. A. *Dilthey: Philosopher of the Human Studies* (Princeton, New Jersey: Princeton University Press, 1975).

Marcuse, H. Contribution to a Phenomenology of Historical Materialism, *Telos* 4 (Fall), 1969, pp. 3–34.

May, R. *Heidegger's Hidden Sources: East Asian Influences on his Work*, tr. with a complementary essay by G. Parkes (London: Routledge, 1996).

Nietzsche, F. *The Birth of Tragedy and The Case of Wagner*, tr. W. Kaufmann (New York: Vintage, 1967).

Nietzsche, F. *The Gay Science*, tr. W. Kaufmann (New York: Vintage, 1974).

Nietzsche, F. *Twilight of the Idols: Or, How to Philosophize with the Hammer*, tr. R. Polt (Indianapolis, Indiana: Hackett, 1997).

Ortega y Gasset, J. *Meditations on Quixote*, tr. E. Rugg & D. Marín (New York: W. W. Norton, 1961).

Orwell, G. *1984* (New York: New American Library, 1961).

Parkes, G. (ed.) *Heidegger and Asian Thought* (Honolulu, Hawaii: University of Hawaii Press, 1987).

Pascal, B. *Pensées*, tr. A. J. Krailsheimer (Harmondsworth: Penguin, 1966).

Petzet, H. W. *Encounters and Dialogues with Martin Heidegger, 1929–1976*, tr. P. Emad & K. Maly (Chicago, Illinois: University of Chicago Press, 1993).

Plato. *Meno*, tr. G. M. A. Grube, 2nd edn (Indianapolis, Indiana: Hackett, 1981).

Plato. *Republic*, tr. G. M. A. Grube & C. D. C. Reeve. In Plato, *Complete Works*, J. M. Cooper (ed.) (Indianapolis, Indiana: Hackett, 1997).

Polt, R. Heidegger's Topical Hermeneutics: The *Sophist* Lectures, *Journal of the British Society for Phenomenology* **37** (1), 1996, pp. 53–76.

Quine, W. V. *Ontological Relativity and Other Essays* (New York: Columbia University Press, 1969).

Rorty, R. Taking Philosophy Seriously, *The New Republic* **88**, April 11, 1988, pp. 31–4.

Russell, B. *Wisdom of the West* (New York: Crescent Books, 1989).

Sacks, O. *The Man Who Mistook His Wife for a Hat and Other Clinical Tales* (New York: Harper & Row, 1987).

Sartre, J-P. *Being and Nothingness*, tr. H. E. Barnes (New York: Washington Square Press, 1966).

Sartre, J-P. *Essays in Existentialism*, W. Baskin (ed.) (New York: Citadel Press, 1990).

Scheler, M. *Formalism in Ethics and Non-formal Ethics of Values: A New Attempt Toward the Foundation of an Ethical Personalism*, tr. M. S. Frings & R. L. Funk (Evanston, Illinois: Northwestern University Press, 1973).

Schneeberger, G. (ed.) *Nachlese zu Heidegger: Dokumente zu seinem Leben und Denken* (Bern, 1962).

Sieg, U. Die Verjudung des deutschen Geistes: Ein unbekannter Brief Heideggers, *Die Zeit* **52** (22 Dec 1989).

Sluga, H. *Heidegger's Crisis: Philosophy and Politics in Nazi Germany* (Cambridge, Massachusetts: Harvard University Press, 1993).

Sobel, D. Among Planets, *The New Yorker*, December 9, 1996.

Spiegelberg, H. *The Phenomenological Movement: A Historical Introduction*, 3d edn (The Hague: Martinus Nijhoff, 1982).

Unamuno, Miguel de. *The Tragic Sense of Life in Men and Nations*, tr. and ed. A. Kerrigan (Princeton, New Jersey: Princeton University Press, 1972).

Villa, D. R. *Heidegger and Arendt: The Fate of the Political* (Princeton, New Jersey: Princeton University Press, 1996).

Wittgenstein, L. *Tractatus Logico-Philosophicus*, tr. D. F. Pears & B. F. McGuinness (London: Routledge & Kegan Paul, 1961).

Wittgenstein, L. *Philosophical Occasions, 1912–1951* (Indianapolis, Indiana: Hackett, 1993).

Index

aletheia see unconcealment

analytic philosophy 11, 39–40, 74, 122–3, 179

Angst see anxiety

animals 45, 78, 97, 128, 155

anticipation 88, 95, 99

anti-Semitism 156–7

anxiety 76–9, 88, 90, 99, 124–6, 139

appearance 38–9, 131

appropriation 134, 143, 145–8, 178

Aquinas, T. 19, 27

Arendt, H. 20, 156

Aristotle 10–11, 21, 32, 37, 105, 170

art 45, 134–40, 149, 151

assertion 68–9, 73–4, 131

assignment *see* reference

atheism 152, 165

attunement 64–8, 89

Augustine, St. 13, 75, 106

authenticity 22, 36, 61–3, 75–6, 177
  and death 87–8, 95
  and ethics 91–2, 161
  and everydayness 45, 94
  general explanations of 5–6, 44, 90
  and guilt 90–1, 95
  as requirement for philosophy 93–4, 160
  and temporality 99–101, 108–9
  and understanding 70, 94, 104
  see also anticipation; repetition; resoluteness

Basic Problems of Phenomenology 24, 37, 110–12, 117

Beaufret, J. 115, 164

becoming 130–1

Being 15, 26–7, 41–2, 144, 168
  general explanations of 2–3, 28, 40, 81
  historicity of 5, 104–5, 119, 130–2, 147–8, 173
  meaning of 5, 10, 28, 72
  question of 3–4, 24, 109
  relation to Dasein 30, 33–5, 84, 118, 168–9
  self-concealing 5, 149
  understanding of 4, 27–9, 35, 40, 70, 72, 81–2
  see also beings; essence and existence; ontological difference; ontology

Being and Time 14, 23–113, 117–18, 121, 142, 170
  composition 5, 22, 25, 166
  method 31, 38–42, 92–4
  political implications 155, 161–3

Being-in 46, 64, 77

Being-in-the-world 42–3, 46–8
  see also world

beings 2, 142, 149–51
  relation to Being 3, 28, 41–2, 145
  see also ontical; ontological difference

Being-with 61–4, 136

Binswanger, L. 115

Blochmann, E. 156
Boss, M. 114–15
Braig, C. 10
Brentano, F. 10
Buddhism 96
Bultmann, R. 20

care 46–7, 50, 89, 96, 108, 154
    general explanations of 65, 78–80
    as historical possibility 120, 150
    taking care *see* concern
Carnap, R. 122–6
categorial intuition 15
Christianity 75, 88, 101, 142, 168
    Heidegger's personal relation to 9, 13,
    165
    and metaphysics 43, 132
circumspection 51
clearing 9, 57, 64, 149, 167
communism 114, 157, 162–3
concern 46–9
conscience 88–91
consciousness 14–15, 55
Contributions to Philosophy 69, 114, 134,
    140–52, 155–6, 168–9

Dasein 42–5, 64, 118, 127–30, 148, 167
    general explanation of 29–30
    as possibility for human beings 120,
    150
    relation to Being 30, 33–5, 84, 118,
    168–9
    see also Being-in-the-world; care;
    existence; temporality
death 85–8, 95–6, 99, 112, 166
deconstruction 22, 37, 102, 179
deficient modes 47, 62
democracy 114, 162–4
Derrida, J. 37
Descartes, R. 25–6, 33, 37, 67–8, 87
    and problem of external world 47–9,
    55–6, 58–9, 80–1
    and subject-object distinction 60, 84,
    142
destiny 102–3
Dewey, J. 46
Dilthey, W. 13, 15–16, 22, 100, 103
discourse 65, 74–5
distantiality 62

Dostoyevsky, F. 13
dwelling 46–8, 64, 77–8, 148, 177–8

earth 136–40, 149–50, 171
Eastern thought 102, 115
Eckhart 121
Einstein, A. 84, 125
ek-sistence 34, 127, 129, 167–8
enframing 142
    see also technology
entanglement *see* falling
entities *see* beings
environment 49–50, 52, 55
epistemology 47–8, 80
equipment 49–51, 151
errancy 129–30
    see also untruth
Ereignis see appropriation
essence and existence 29–30, 44, 63–4,
    164, 167
essential unfolding (*wesen*) 64, 144–5
ethics 61, 92, 159–61, 166–7, 169–71, 179
    see also conscience; values
etymology 11, 133
everydayness 36, 43, 45, 76–7, 94
evidence 14–15, 70
evil 158, 170
existence 34–5, 43–5, 93, 111
    see also essence and existence;
    ek-sistence
existentialia 43–4, 63–4, 119
existentialism 22, 44, 77, 121–2, 164–8,
    179
existentiality 79, 89
existentiell 35, 63–4, 93, 113, 119
external world 47–9, 55–6, 60, 80–1

facticity 17, 46, 66–7, 79, 89, 95
falling 36, 65, 75–7, 81, 103, 106
    as in-sistence 129
fascism *see* National Socialism
fate 102–3
fear 66
formal indication 17–18, 40
for-the-sake-of-which 53–4
Foucault, M. 37
fourfold 152
freedom 102–3, 126–8, 164, 167
Frege, G. 11

friendship 92
Fundamental Concepts of Metaphysics
77, 97, 117
future 3, 34, 65, 79, 89, 111
  and historicity 5, 101, 103
  and temporality 96, 99–100, 107–8
  see also possibility; projection;
    temporality; time; understanding

Gadamer, H-G. 19, 21, 33, 105, 115–16,
  152
Galileo 105
George, S. 177
Gesamtausgabe (collected edition) x, 1,
  116, 181–2
God 1, 88, 142, 165, 168, 180
  distinction from Being 3, 28
  metaphysical view of 4, 144
gods 45, 142, 152, 165
guilt 89, 95, 166

handiness *see* readiness-to-hand
Hawking, S. 2
Hebel, J. 9
heedfulness *see* concern
Hegel, G. 19, 167
Heidegger
  life 8–10, 19–22, 113–16
  politics 113–14, 152–64
Heraclitus 114, 131, 138
heritage 101–2, 162
hermeneutic circle 31, 71, 93, 98
hermeneutics 13, 17, 41, 179
historicism 14, 103–6
historicity 5, 37–8, 78, 100–6, 120, 162
History of the Concept of Time 24
Hitler, A. 21, 154–7, 160–2
Hölderlin, F. 114, 152, 174, 177–8
Holocaust 157–8, 172, 174
Holzwege 7
Homer 132
horizon 25, 105, 110–12
horizonal schema 110–12
humanism 163–4, 166–9
Hume, D. 131
Husserl, E. 21, 41, 58, 70, 156
  influence on Heidegger 11–16, 32, 38,
  119
Huxley, A. 172–3

idle talk 162, 176–7
inauthenticity *see* authenticity
in-order-to 51
intentionality 14
interpretation 5, 69–72, 98, 138
Introduction to Metaphysics 2, 77,
  130–4
intuition 15, 70–1
involvement 53–4

Jaspers, K. 22, 114, 166

Kant, I. 11, 26, 37, 96, 109, 117
  ethics 61, 88, 169
  influence on Heidegger 22, 41–2, 109,
  110–11, 119
Keeler, H. S. 141
Kierkegaard, S. 6, 13, 26, 109, 165–6
knowledge 47–8, 70–1, 80
  see also theory; science
Kuhn, T. 33
Kreutzer, C. 8

language 18, 27, 74–5, 119, 125, 174–8
leaping in and leaping ahead 61, 92, 161
"Letter on Humanism" 115, 117–18,
  164–71, 173, 175
Levinas, E. 171
liberalism 156–7, 162–3
lifeworld 58–9
Lin, M. 135
lived experience 134, 142–3
logic 11–12, 16–18, 73, 125–6, 131, 154,
  175–6
logical positivism 122, 125–6
logos 38–9, 73, 131, 134
Löwith, K. 19–21, 62, 156, 162
Luther, M. 13

machination 142, 151, 171
  see also technology
Marcel, G. 165
Marcuse, H. 157, 162
Marx, K. 162
meaning 24, 28, 72, 167
Metaphysical Foundations of Logic 117
metaphysics 114, 119, 123, 168
metaphysics of presence 5, 38, 70, 100,
  132, 163, 180

method 31, 33, 38–42, 92–4
Mill, J. S. 27
mind 5, 55–6, 64–5
mineness 44
modernity 55–8, 142–3, 171
moment of vision 100
moods 64–8, 124–6
    see also anxiety; attunement
Mussolini, B. 155

National Socialism 114, 153–64, 169, 172
Natorp, P. 21
nature 51, 137–9, 171–3
Neurath, O. 125
Newton, I. 84
Nietzsche, F. x, 6, 36, 145, 166
    Heidegger's critique of 114, 131, 144
    influence on Heidegger 13, 139–40
nihilation 124–6, 170
nihilism 155, 158, 164, 170
nothing 1–3, 121–7, 130

objects 4, 55–7, 142
objective presence, see presence-at-hand
objectivity 56–8, 66–7, 71, 79, 106–9,
    125
"On the Essence of Truth" 118, 121,
    126–30, 167
ontical 34, 43, 93
ontological difference 28, 111
ontology 34–5, 40–1, 80, 93
onto-theology 144
"The Origin of the Work of Art" 134–40,
    149, 151, 171
Ortega y Gasset, J. 30
Orwell, G. 172

Parmenides 114, 131
Pascal, B. 6
past 3, 5, 37, 42, 89, 103
    and temporality 99–101, 107–8
    as thrownness 65–6, 76, 79, 96–7
    see also attunement; facticity;
        temporality; thrownness; time;
        tradition
Paul, St. 13
phenomenology 14, 38–40, 119
physis 132
Plato 24–5, 31, 95, 117, 130–2, 169

poetry 119–20, 134, 175–8
possibility 3, 68–70, 86–7, 112
postmodernism 163–4, 179
potentiality-for-Being 69, 89, 96
pragmatism 179
presence 3–5, 70
    see also metaphysics of presence
presence-at-hand 58, 81, 108
    distinguished from existence 43–6, 97
    as dominant meaning of Being 70,
        109–10, 142
    relation to readiness-to-hand 50, 52
present 42, 97, 99–101, 107–8, 111
    see also temporality; time
projection 69–70, 89, 139
psychologism 12, 125

"The Question Concerning Technology"
    151, 171–4
Quine, W. V. 131

racism 155–6
readiness-to-hand 45, 49–50, 52, 55, 57
reality 81–2
reference 51–4, 72, 90
relativism 14, 68, 71–2, 103–6, 125
releasement 58, 121
relevance 53
repetition 91–2, 99–101
representation 5
resoluteness 63, 90–1, 95, 103, 121, 161
retrieve see repetition
Rickert, H. 11, 12, 14, 169
Rilke, R. M. 177
Rorty, R. 160
Russell, B. 11, 122–4, 176
Ryle, G. 159

Sacks, O. 50
Sartre, J-P. 87, 115, 164–8
Scheler, M. 169
Scholasticism 41, 56
science 1, 13, 56–8, 100, 122–3
    presuppositions of 32–3, 43, 71, 104,
        125–6
    relation to philosophy 34, 97
    see also knowledge; theory
selfhood 55, 63–4, 90, 95–6, 126
sheltering 149–51, 169

significance 53–4, 57
signs 53
silence 74–5, 89, 91, 157
situation 90–1, 100
skepticism 14, 68, 71–2, 80–1
  see also external world
Socrates 31, 95, 136
solipsism 61
Sophocles 131
space 59
state-of-mind *see* attunement
subject 5, 60, 80, 142, 167
subjectivity 55–7, 60, 66, 74, 118, 142–3
substance 4–5, 144, 151, 166
surrounding world *see* environment

technology 5, 56, 58–60, 132, 142, 171–4
temporality 5, 36, 85, 94–101, 106–11, 154
  ecstatical 34, 97–8, 100, 110
Temporality 110–11
theory 11–12, 16–18, 49–50, 52, 100
  see also knowledge; science
"they" 62–4, 75–6, 91, 161
they-self 63, 75, 89, 161
thing 151–2
thrownness 65–7, 76, 79, 89, 96, 139, 167
  see also past
Tillich, P. 20
time 3, 16, 42, 59–60, 96
  as horizon of Being 25, 36–7, 82, 110–12, 119
  ordinary concept of 96, 106–9
  see also future; past; present; temporality; Temporality
towards-which 51, 54
tradition 37–8, 67
Trakl, G. 177

transcendence 42, 111, 126–7
transcendental knowledge 41–2, 111, 119
truth 5, 15, 82–4, 126–30, 149–50
  see also unconcealment; untruth
turn 42, 117–21, 129, 163–4

Unamuno, M. 6
unbeings 142, 150
unconcealment 125, 129, 132–3, 135, 167, 149–51
  as primary phenomenon of truth 15, 82–4
  relation to propositional truth 12, 18, 83–4
  see also truth; untruth
understanding 5, 30, 54, 65, 68–72, 89
  see also Being, understanding of
untruth 15, 83, 129–30, 162

validity 11–12, 16–17, 73, 82
values 56, 76, 131, 141–2, 164, 169–70
Van Gogh, V. 137

Weiss, H. 154, 156
"What is Metaphysics?" 2, 77, 121–6, 170
Wittgenstein, L. 2, 18, 68, 81, 174
world 90, 136–40
  general explanations of 49, 52, 54, 60, 72, 136
  as part of the Being of Dasein 5, 30, 35, 42, 46, 80, 84
  see also Being-in-the-world; environment; external world
"world" 49, 80
worldhood 49–50, 52, 54–5
  see also world
worldliness *see* worldhood